Phulkari
फुलकारी

from the realm of women's creativity

A Tradition of Handmade Embroidery of Punjab and Haryana

PHULKARI
From the Realm of Women's Creativity

ISBN: 978-81-7305-465-5

Text: Krishna Lal
Design: Neeraj Sahai

First Published in **2013** by:
Indira Gandhi National Centre for the Arts
Central Vista Mess, Janpath, New Delhi - 110 001 (India)

Printed and Distributed by:
Aryan Books International
Pooja Apartments, 4B, Ansari Road, New Delhi-110 002 (India)
Tel.: 23287589, 23255799; Fax: 91-11-23270385
E-mail: aryanbooks@gmail.com
www.aryanbooks.co.in

Phulkari

फुलकारी

from the realm of women's creativity

A Tradition of Handmade Embroidery of Punjab and Haryana

Selected Pieces from the Archives of IGNCA

Indira Gandhi National Centre for the Arts
New Delhi

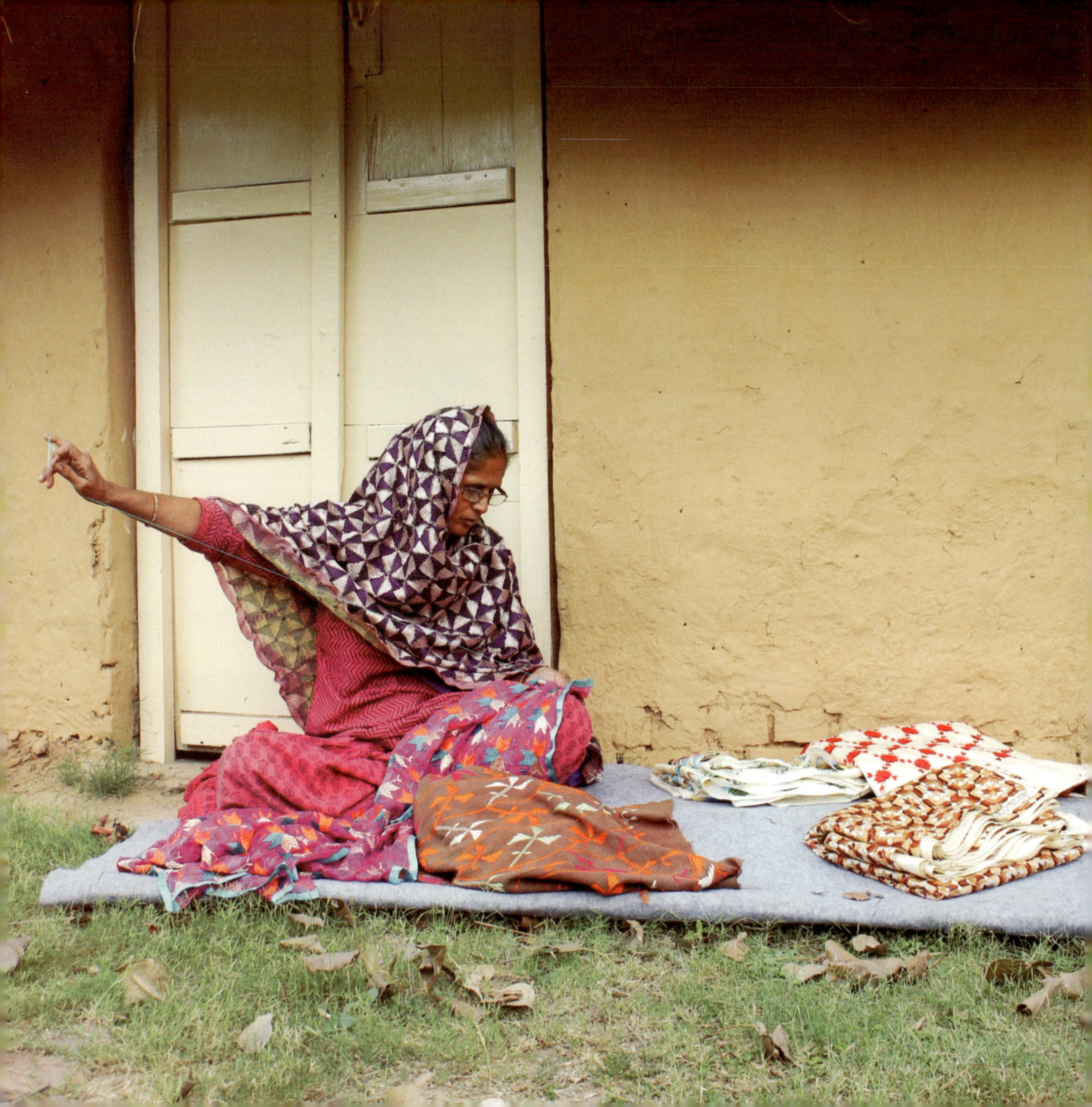

INTRODUCTION

The Indira Gandhi Centre for the Arts (IGNCA), was established in the memory of Late Smt. Indira Gandhi and is visualized as a centre encompassing the study and experience of all the arts, each form with its own integrity yet within a dimension of mutual interdependence, interrelated with nature, social structure and cosmology.

The Janapada Sampada division of the IGNCA undertakes research of the Indian cultural phenomenon in its totality and builds core collection of material and documentation on folk and tribal arts through multidisciplinary approach. One of the major programs of the division is Ethnographic Collection under which creativity at different levels is explored, researched and documented. This collection involves ritual objects, masks, puppets, musical instruments and textiles collected from various regions of the country, out of which among these fifty two rare pieces of Phulkari collection were also acquired.

Phulkari is a very refined embroidery work of Punjab and Haryana. India has a great tradition of embroidery in different parts, and phulkari stands out among these. It has more emotional, social and cultural value which is very rare. Embroidered with silk thread on cotton base, phulkari is a shawl made by the mother for her young daughter or daughter-in-law. Phulkari literally means floral work and is also called *Bagh*, which literally means a garden.

In the olden times, accomplishment of a bride and her mother was judged by the beautiful phulkari and bagh they made. Even the affluence of the families was judged by the number and work of phulkari and bagh they gave to their daughters in their trousseau. They also made ceremonial pieces which were used in marriages, at the time of birth of a child and during festive occasions. Phulkaris are known for their vibrant colours, geometric pattern and gaiety which are an integral part of the life and tradition of the people of Punjab.

The IGNCA has completed twenty five years and is celebrating its silver jubilee by holding seminars, conferences, and exhibitions on various dimensions of Indian arts and culture.

Keeping with this spirit, the centre is organizing an exhibition of its collection of the embroidery art of Punjab entitled, **'Phulkari: from the realm of women's creativity'.** The event encompasses interactive workshop with the women artisans of this craft display their work on phulkari; special lectures by noted scholars; and an evening of cultural performance.

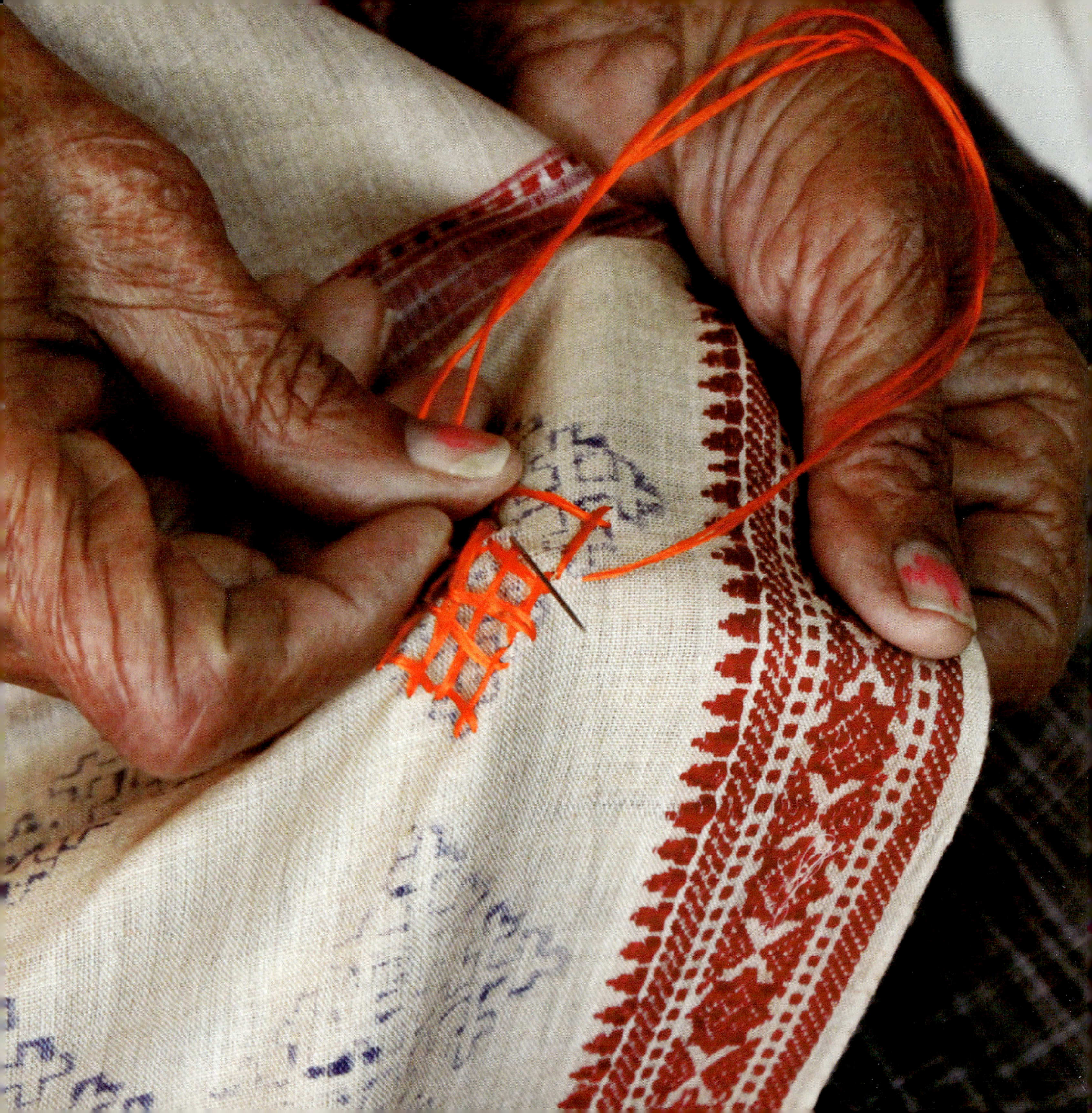

PHULKARI: from the realm of women's creativity

Embroidery is defined as the addition of pattern or other ornamental embellishment to a fabric by the use of needle and thread. Embroidery has a very rich and continuous tradition in India dating back to prehistoric period. The embroidered craft continued for centuries. We find samples of embroidery in various museums across the country.

Bronze needles excavated at Mohenjodaro (2700 BC); and the numerous terracotta figurines, as well as the textual reference of the "never breaking needle" and "coat of armour" in the *Rigveda* and *Aitharya Brahmana*, clearly indicate the importance of needle as a symbol of fine workmanship in ancient Indian society. The figures on the railings and pillars of the stupas at Sanchi and Bharut in Madhaya Pradesh (1st–2nd century BC), display embroidered veils and headbands. The frescoes of Ajanta and Ellora (2nd–5th century AD) are exquisite examples of beautifully embroidered jackets, tunics and robes reflecting excellent workmanship on the sleeves, yokes, hem and necklines of these garments. Ancient Sanskrit literature is replete with references to embroidery. While Kalidasa (4th–5th century AD) describes numerous costumes worn by various characters in his works, Bana Bhatta in his *Harsh Charita* (6th–7th century AD) mentions embroidered *odhani*, bodices, short jackets with pearl embroidery and even describes "a divine woman wearing a dazzling muslin robe with hundreds of diverse embroidered flowers and birds, gently rippled by breeze."

India has a great tradition of embroidery prevalent in each and every region; each of them different from the other. There are several embroidery styles, which have become popular nationally and internationally and have become synonymous to the region they come from. For example, Kashmir is known for *amlikar* work on shawls, Himachal Pradesh for chamba *rumal*, Uttar Pradesh for *chikan* work, Gujarat for *mochi* work and Punjab for *phulkari*. Each one has its own characteristics and phulkari stands out to be different among all these.

Origin and History

There is not much known about the origin of phulkari. It is said that this tradition was brought by the Persians to Kashmir, where this type of work is known as *gulkari*, where *gul* means flower; and *kari,* working style. The term phulkari also refers to the 'flower' (*phul*) work. However, Kashmir embroidery is very different from the stitch craft of Punjab and Haryana where this art form is still prevalent.

It is also believed that the *Jats* or *Gujjars* came to India from Central Asia and brought the stitch craft of phulkari with them. It is a well known fact that Persian and Central Asian nomads were weavers. Perhaps the sense of colour might have been inspired from these nomads, but the embroidery on home spun, woven *khaddar* was very much Indian. The earliest references to phulkari are found in holy book of the Sikhs, the *Guru Granth Sahib* among others. *Heer Ranjha*, the famous love story of Punjab written by Waris Shah (1725 – 1790), is another example, where the trousseau of Heer is mentioned as a clothing article.

Tradition and Meaning

The art of embroidery in Punjab is centuries old as it was a part of girl's education. In the *Granth Sahib*, the religious book of the Sikhs, Guru Nanak (the first Guru of Sikh, 1469-1539) wrote;

> *"Kadd kasidha paihreh choli, tan tu jane nari."*

Translation:

> "When you have embroidered a *choli* (blouse) then only
> you will be recognized as an accomplished woman."

Phulkari, floral work is also called *bagh*, which literally means a garden. Phulkari is an embroidered shawl worn by the women of Punjab. These shawls are embroidered with beautiful and colourful variety of geometrical motifs which gives an appearance of a garden; hence they are called phulkari or bagh.

Phulkari is a covering for head made by the mother for her young daughter or daughter-in-law. Richly embroidered phulkaris are an integral part of the life and tradition of the people of Punjab. In the olden days, accomplishment of a bride and her mother was judged by the beautifully embroidered phulkaris . Even the affluence of the families was judged by the number and work of phulkari and bagh they gave to their daughters in their trousseau. Many a time, as many as fifty one or even more phulkaris were given to the daughters and daughters-in-law at the time of their marriages. Ceremonial pieces were made during marriage ceremonies, birth of a child, festive occasions; and also at the time of death.

Phulkaris are of three types. First, where the pattern is dispersed at intervals over the entire cloth. Second is called bagh or garden where the whole surface of the material is decorated with patterns closely connected with each other; and where the ground or base material cannot be seen. Bagh was earlier used as a covering for head, and as shawls for ceremonial use. Closely embroidered as tapestries, bagh do not have pallus, and the main pattern is often repeated, however being placed differently.

The third type is called *chhope*, where the field remains plain and only the edges are embroidered in double-sided (reversible) running stitch, which gives a much sparser effect to the cloth. Chhope is held in high regard and plays an important part in wedding rituals. The designs are almost exclusively geometrical and worked out on a coarse hand-made cotton fabric with floss silk, embroidered with simple darn stitch, worked entirely on the wrong side of the material.

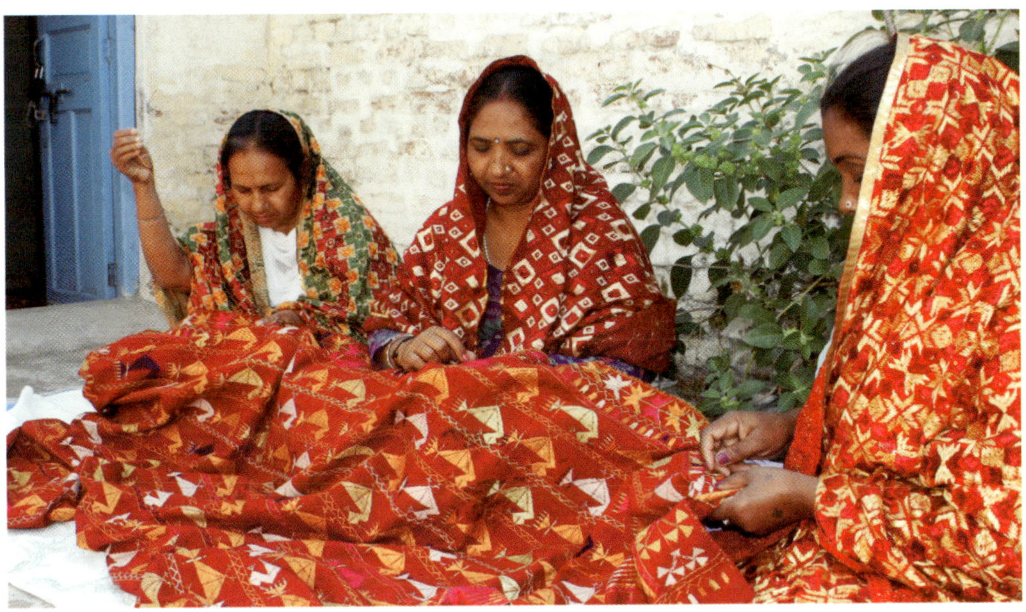

Phulkari embroidery is done exclusively by the women in their free time often competing with each other to produce better pieces. This art form provided a canvas for the women for maximum expression of their imagination and skill. Young girls were taught by their mothers at a very young age and by the time they reached marriageable age they were accomplished artists in this craft.

Auspicious time as per the almanac was chosen to start the embroidery with appropriate ceremony and prayers. Sweets and *prasad* were offered before embroidering the phulkaris or bagh by the mother or the grandmother. Almost from the time of the birth of a girl child, the grandmother would begin to work upon a bagh. After attaining marriageable age, the same bagh was given to the bride as her wedding trousseau.

Phulkari or bagh were made only for personal use. Phulkari (flowering work), was originally applied on cloth made for everyday wear, on which designs were sparsely embroidered on a coloured coarse cotton fabric known as *khaddar*. Phulkaris have richly embroidered *pallus* with striking designs in silk thread. The most interesting aspect of phulkari is that it does not have any commercial angle; rather it has more emotional value. Besides emotional, it has many social and cultural values too, which is rare among the embroidered art forms.

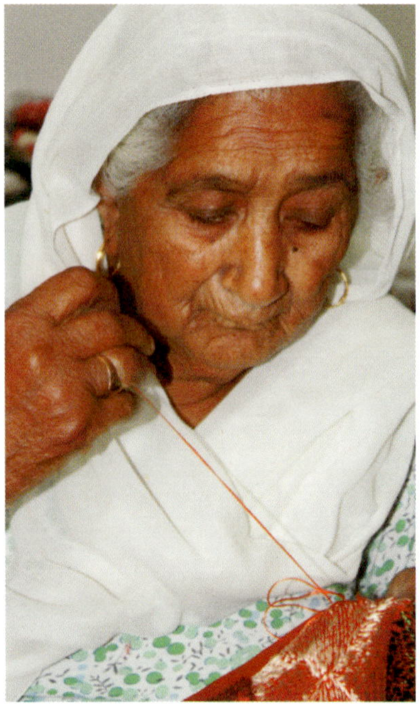

Methods and Techniques Used for Phulkaris

Phulkari or bagh were embroidered on coarse cotton cloth known as *khaddar*. The cotton yarn for base material was mostly spun on *charkha* (spinning wheel) by the women at home. It was sometimes also woven by the village weavers on small looms. Two or three pieces were joined lengthwise to get the required width of the head covering. The workmanship depended on the careful counting of the threads of the base fabric i.e. khaddar which was used for better effect of the embroidery.

Khaddar was mostly dyed in different shades of red by the women at home. Great care was taken while dyeing the khaddar in order to bring out the beauty of the embroidery which reflected on the richness of colour of the background cloth. Women of the house and *rangrez* (dyer) prepared the dyes at home, which were extracted from barks, leaves and roots of trees and plants. These dyes were fast in colour and less expensive. Some dyes were made from the *palash* flower (flame of forest), bark of *kikar* (acacia) tree and the roots of *manjheet* plant (madder) and were popularly used to obtain desired colours.

Manjheet is a creeper which grows in the north-west hilly region up to the north-east border of India. The roots of this plant were grounded into coarse powder and boiled for 2 – 3 hours to obtain different shades of red, chocolate brown and yellow. Indigo was also used for obtaining blue dye. Red was considered as an auspicious colour. Yellow, crimson, blue, white, brown, orange, violet, black and green colours were popularly used for making beautiful coverings for head. Copper and earthen pots were generally used to prepare the dye.

In Punjab, before dyeing, the cloth was soaked in a decoction of *tamarisk* (a form of deciduous tree) which acted as a dye resist. The cloth was then dipped in manjheet solution, small amount of alum was added to act as mordant; the dye was boiled again and a few grains of wheat were added. When the grains became soft, it was an indication to remove it from fire. The cloth was left to soak for few hours before drying. Earlier embroidery was done with soft untwisted silk thread called *patt*, which usually came from Kashmir, Afghanistan and Bengal. Sometimes it was also imported from China. Before independence, best phulkaris and bagh were made in west Punjab (now in Pakistan), in the districts of Sialkot, Peshawar, Jhelum, Ravalpindi and Hazara.

These days phulkaris are made in Gurdaspur and Patiala in Punjab, and in Haryana. While working on a phulkari, utmost care and attention is required. Designs on phulkari are floral in character but sometimes geometrical designs are also embroidered. Embroidery is done with a single thread, in darn stitch from wrong side of the cloth and by placing the needle in different directions i.e. horizontal, vertical and diagonal. Pattern in phulkari is controlled by counting the thread, very often embroidered with a green outline. Besides darn stitch, stem, herringbone, satin, straight, back, running, blanket, split, cross and chain stitches are also used in the embroidery.

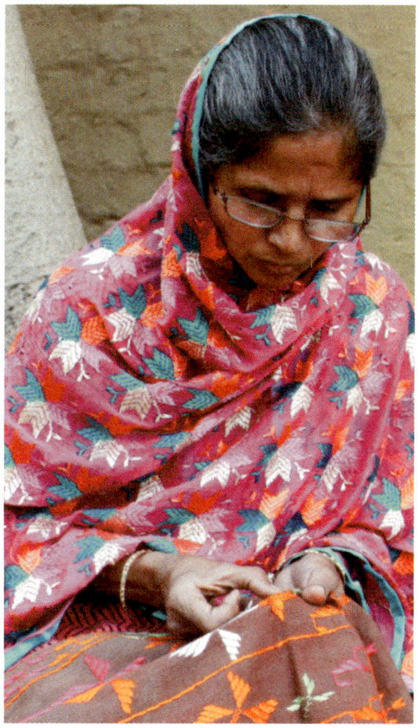

The coarse cotton cloth that was used earlier for making phulkaris is now being replaced by other fabrics; hardly any of the earlier embroidery has survived except for those kept in museums and private collections. Unfortunately, traditional phulkari designs used earlier, are no longer in use. Phulkari artists are now experimenting this craft on different fabrics to give a new look to the traditional art form.

Different Types of Phulkaris :

1. *Vari da Bagh* is made and presented by the grandmother of the bridegroom to the bride. Embroidered on a red *khaddar* (coarse cloth) with yellow colour, it symbolizes happiness and fertility. It is embroidered with great care and skill. The entire field is embroidered with designs such as lozenges enclosing other smaller lozenges. The side borders and *pallus* on two sides have different designs. The work being very fine, sometimes it takes more than a year to complete.

   This kind of embroidery is draped around the bride immediately after the marriage ceremony. A married woman is often seen wearing the bagh on all festive occasions and during *karva chauth*, when she observes a fast for the long life of her husband.

2. *Ghungat Bagh* is a veil or shawl. It is embroidered with a triangular motif on the portion of the Phulkari that covers the head. In such shawls normally two triangular motifs are embroidered with decorative edges.

3. *Sar-pallu* mostly corresponds well with Ghughat Bagh. The only difference is that it is more richly embroidered with large pallus. Two panels on two sides are fully embroidered in bagh style while the centre panel of the sar-pallu has various floral, animals, birds, human and jewel motifs in between.

4. *Chhope* is a wedding phulkari given to the girl at the time of her marriage by the maternal grandmother. Chhope is larger than an ordinary phulkari. It is very laborious to embroider a chhope as both sides must look similar in design. It is done with a double darn stitch on a rich red colored background with yellow silk thread embroidery. The outer two panels are embroidered with borders and two large-sized triangles with their base towards opposite directions. The main surface of the shawl is left undecorated. The ends are also kept plain to bring her unlimited prosperity and happiness. Chhope is wrapped around the bride-to-be when she is made to wear *choodha* (ivory bangles). This ceremony is called *choodha chandhaava* which takes place a few hours before the marriage rituals. This ceremony is still prevalent in the orthodox Punjabi families when all the close relatives of the bride sit around, while the maternal uncle gives jewellery and ivory bangles to her and the ladies sing *sohag* (marriage) songs.

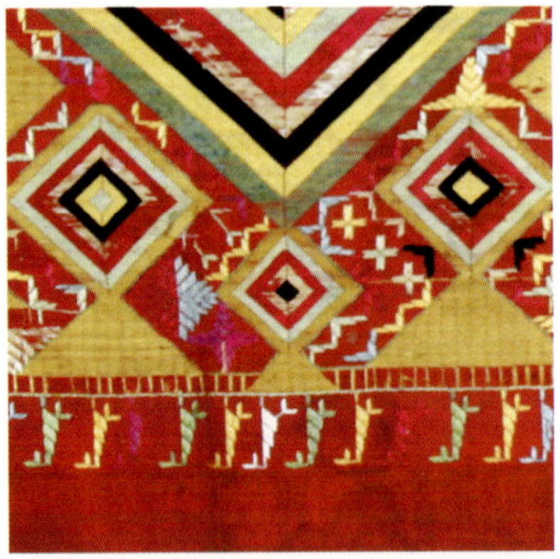

Sar-pallu

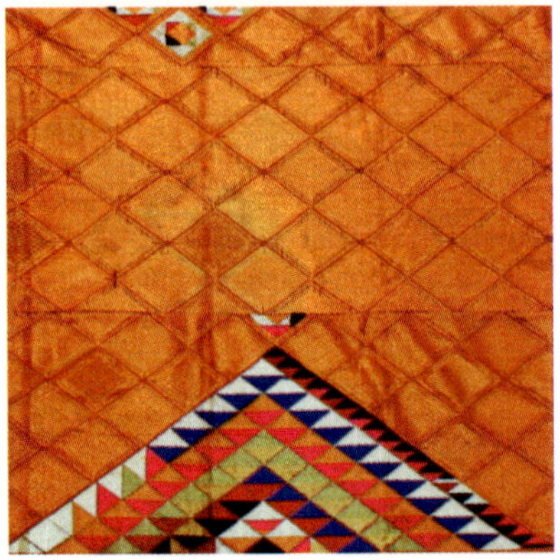

Ghungat Bagh

Chhope is pride of the grandmother or the mother of the bride. An auspicious date and time is worked out to start the embroidery. The courtyard is cleaned, *durries* (floor mats) are spread, relatives and close friends gather together for the ritual. With a prayer on her lips, the young bride distributes *gur* (jaggery) and ties *kalava* (sacred thread) on everyone's wrist. *Sohag* songs are sung by the ladies. A chhope is thus born in an atmosphere of love, goodwill and friendship with the grandmother's blessings. Later, with tender care and ardent faith, it grows into a lovely and magnificent shawl.

5. *Suber* is a phulkari and is made on red khaddar with yellow thread. It has fine floral motifs in each corner; rest of the field is left plain. It is considered an auspicious phulkari and is worn by the bride at the time of *pheras*, a sacred marriage ritual observed by the Hindus and the Sikhs.

6. *Til Patra* means sprinkled sesame seeds. These phulkaris are made on inferior quail of khaddar and are very sparsely embroidered. They are for domestic use and are given away at the time of marriage to the servants. Many a times these are made by hired labours.

7. *Chhamas* or *Shishedar* phulkaris are embroidered all over with small circular dull pieces of glass on red or dark brown ground with yellow yarn, giving a lot of depth and ornamental look to the embroidery. This type of phulkari is very popular in Rohtak, Hissar, Gurgaon and Delhi.

8. *Thirma* is a shawl embroidered on white base. It could be either a bagh or a phulkari. There is a good collection of thirma in the National Museum, New Delhi. Mainly done with dark maroon color, thirma was an essential part of a girl's trousseau.

9. *Nilak* is another attractive phulkari, popular among both Muslim and Hindu women. It is embroidered on a navy blue or black coloured khaddar with yellow and red threads. Khaddar is mostly dyed at home with indigo mixed with a little iron to give it a black colour. Nilak phulkaris are not worn during marriage ceremonies, but are used during other festive occasions.

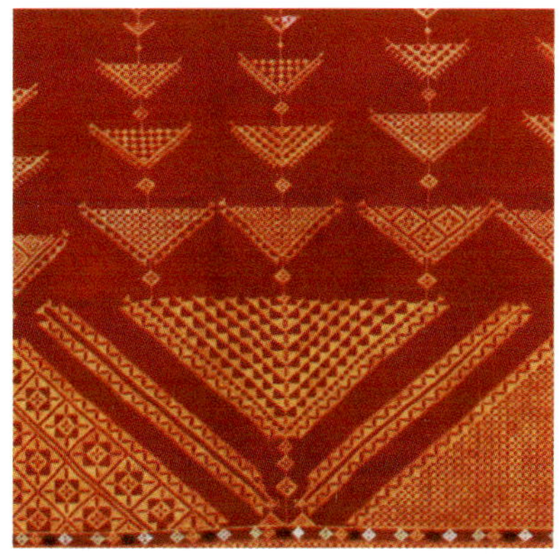

Chhope

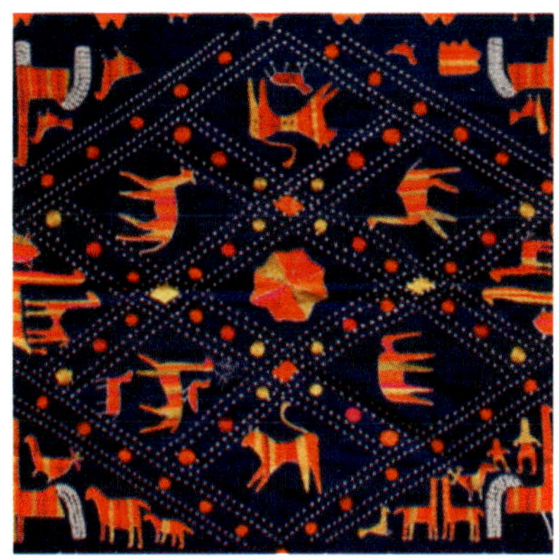

Sainchi Phulkaris

10. *Sainchi Phulkaris* are very popular in Bhatinda and Faridkot districts, and are embroidered with scenes from day-to-day life. The designs are first drawn and traced with ink on the cloth and then embroidered with simple darn stitch and satin stitch. The designs are imaginary and express the creativity of women embroiderers.

    Sainchi phulkari is embroidered with birds, animals and village scenes such as women churning curd, spinning, grinding; a man ploughing, wrestling, Shraman Kumar carrying his parents in baskets on his shoulders etc. Other depictions include scenes as varied as a man lying on a cot, women in conversation, quarrelling, man and woman wearing western clothes, man holding a stick, swordsman sitting on a chair attended by a woman who is holding a fan, men playing *chaupar* (dice game), a trainer with a lion and a stick, woman visiting a *sadhu*, train with black engine and several compartments, solders catching a thief, kitchen accessories like *belan*, utensils, half-filled *matka* (pitcher), vegetables like brinjal, pumpkins, chilies, etc. Things of daily use such as comb, mirror, toys, rattles, besides items of jewellery like *karna phool* (ear rings), *kangan* (bangles), *jhumka* (danglers), bracelets, *nath* (nose ring), *tika* (forehead ornament), etc., are embroidered with great love and care. All the jewellery items are embroidered with golden thread, but never in silver. In some phulkaris, lotus flower is embroidered in the centre symbolizing the manifestation of the universe. It is surrounded by birds and animals like elephant, cow, buffalo, deer, camel, horse, goat, donkey, pig, snake, frog, tortoise, fish, mouse, scorpion, cat, squirrel, pigeon and sparrow.

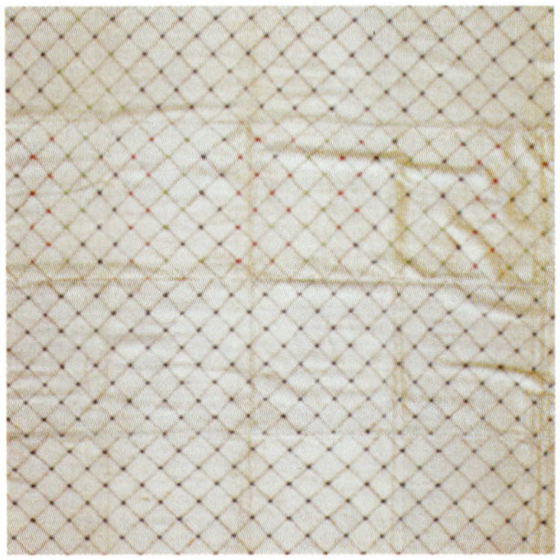

Reshmi Sheesh Bagh

11. *Reshmi Sheesh Bagh* is embroidered with very fine and delicate work but only with white coloured silk threads which makes it look like a mirror.

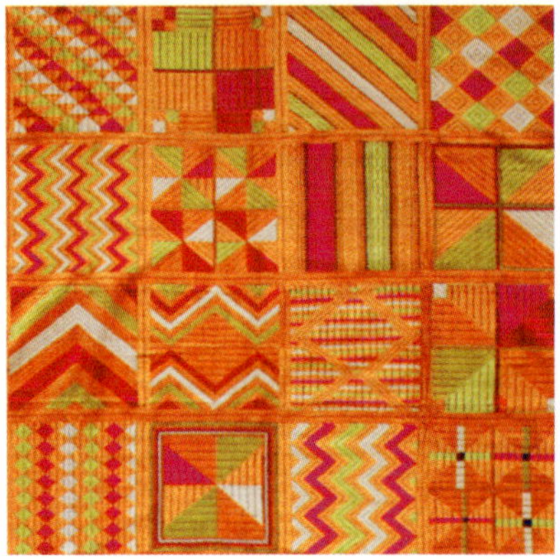

Bawan Bagh

12. *Bawan Bagh* is mostly embroidered with fifty-two designs. The field is divided in to forty-two to fifty-two square and rectangular enclosures, each with different design. The designs on *pallus* and border are different from each other. Embroidery is done with colourful threads. At times, there are only forty-two to forty-nine enclosures depicting different designs, but are still called bawan bagh.

13. *Darshan Dwar* are baghs embroidered on red khaddar made for offerings in the temples and religious places after one's wish is fulfilled. These baghs are embroidered with architectural designs with gates on both the outer panels with their bases facing each other. The central longitudinal panel is mostly

embroidered with human figures, birds, animals, flowers and plants; giving the impression of passing through a crowded street. The gates have pointed tops. The number of gates depends on the size and space on the field. Usually four to seven gates are embroidered inspired by arched verandahs of the temples.

14. There are baghs, which are distinguished by the colours for e.g. *panchranga* bagh, embroidered with five colours; *satranga* bagh, embroidered with seven colours; *dhoop chhaon* bagh, light and shade designs embroidered with shining shades of yellow and white coloured threads; and *patedar* bagh, embroidered with stripped designs.

15. *Lahriya Bagh* embroidered with patterns depicting waves; and *darya* bagh embroidered with designs depicting waves of river, are inspired by rivers and running water.

16. Some designs are named after vegetables for e.g. *karela* bagh (bitter gourd); *dhaniya* bagh(coriander leaves); *mirchi* bagh(green or red pepper); *kakri* bagh (cucumber); *gobhi* bagh(cauliflower) etc.

17. *Shalimar*, *Charbagh*, *Chamasia Bagh* are designed after well-known Mughal gardens.

18. *Ikka* designs are like ace of diamonds, inspired by playing cards.

19. *Chand Bagh* is a round floral design depicting the moon.

20. *Patanga Bagh* depicts kites embroidered all over the field.

21. *Saru Bagh* is designed like a cypress tree.

22. *Belan Bagh* is a design inspired by the roller which is used in the kitchen to roll *chapattis* (bread).

23. There are phulkaris and bagh that are inspired by flowers such as *surajmukhi* bagh, embroidered with numerous sunflowers with bright yellow colour which gives the cloth a brilliant effect; *genda* bagh are designed like marigold flowers and *chameli* bagh which is embroidered with jasmine flowers all over the field.

Krishna Lal

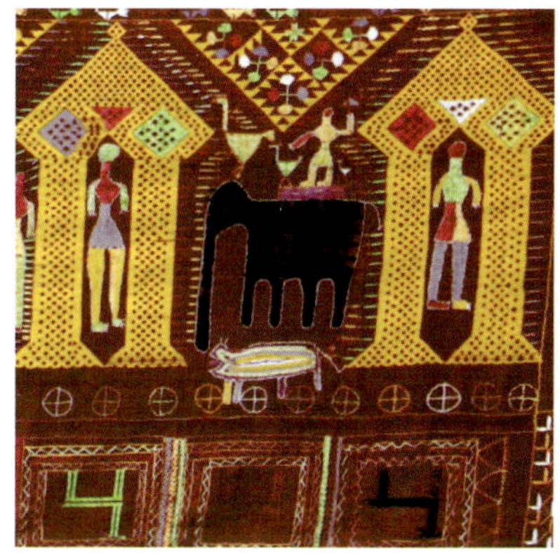

Darshan Dwar

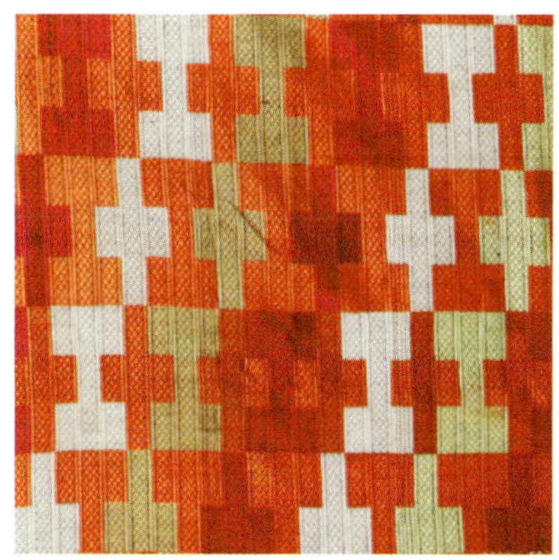

Belan Bagh

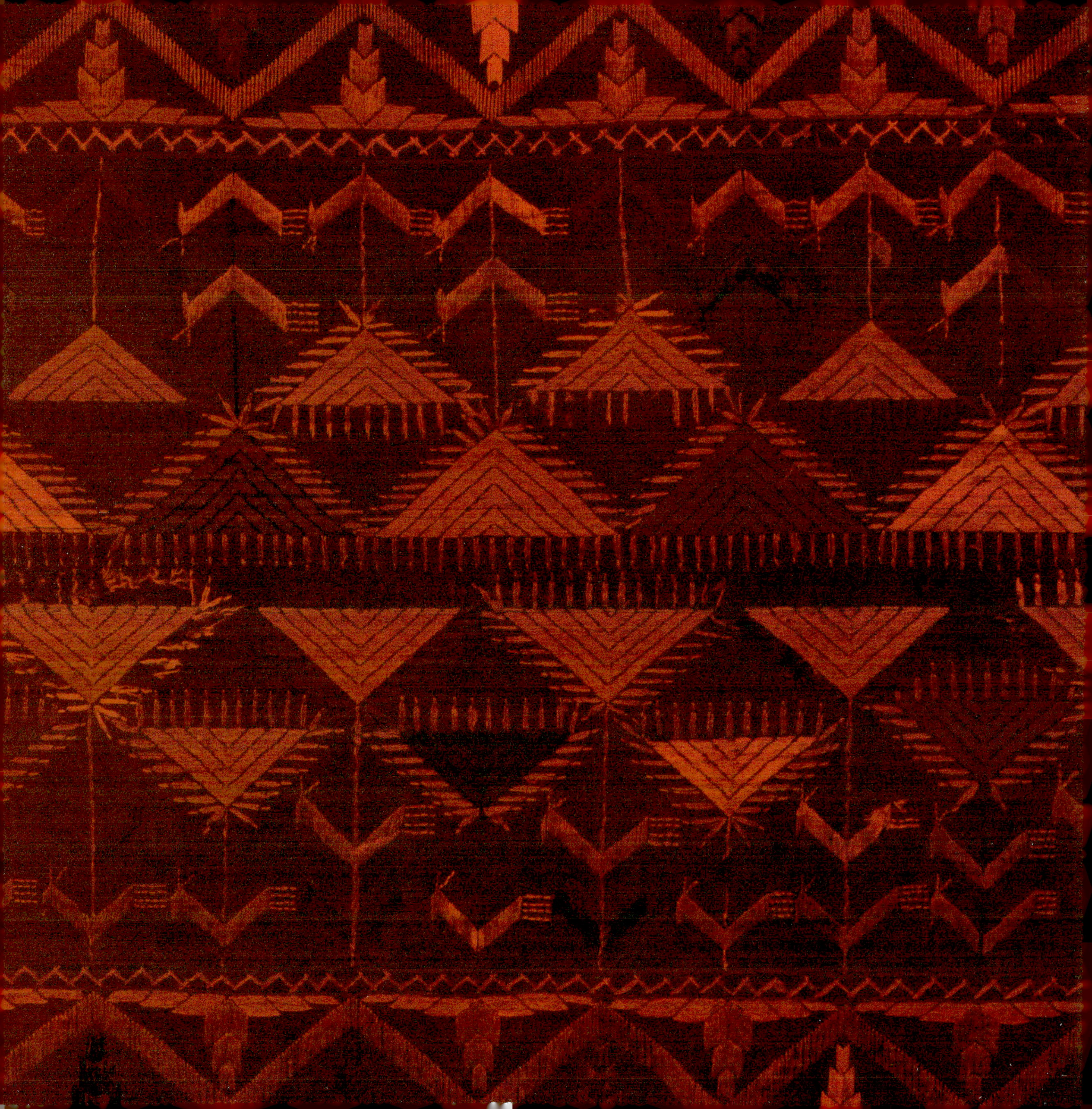

Phulkari

फुलकारी

from the realm of women's creativity

Selected Pieces from the Archives of IGNCA

PHULKARI

Acc. No: 99 .1.PH-1

Phulkari embroidered in squares, each square has eight petals. Stylized floral design and geometrical patterns are depicted on four sides of the border. The *pallu* has a double border.

Early 20th Century; Haryana

Size: L: 235 cm X W: 140 cm

Base fabric: Maroon *khaddar* (hand spun and hand woven coarse cotton cloth).

Light green, orange and magenta silk threads are used in the embroidery.

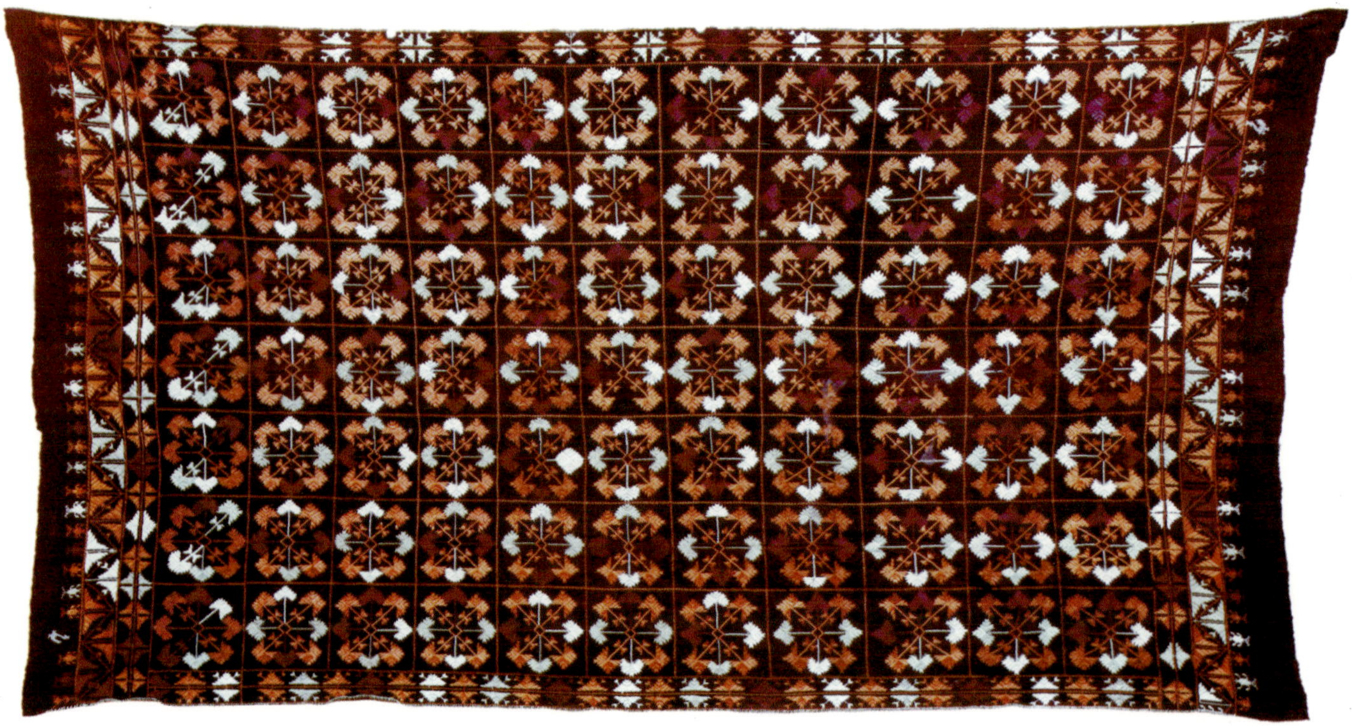

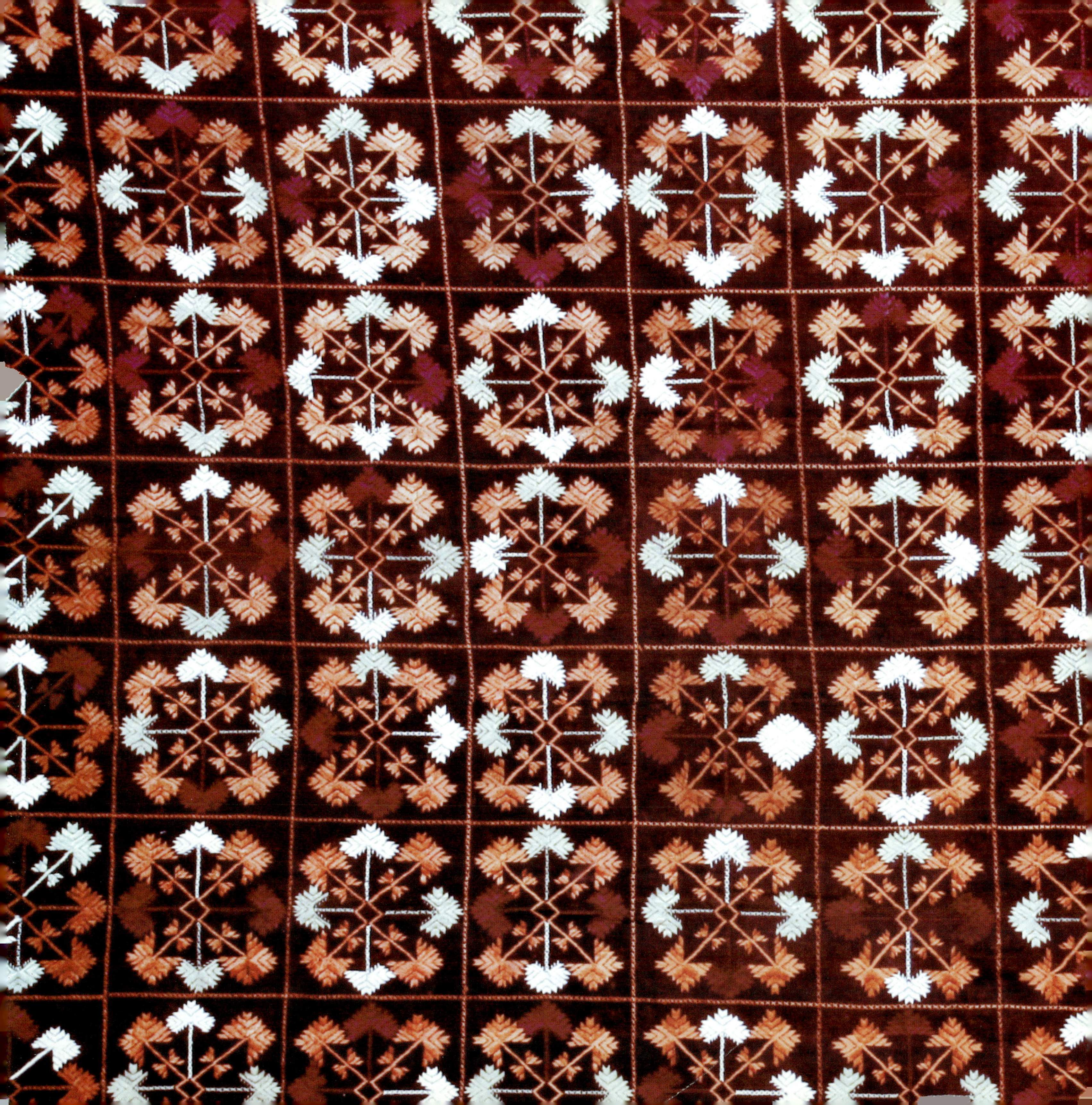

SAINCHI PHULKARI

Acc. No: 99.1.PH-2

Sainchi phulkari, depicting village life surrounded by flora and fauna. The *pallus* on both the sides are embroidered with birds depicting tree of life. The two borders are in multicoloured diamond shaped motifs on yellow embroidered base. Entire field has both small and large birds, human figures, wheat, *nath, kundal* (nose and ear ornaments), triangles and floral pattern.

Late 20th Century; Haryana

Size: L: 241 cm x W: 143 cm

Base fabric: Maroon khaddar.

Yellow, red, green, blue and purple silk threads are used in the embroidery.

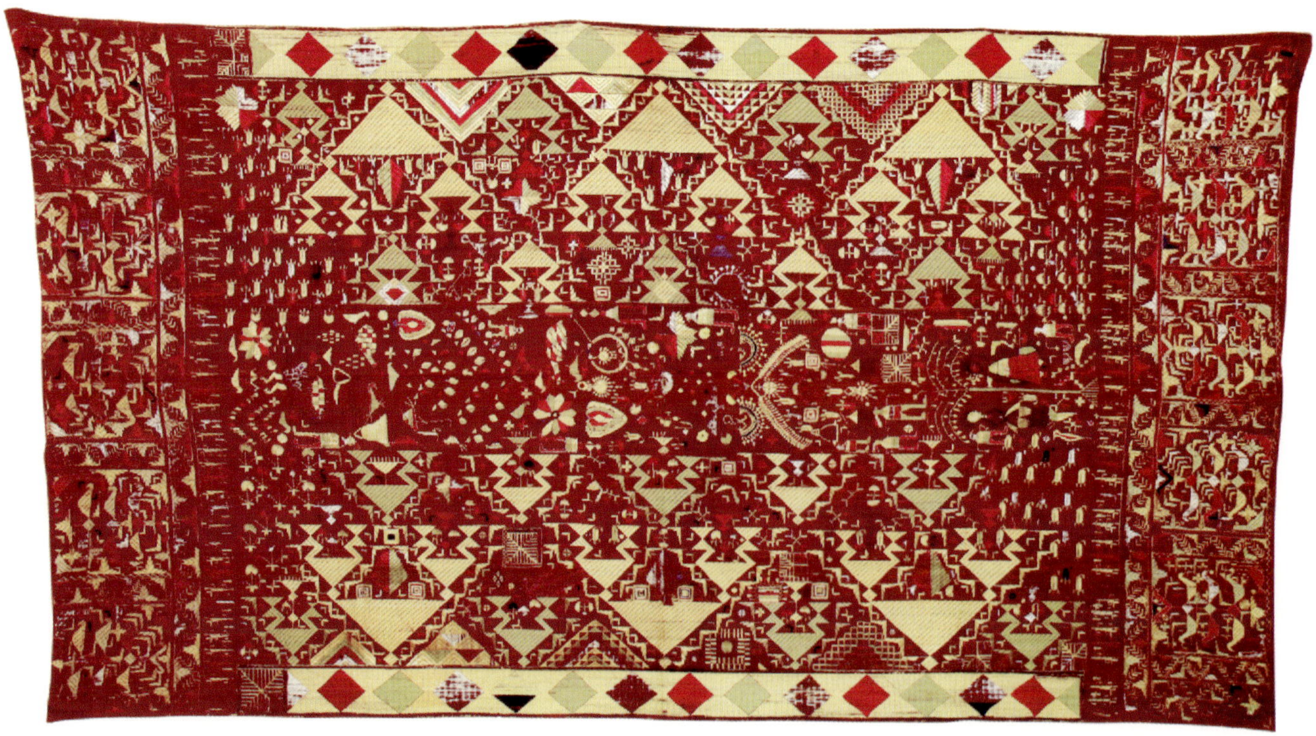

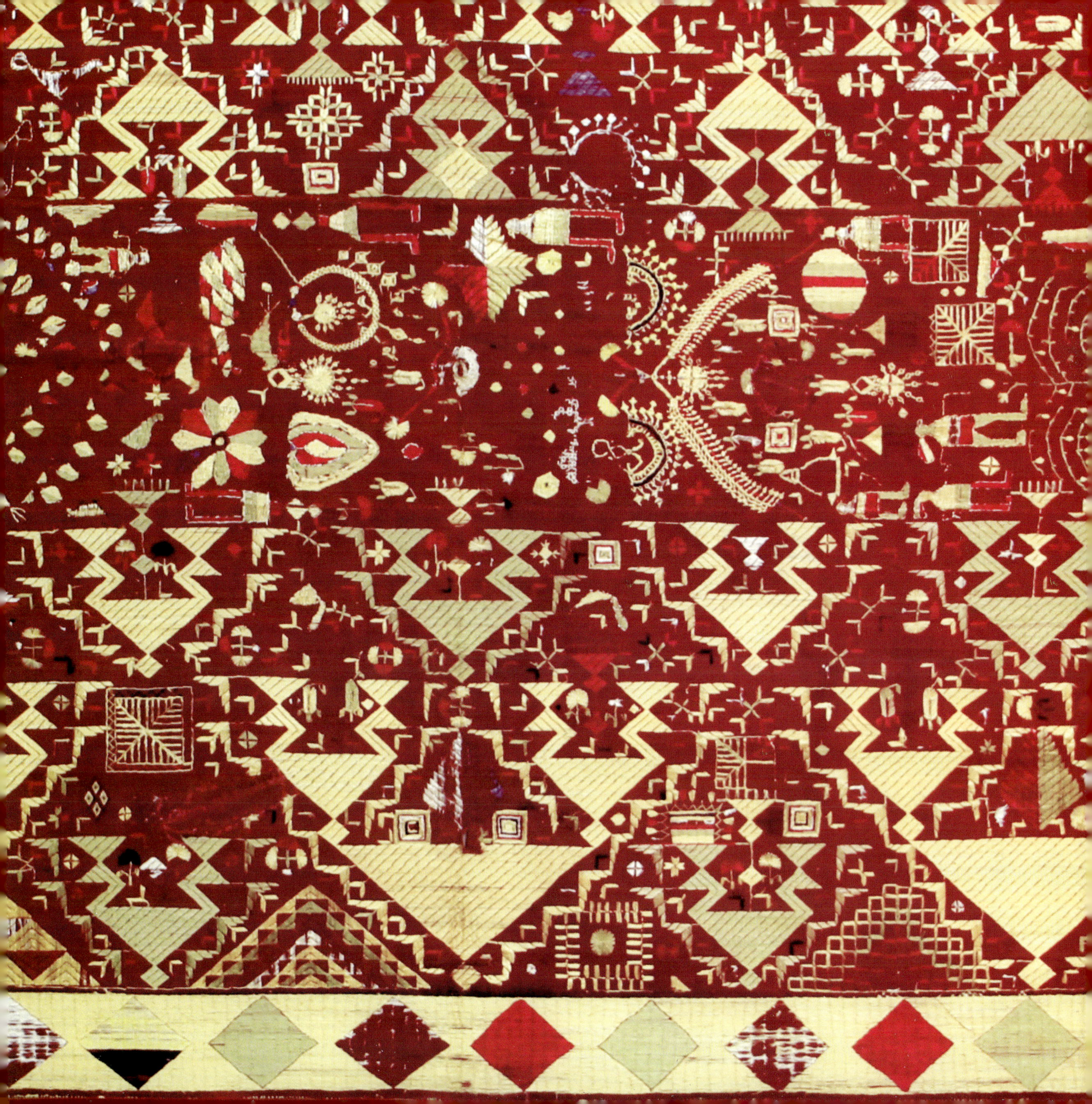

PHULKARI

Acc. No: 99.1.PH-3

Phulkari with two *pallus* and borders in multicoloured diamond patterns in Bagh style. The entire field is covered with *jaal* (lattice work) in diamond shape, each with four-petalled flower.

Late 20th Century; Punjab

Size: L: 214 cm x W: 127 cm

Base fabric: Maroon khaddar.

Yellow, light green, red, purple silk threads are used in the embroidery.

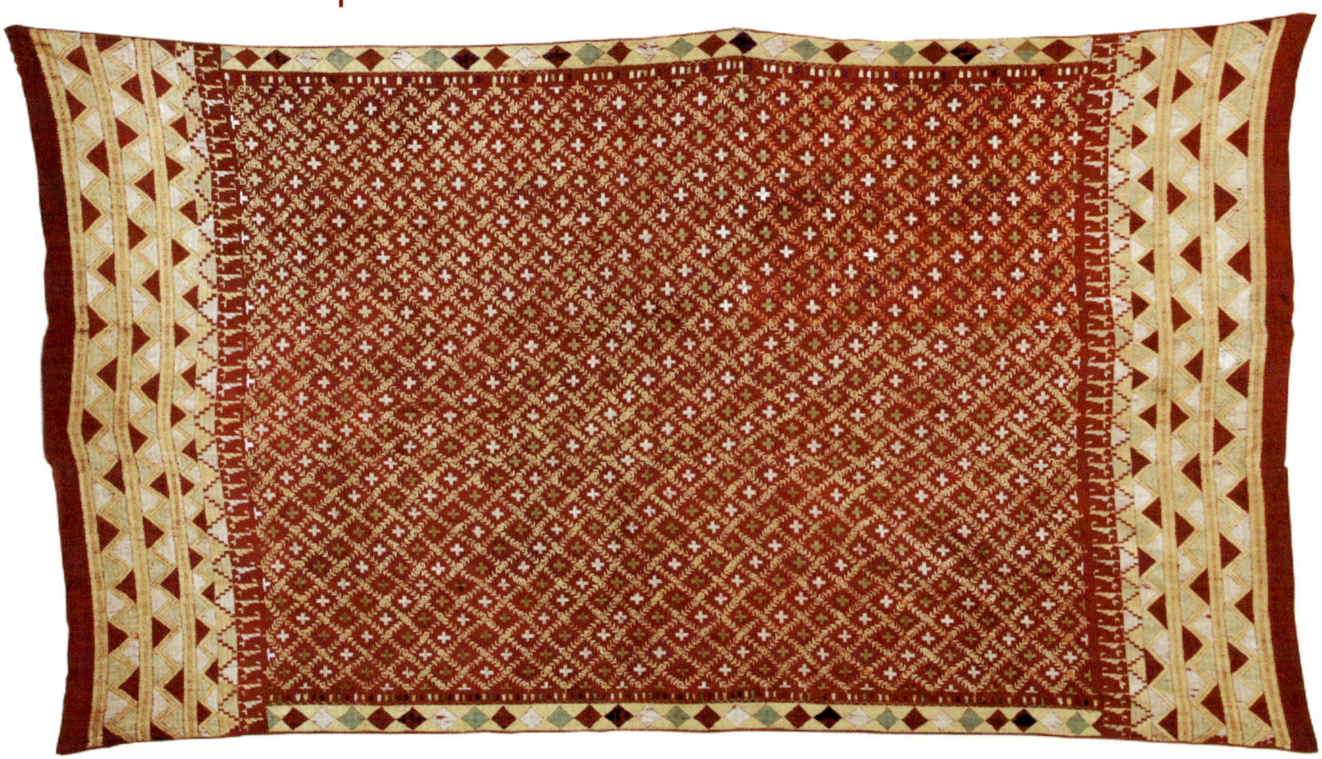

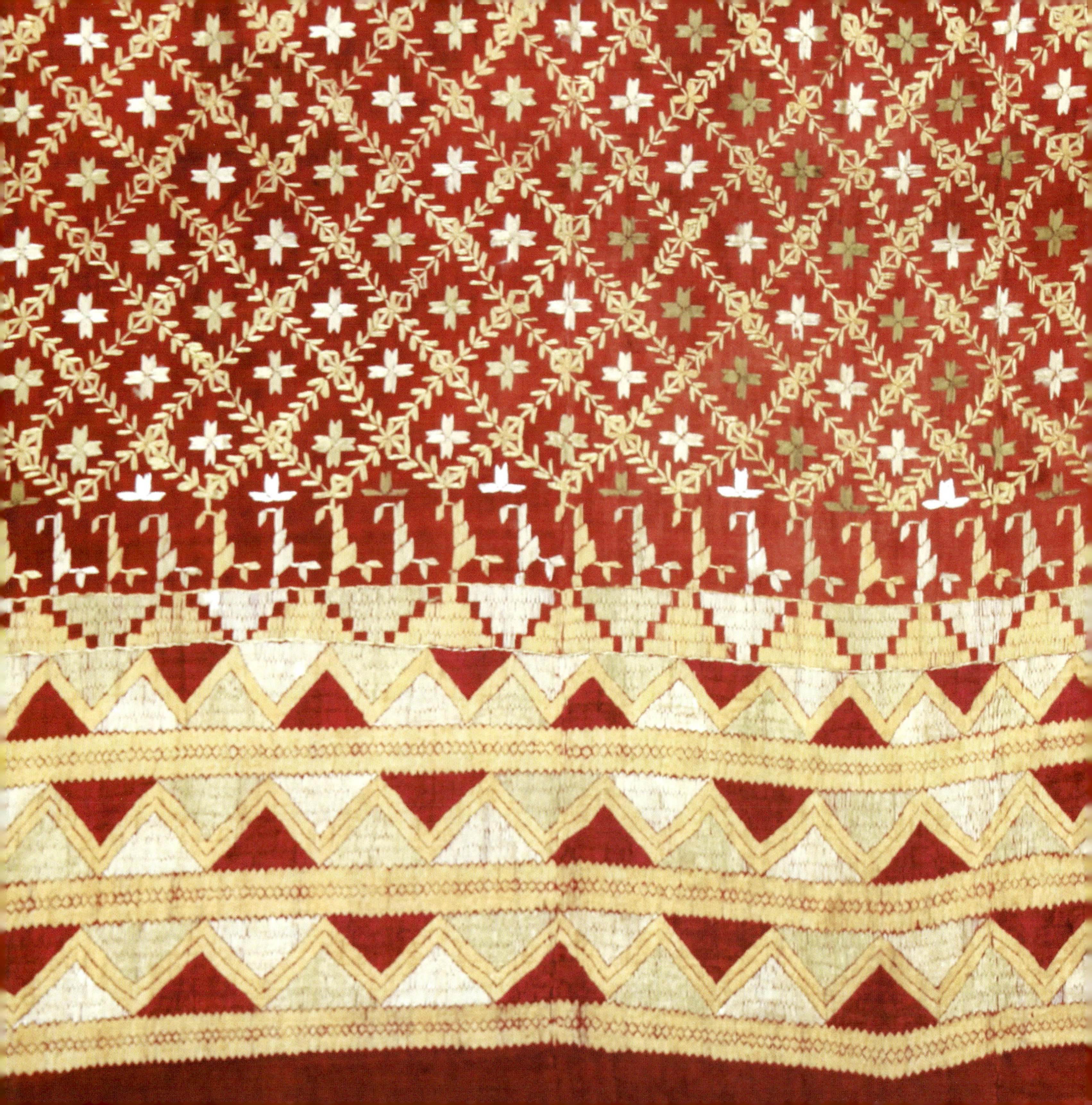

PHULKARI

Acc. No: 99.1.PH-4

Phulkari with two borders embroidered in floral-cum-geometrical pattern. The entire field is covered with stylized geometrical pattern arranged in squares.

Early 20th Century; Punjab

Size: L: 250 cm x W: 144 cm

Base fabric: Red khaddar.

Green, mustard, white and magenta silk threads are used in the embroidery.

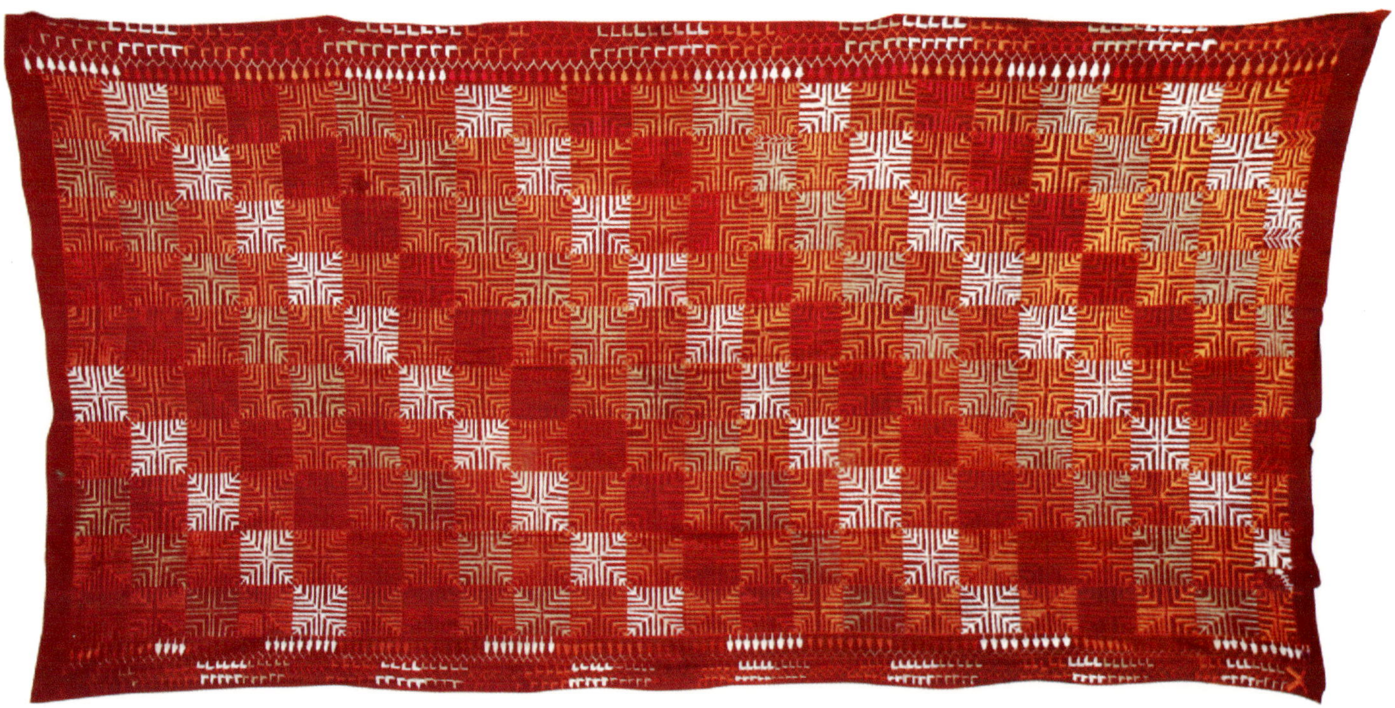

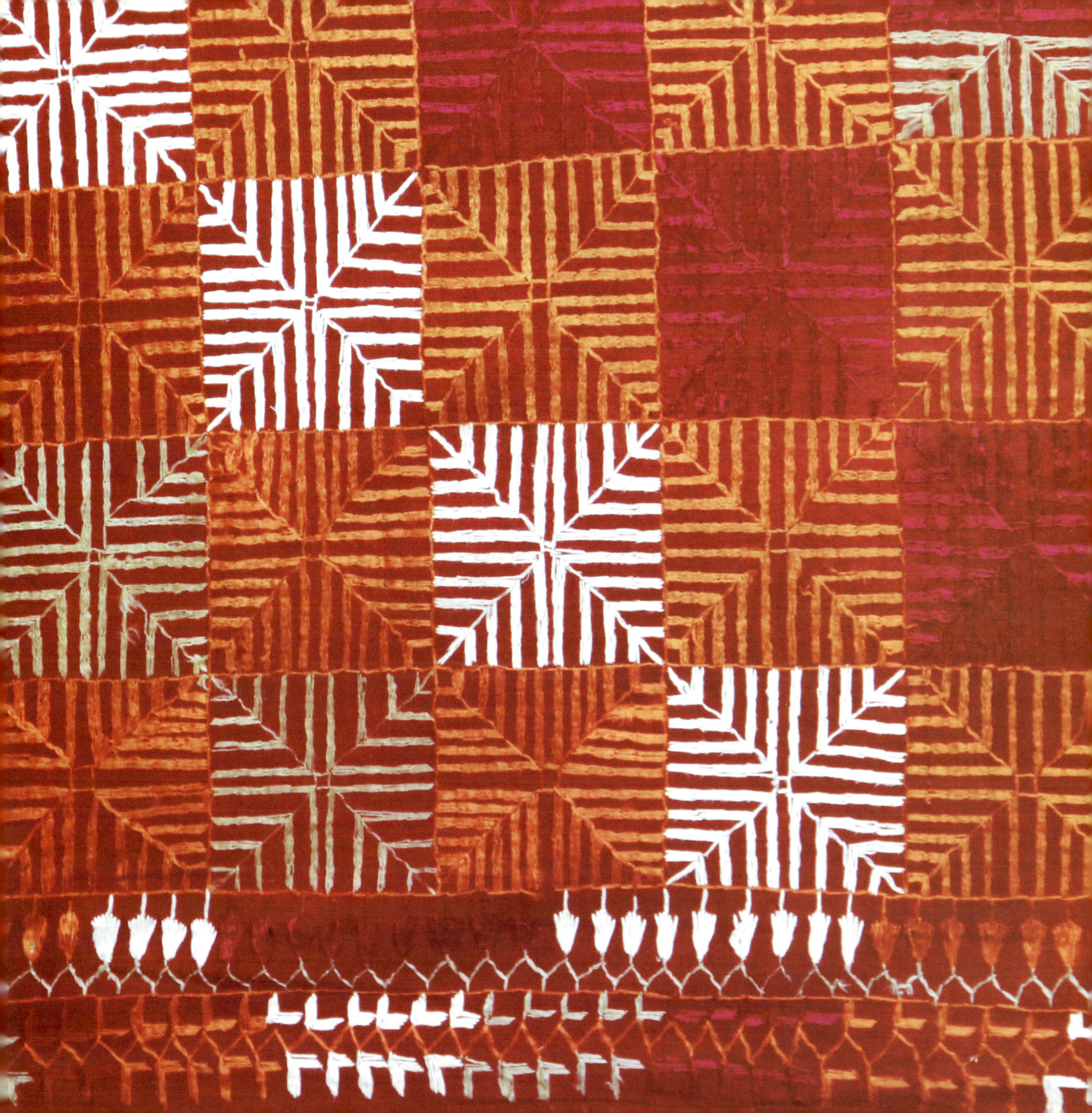

PATANGI PHULKARI

Acc. No: 99.1.PH-5

Patangi Phulkari (kite) in black colour, embroidered all over with multicoloured tasselled kites. On one *pallu,* there is floral-cum-geometrical designs arranged in large squares, with small butis (motifs) arranged in vertical lines. The other *pallu* has similar large squares in the centre with *jaal* and butis on one side and small linear motifs on the other.

Early 20th Century; Haryana

Size: L: 242 cm x W: 133 cm

Base fabric: Black khaddar.

Mustard, white, magenta, orange and green silk threads are used in the embroidery.

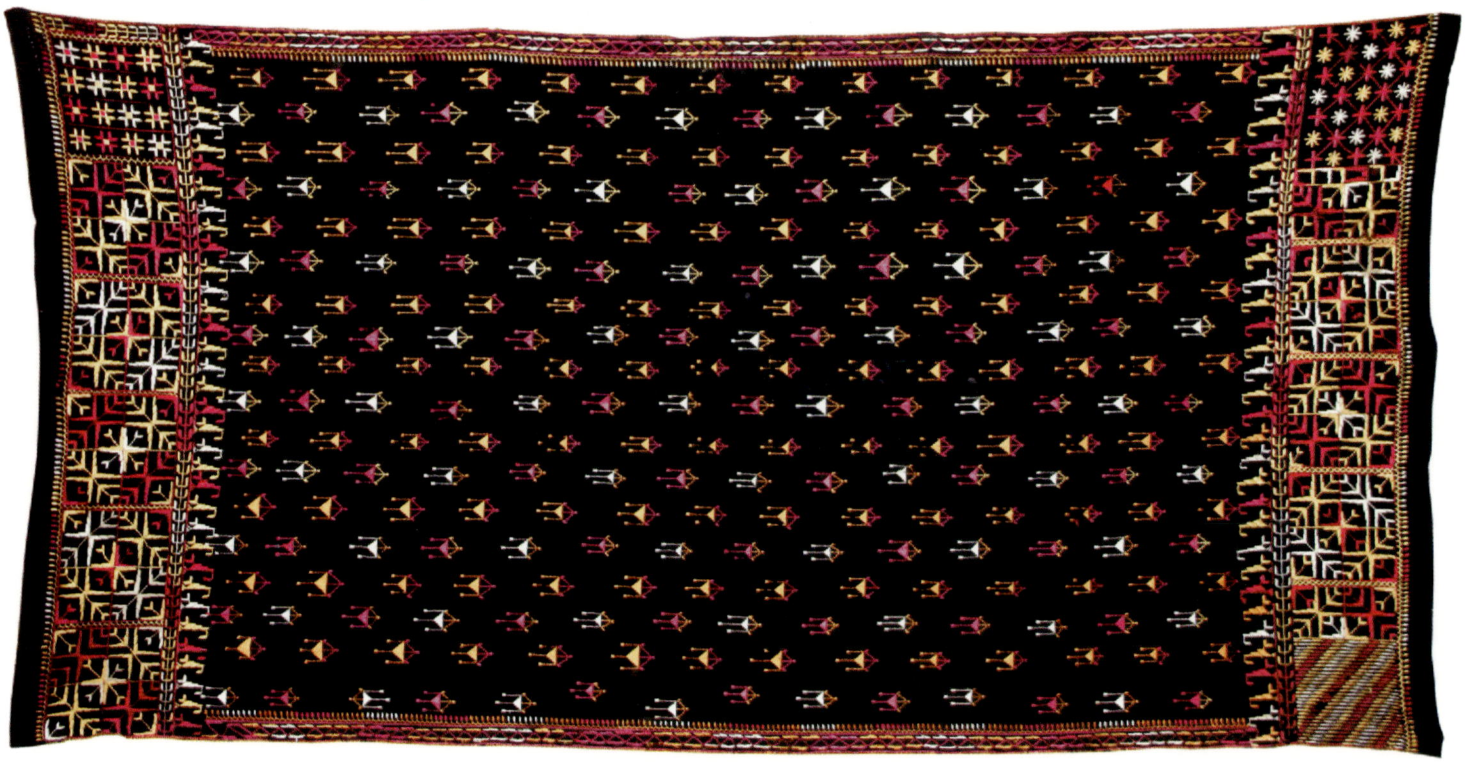

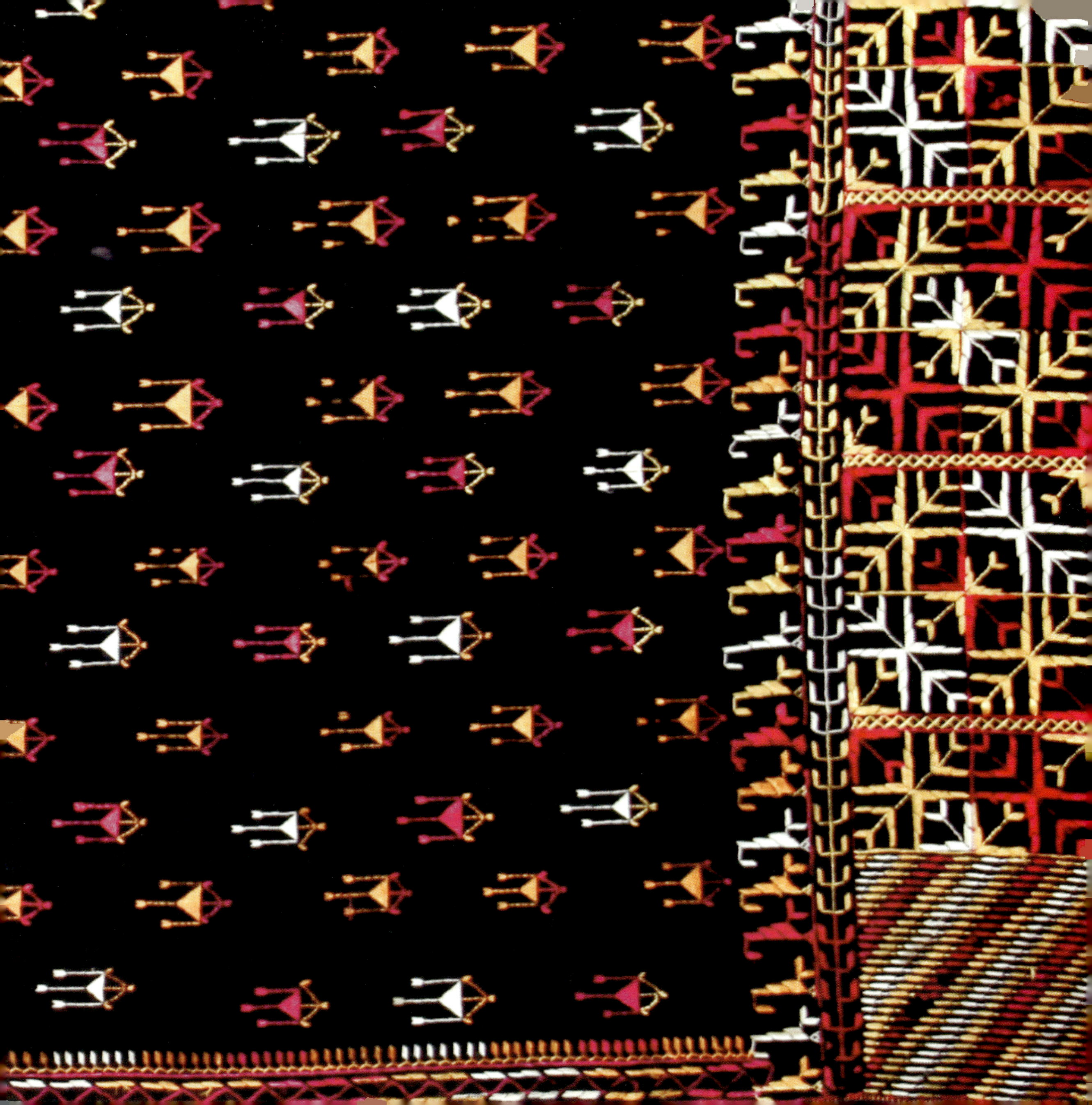

CHHOPE PHULKARI

Acc. No: 99.1.PH-6

Chhope Phulkari. Red symbolizes auspiciousness, and yellow affluence, happiness and fertility. Double side line stitch is used on both the sides signifying good luck to the bride in both the worlds (*loka and parloka*). Side borders are embroidered with triangles. Each triangle is filled with geometrical pattern. They are embroidered in a way that their base is towards the border and pointed inwards.

This particular piece is larger and wider than the other Phulkaris. Lozenges are embroidered in the double sided line stitch on the side borders. There are no *pallus* but the two ends are kept open without any border, signifying unlimited prosperity to the bride.

Late 19th Century; Haryana

Size: L: 286 cm x W: 192 cm

Base fabric: Maroon khaddar.

Yellow silk threads are used on the border with green and purple colours at different places.

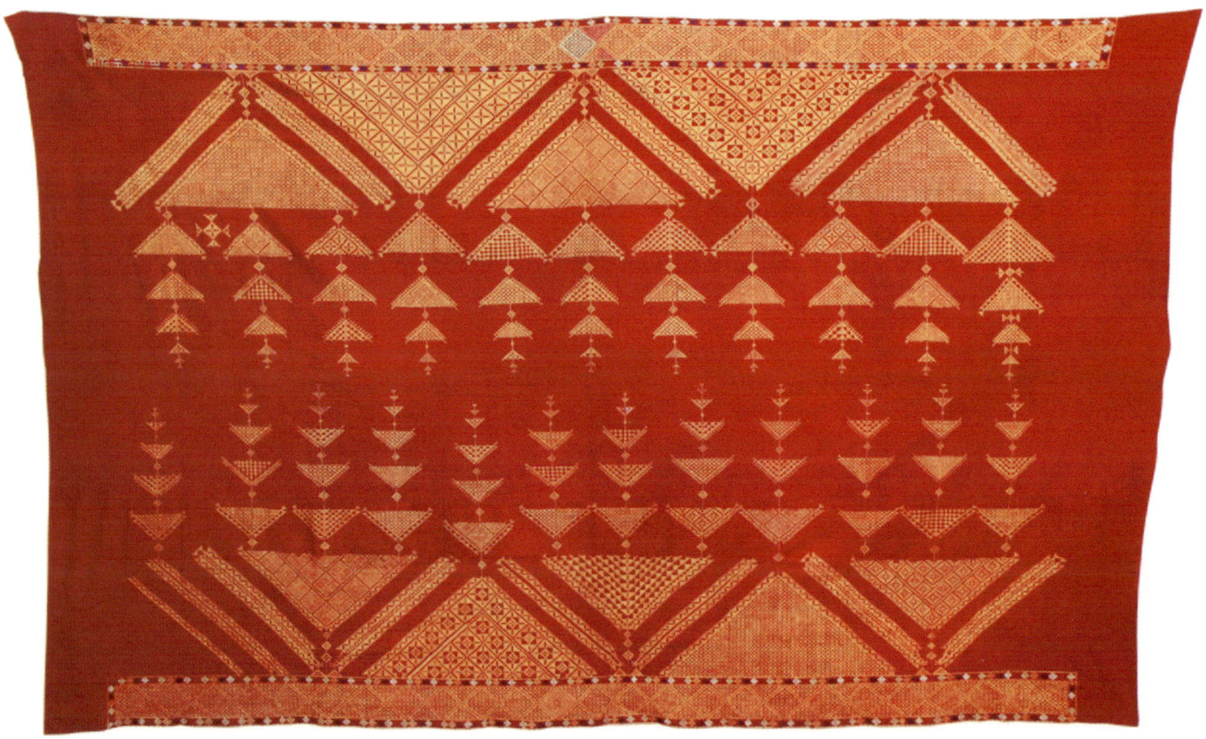

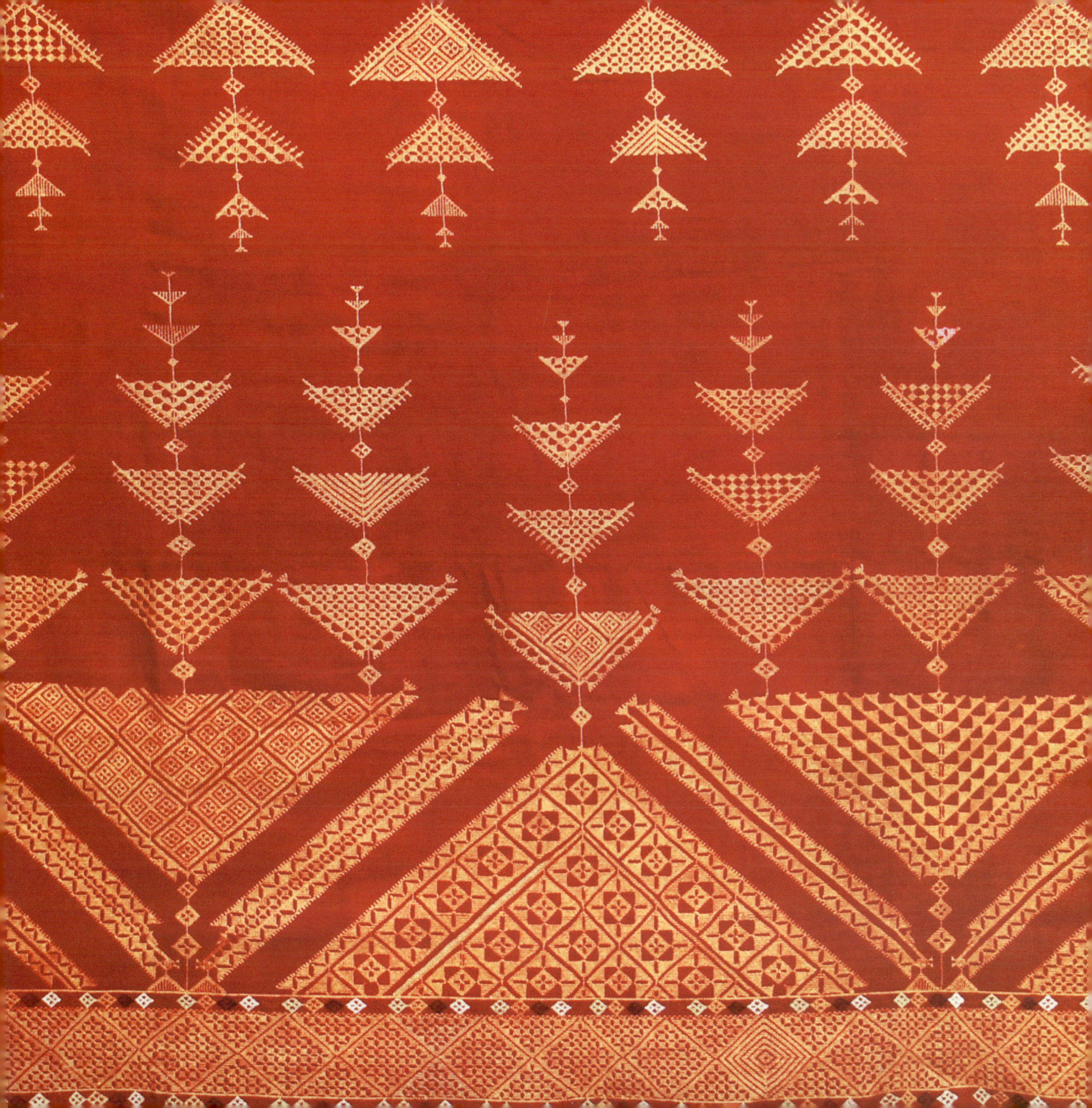

PHULKARI

Acc. No: 99.1.PH-7

Phulkari embroidered with self-coloured silk thread with very intricate zigzag pattern spread uniformly all over the field. The two *pallus* have small triangular motifs arranged in horizontal rows.

Late 20th Century; Punjab

Size: L: 218 cm x W: 143 cm

Base fabric: Maroon khaddar.

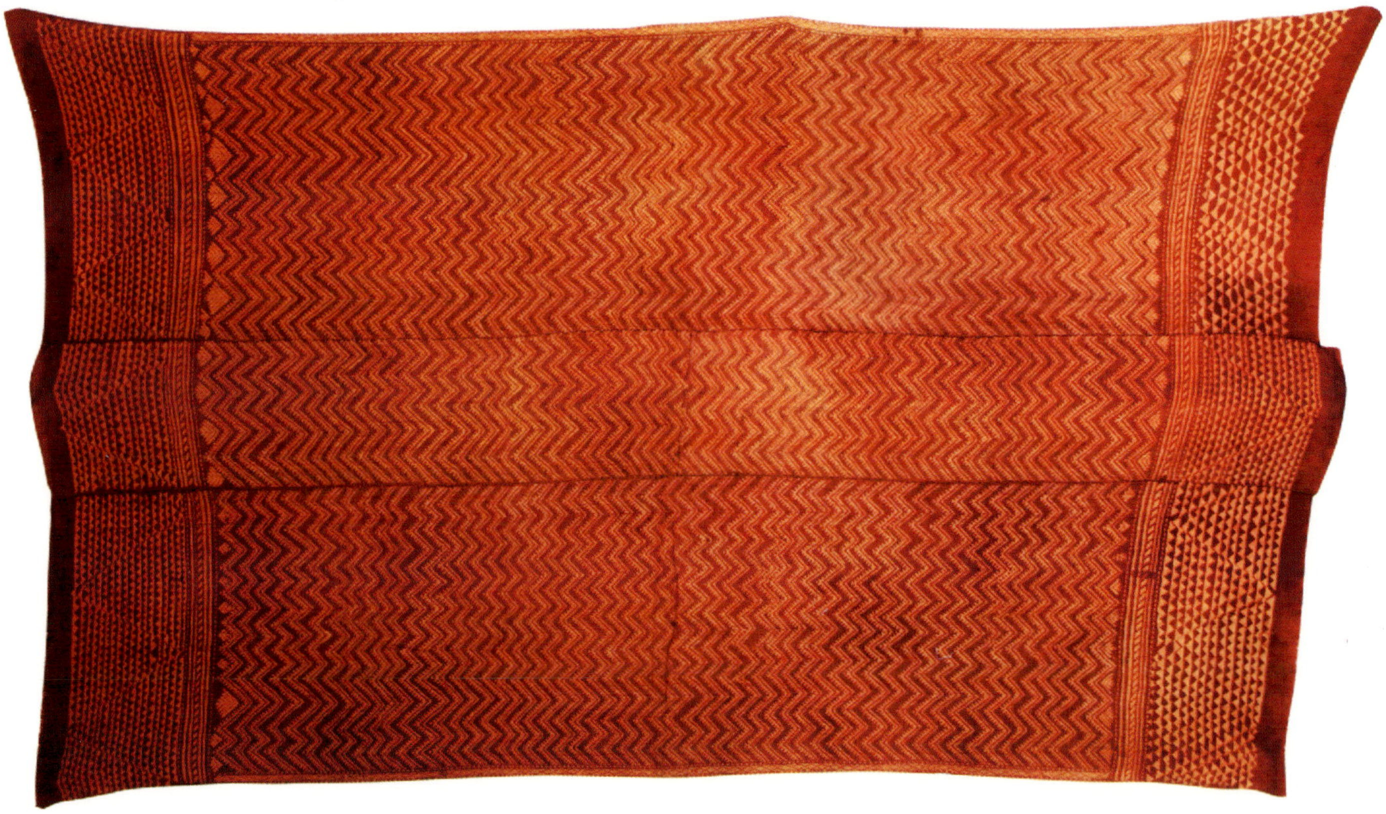

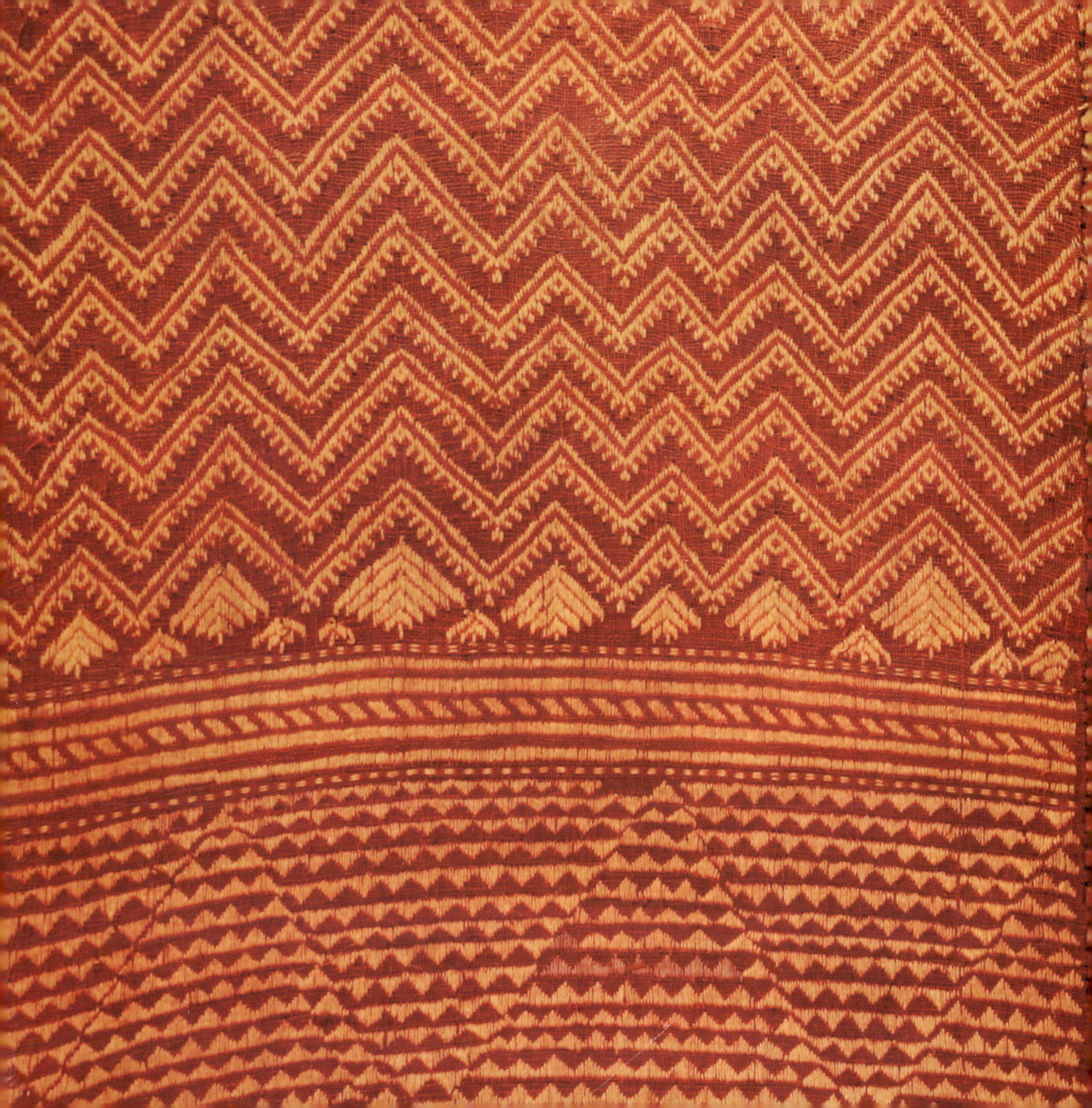

PANCHRANGI PHULKARI

Acc. No: 99.1.PH-8

Panchrangi Phulkari (five colours), with two *pallus*, embroidered in geometrical-cum-multi–coloured floral pattern. Both the *pallus* have four corners in different designs. In one corner, there are *chaar khana* (four square-like pattern), in the other corner there are four pyramids touching each other on top in zigzag pattern. On the other corner of the *pallu* architectural designs are embroidered on one side; and two lotus flowers on the other. One side of the border has small triangular motif, while the other side is embroidered with wheat motifs. The entire field is covered with small four petalled flowers spread uniformly.

Early 20th Century; Haryana

Size: L: 225 cm x W: 129 cm

Base fabric: Maroon khaddar.

White, green, mustard, red and magenta silk threads are used in the embroidery.

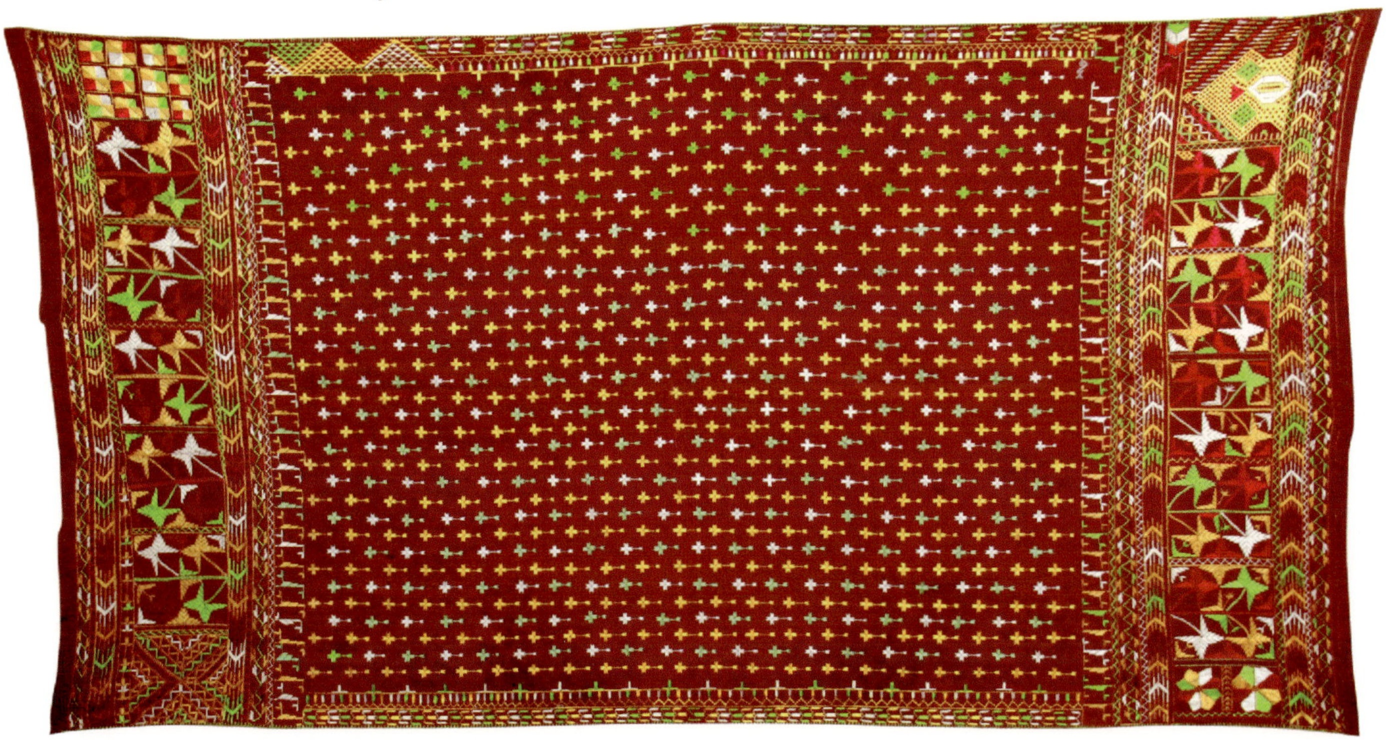

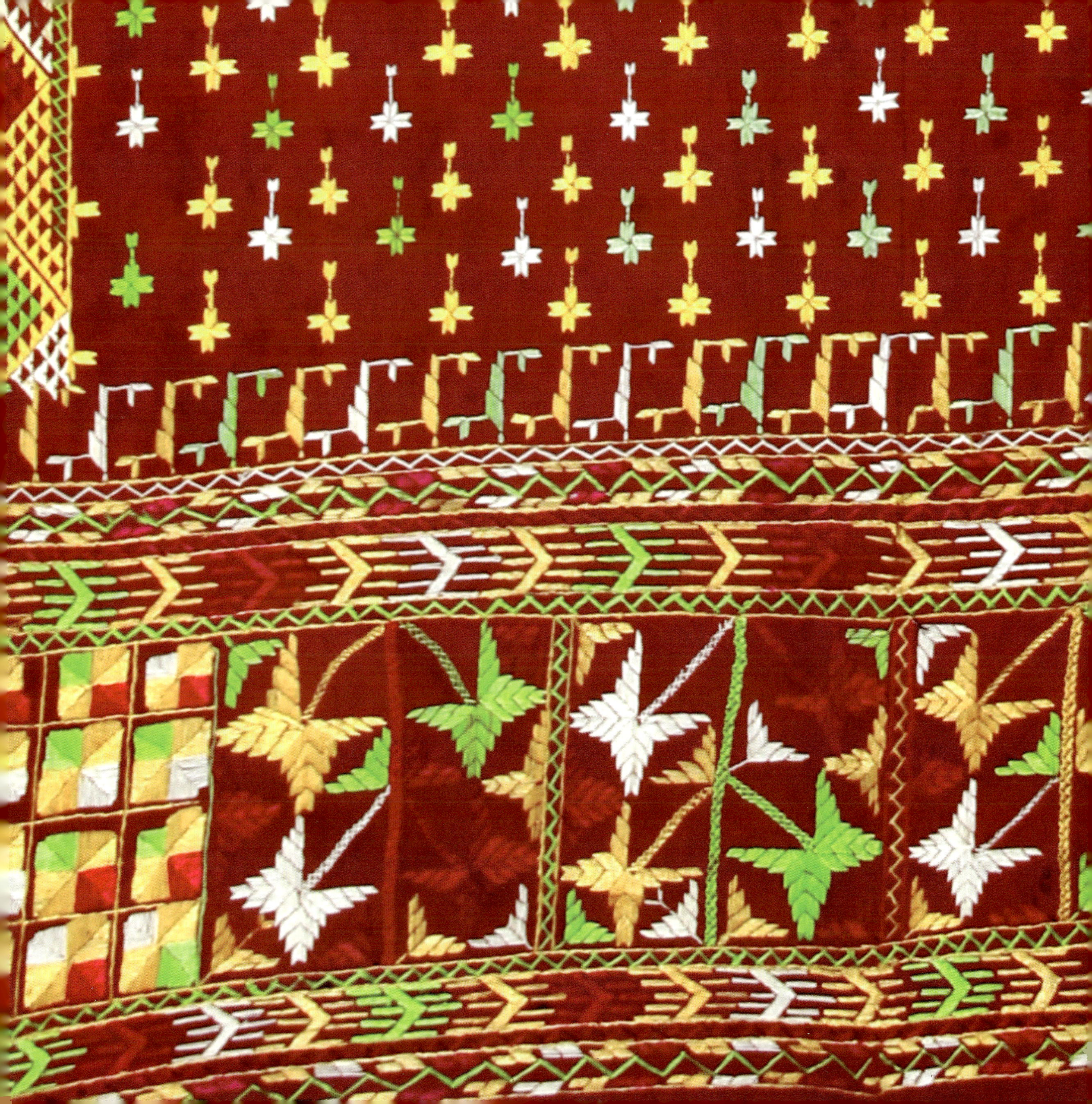

KANKI PHULKARI

Acc. No: 99.1.PH-9

Kanki Phulkari, with floral design on pallus on both the sides. The entire field is embroidered uniformly in kanka (wheat) pattern. Small peacocks are depicted along the borders of the pallus.

Late 20th Century; Haryana

Size: L: 221 cm x W: 144 cm

Base fabric: Maroon khaddar.

Green, yellow, mustard, peach, white and purple silk threads are used in the embroidery.

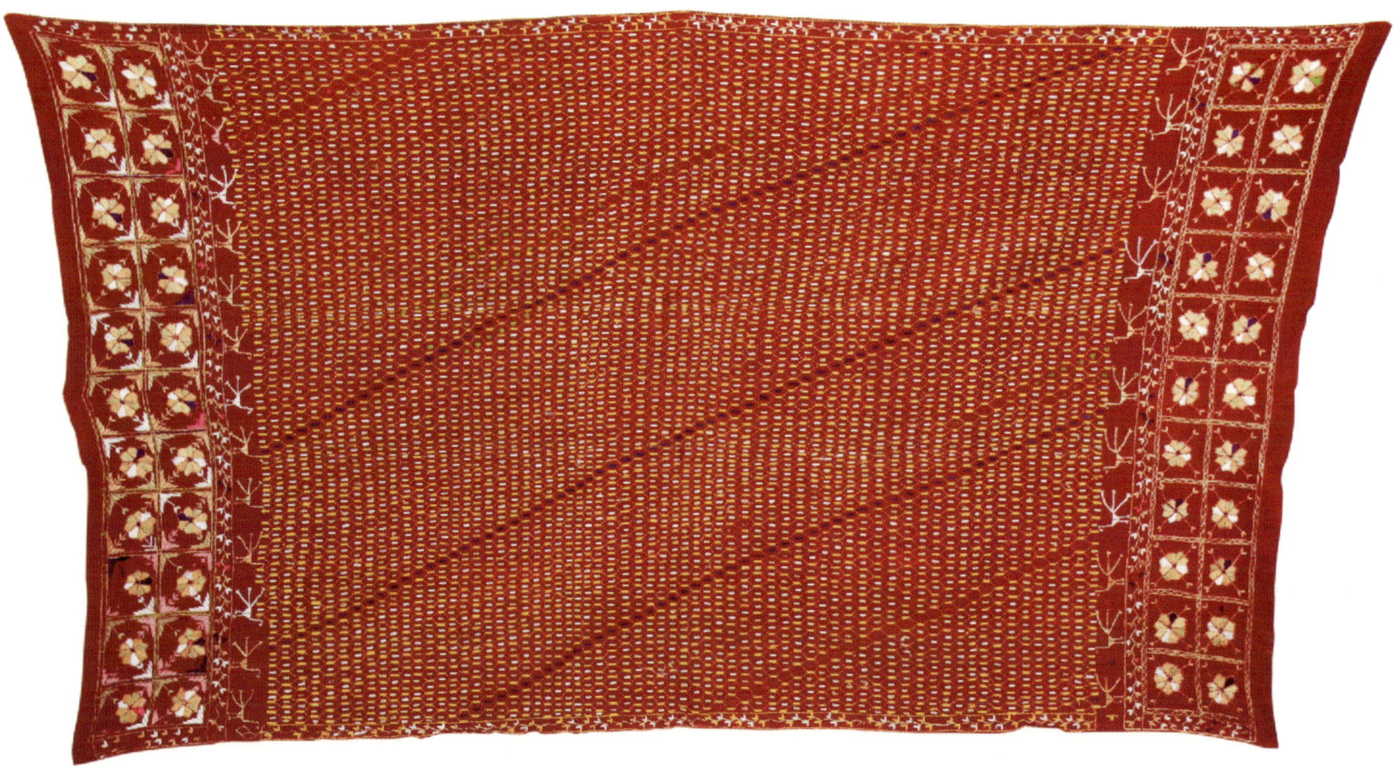

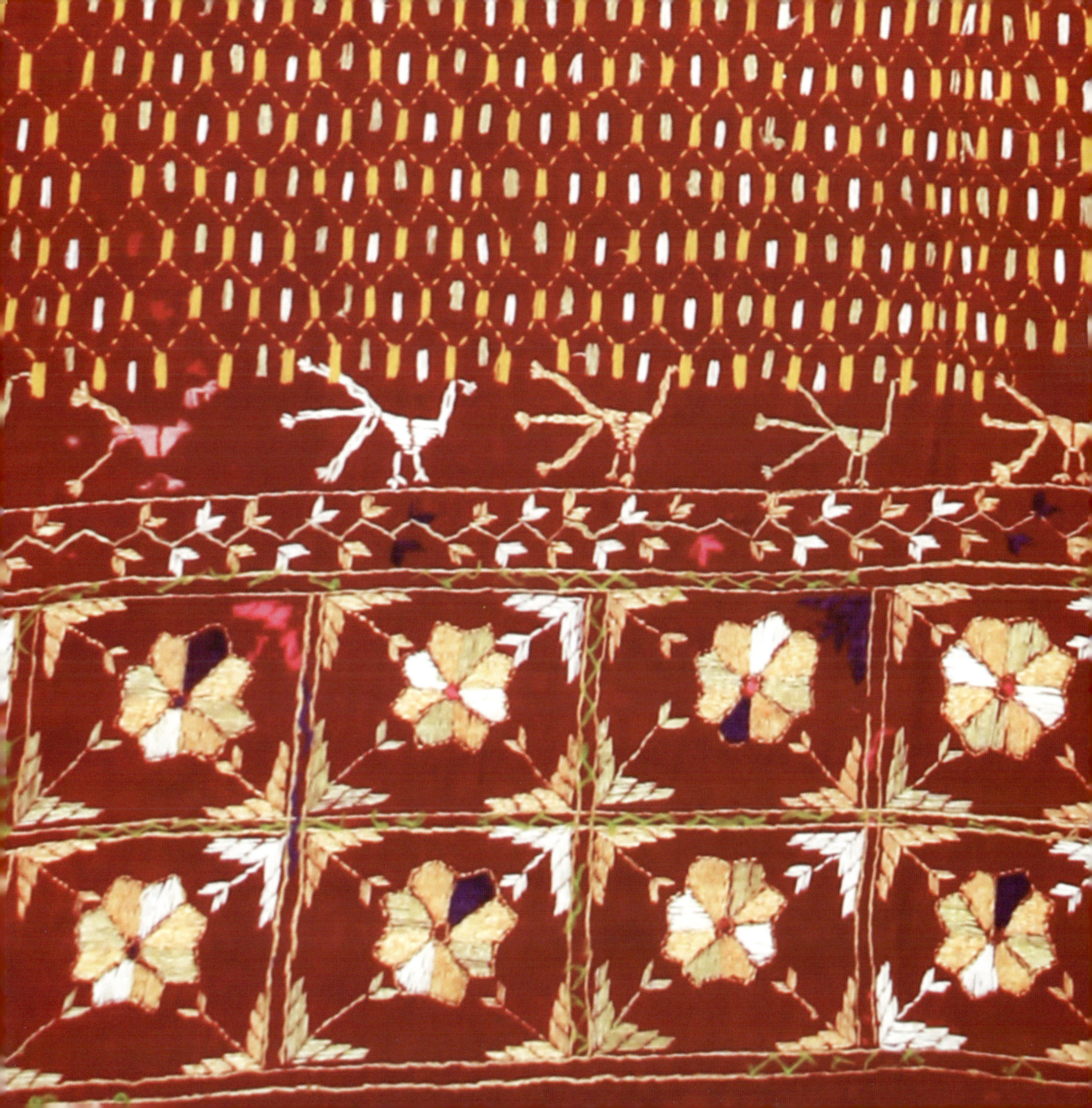

CHHOPE PHULKARI

Acc. No: 99.1.PH-10

Chhope Phulkari embroidered in triangles. Each triangle is filled with geometrical pattern embroidered in a way that their base is towards the borders and pointed inwards i.e., upwards in case of triangles on both sides and downwards on the upper side. Upper and lower points of triangles do not touch each other. The embroidery is done in double sided line stitch on both sides. (Description same as PH-6)

Late 19th Century Punjab

Size: L: 288 cm x W: 172 cm

Base fabric: Maroon khaddar.

The border is embroidered in yellow colour with green and purple silk threads at different places.

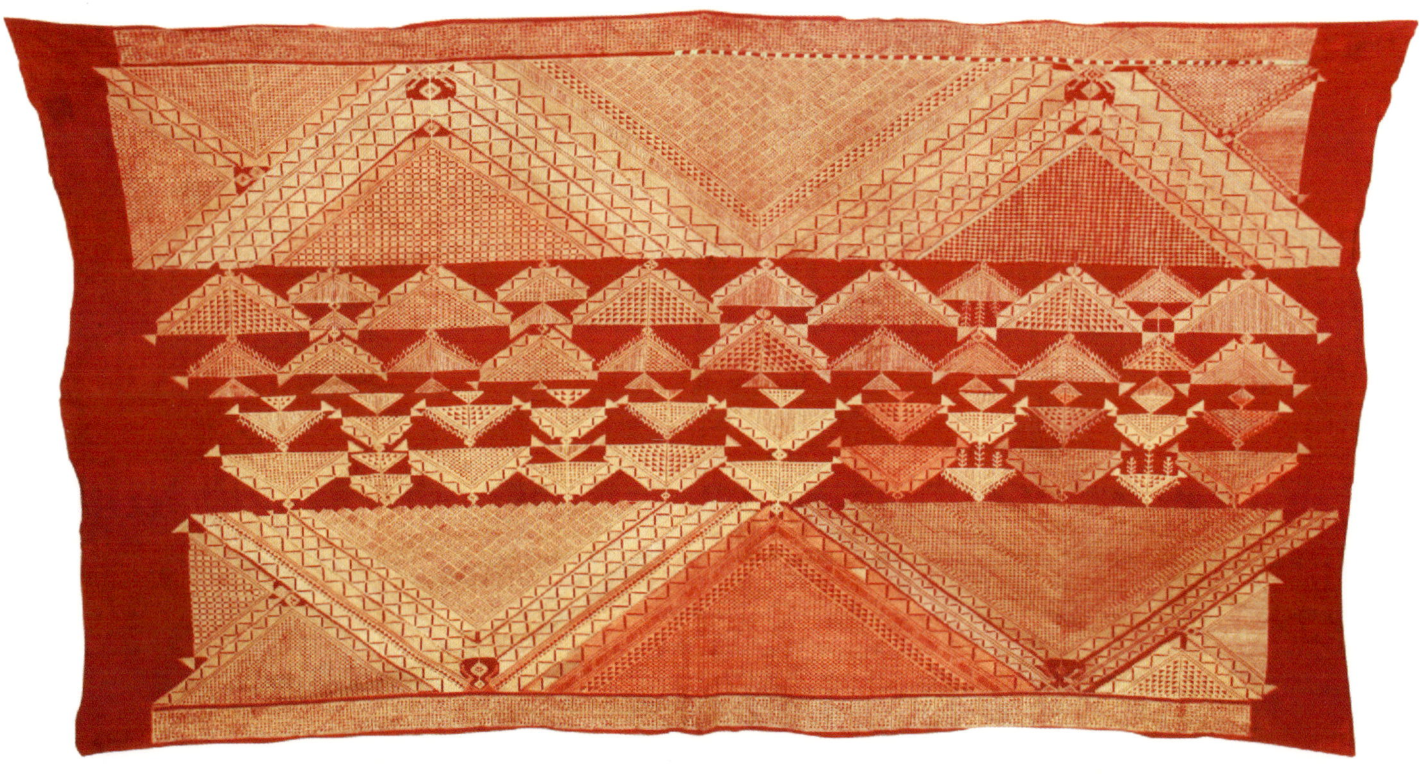

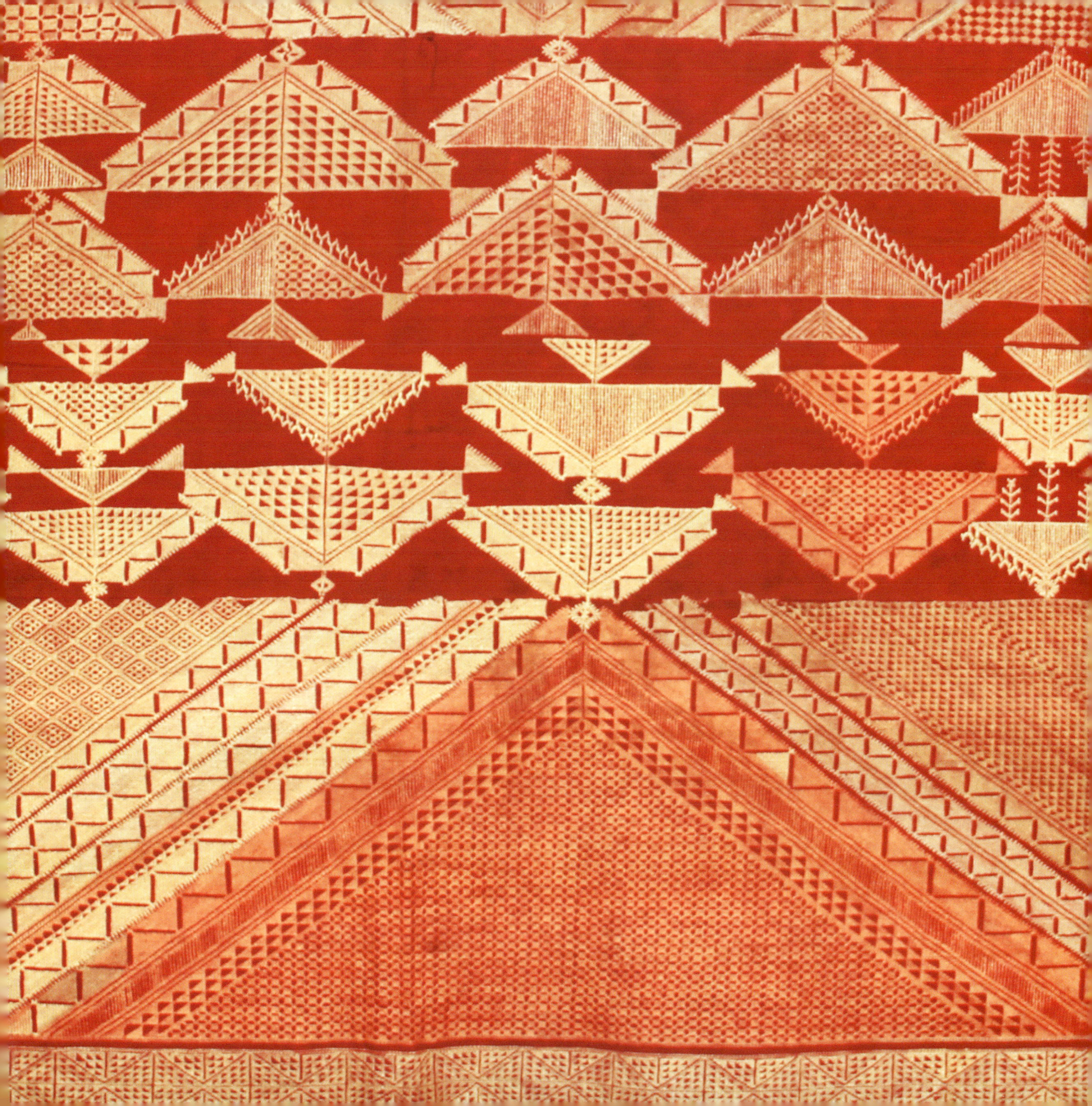

PHULKARI

Acc. No: 99.1.PH-11

Phulkari with two *pallus* embroidered with wheat and floral motifs. One pallu has three acrobats, peacocks and *jhumka (earring)* patterns arranged in a triangle. The entire field has stylized lotuses spread uniformly.

Early 20th Century Punjab

Size: L: 240 cm x W: 136 cm

Base fabric: Maroon khaddar.

Mustard, white, red, with green silk threads are used in the embroidery.

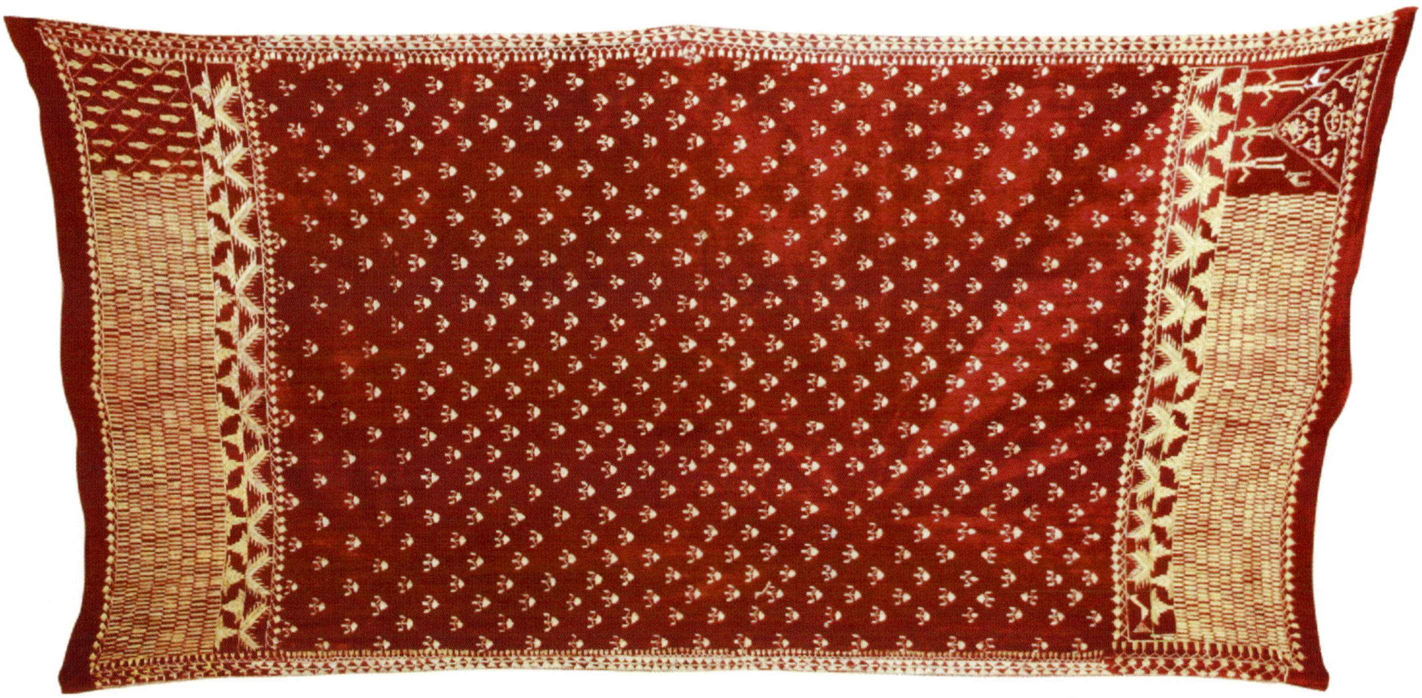

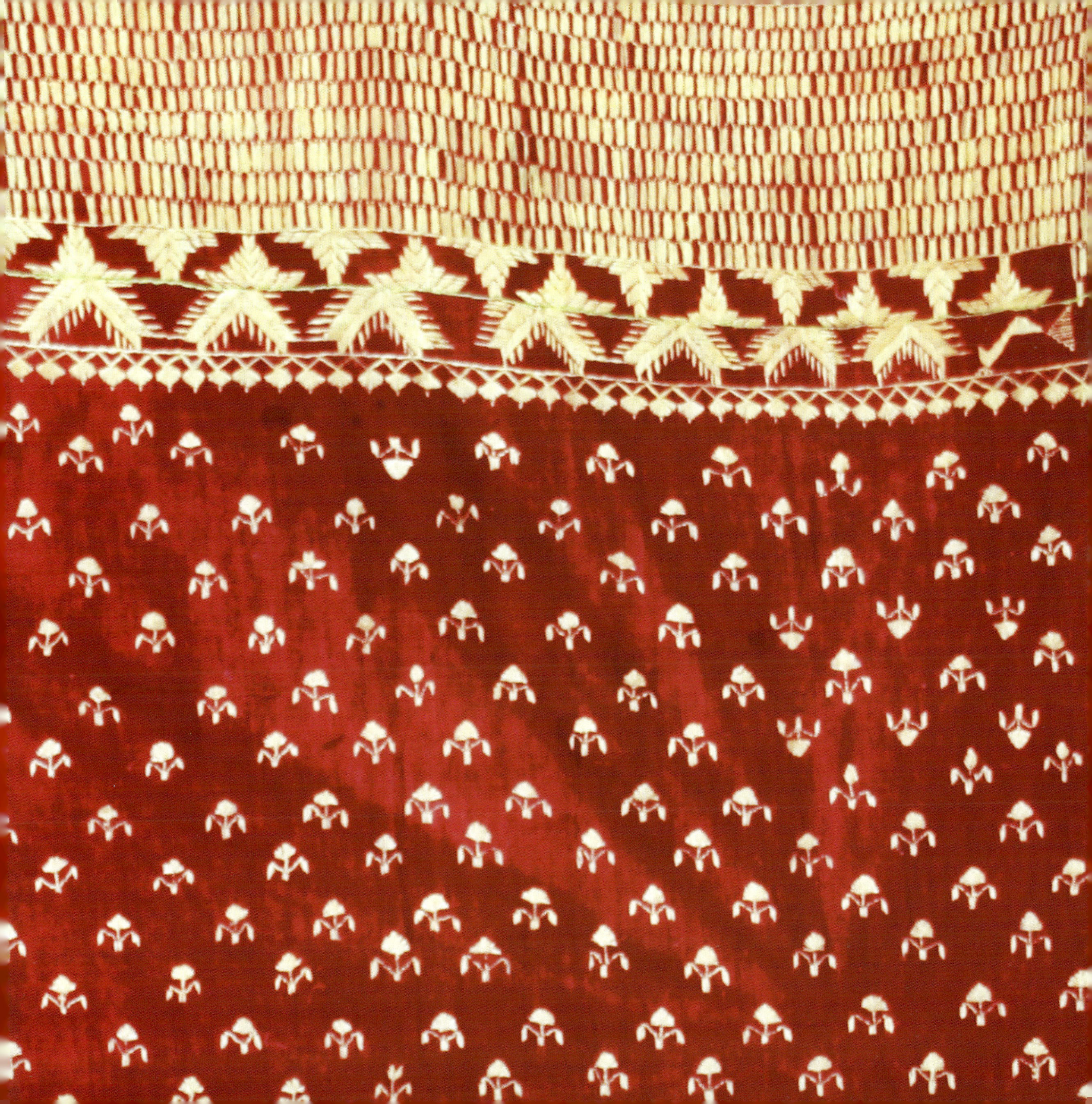

PANCHRANGI PHULKARI

Acc. No: 99.1.PH-12

Panchrangi phulkari embroidered with stylized geometrical, floral and wheat patterns on two pallus. The two borders depict *nakhoon (nail)* pattern arranged in diamonds. The entire field is covered with small four-petalled flowers spread uniformly.

Late 20th Century; Punjab

Size: L: 222 cm x W: 142 cm

Base fabric: Red khaddar.

Pink and mustard silk threads are used in the embroidery.

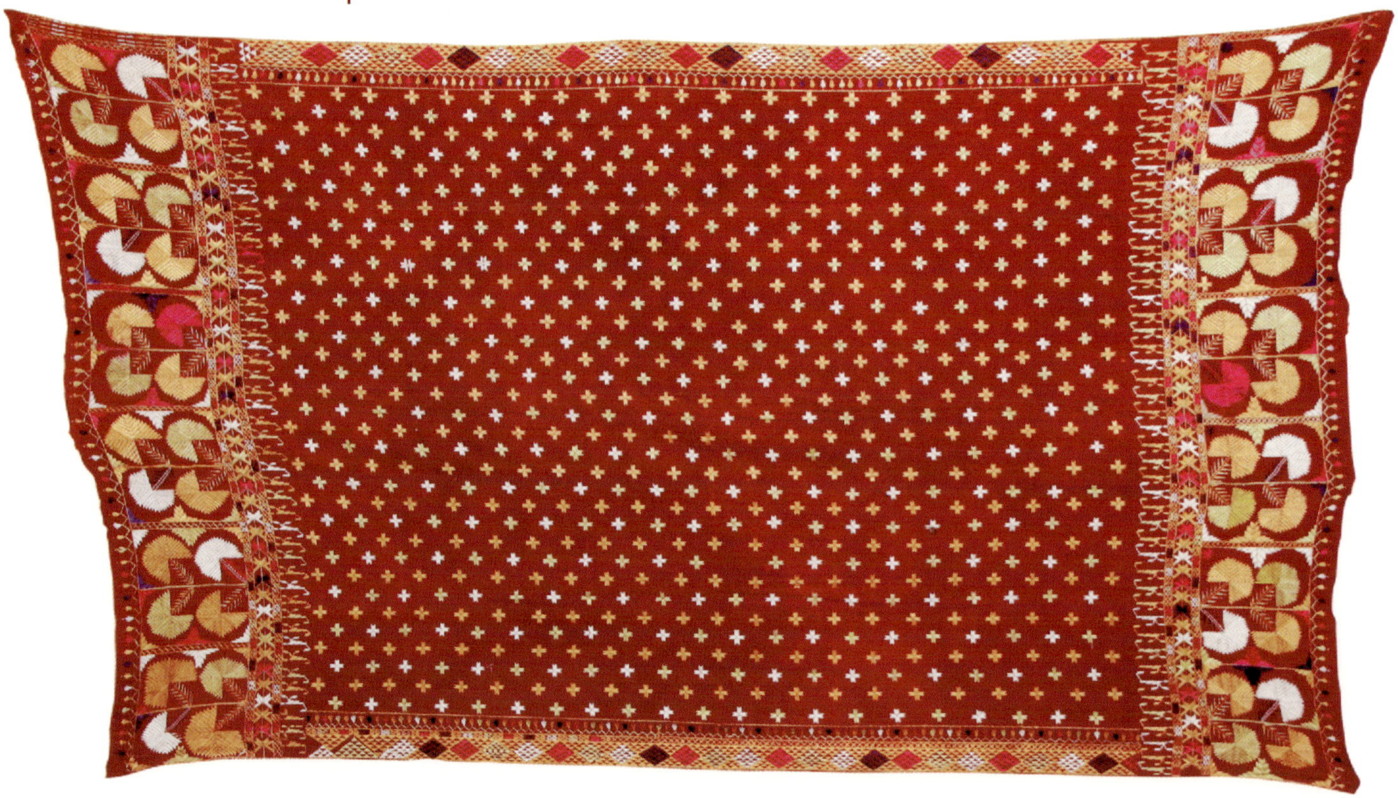

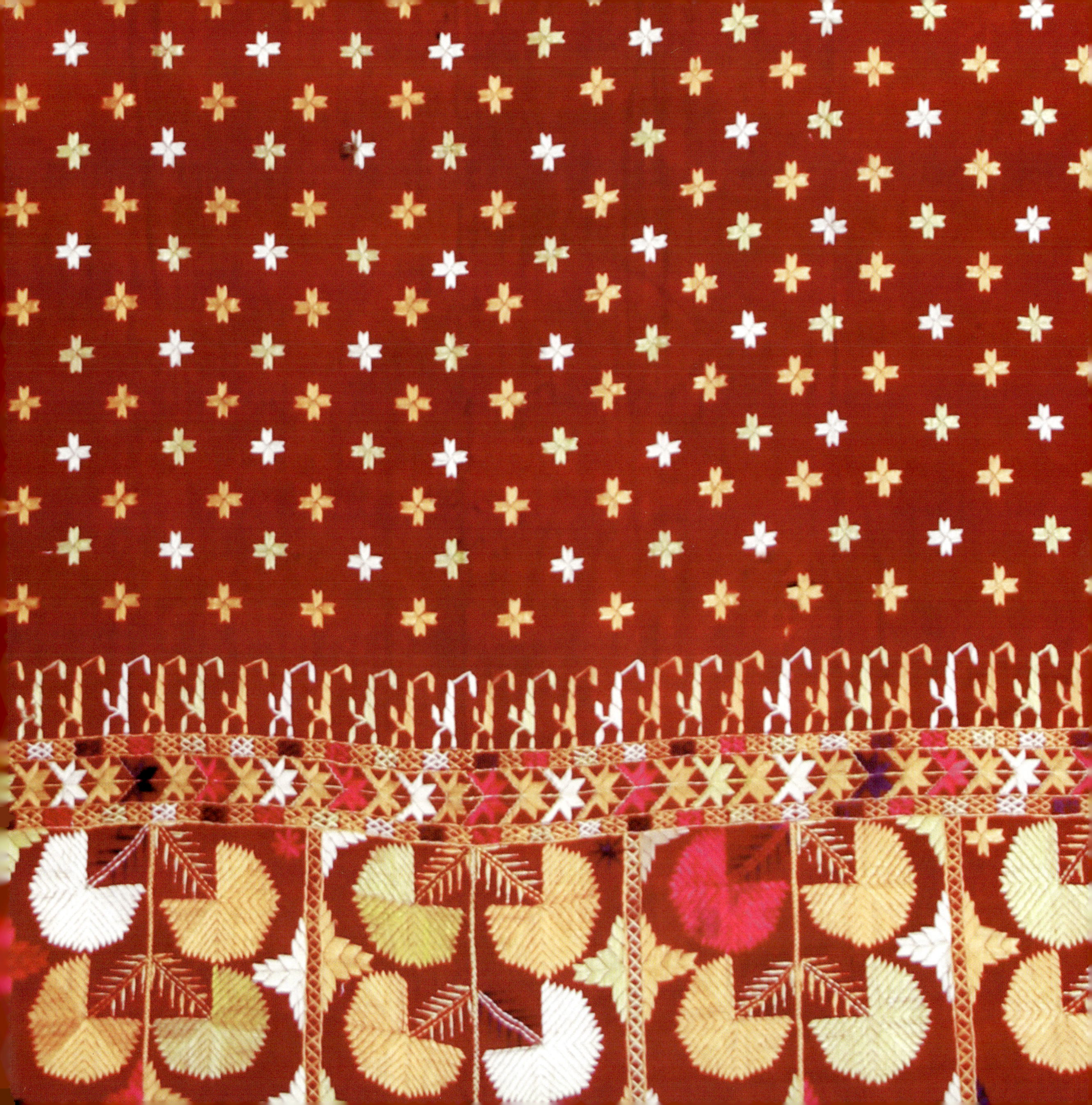

MOR PHULKARI

Acc. No: 99.1.PH-13

Mor (peacock) phulkari, richly embroidered with stylized peacocks, arranged in horizontal rows. The *pallus* are embroidered with stylized geometrical floral patterns arranged in squares. It has double border with wheat and foliage patterns.

Late 20th Century; Haryana

Size: L: 218 cm x W: 143 cm

Base fabric: Maroon khaddar.

Mustard, green, magenta, orange and white silk threads are used in the embroidery.

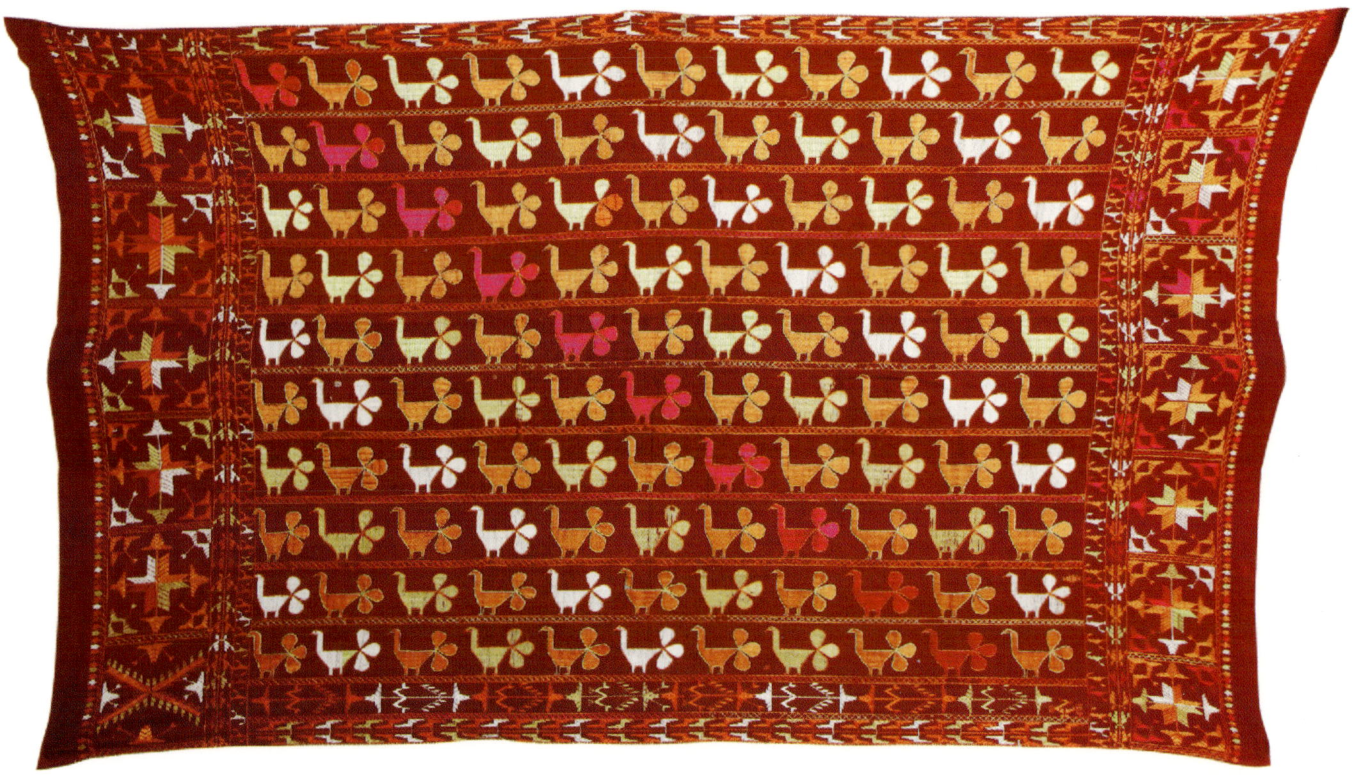

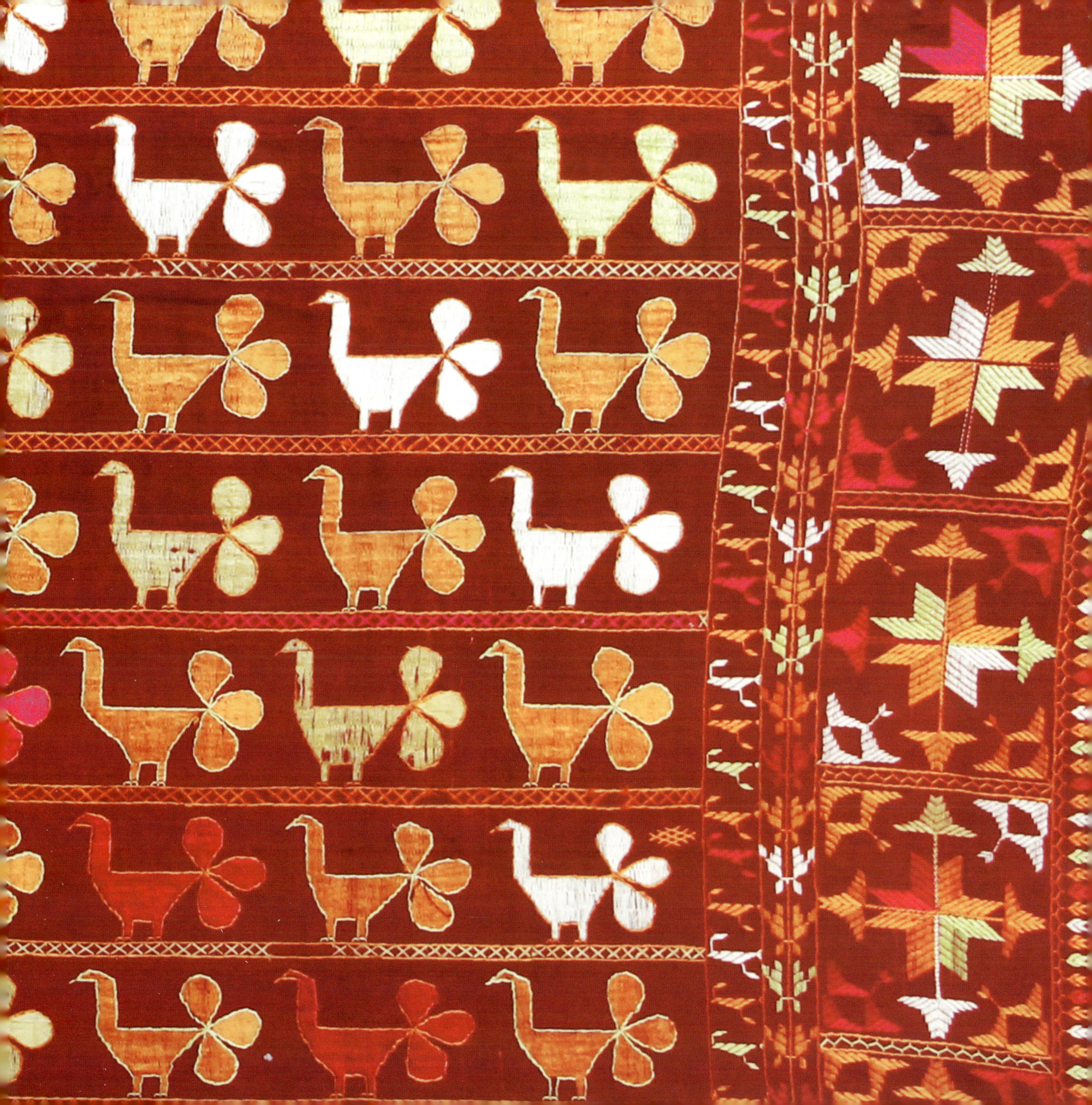

PAAN PHULKARI

Acc. No: 99.1.PH-14

Paan (beetle leaf) phulkari with two borders. One side has small multicoloured pyramids with a small creeper, while the other has diamonds and triangular motifs embroidered in Bagh style. The entire field is divided into squares with stylized floral motif at the centre and four beetle leaf motifs on four corners, alternating with bud pattern.

Early 20th Century; Punjab

Size: L: 235 cm x W: 126 cm

Base fabric: Maroon khaddar.

Mustard, white, magenta, green and blue silk threads are used in the embroidery.

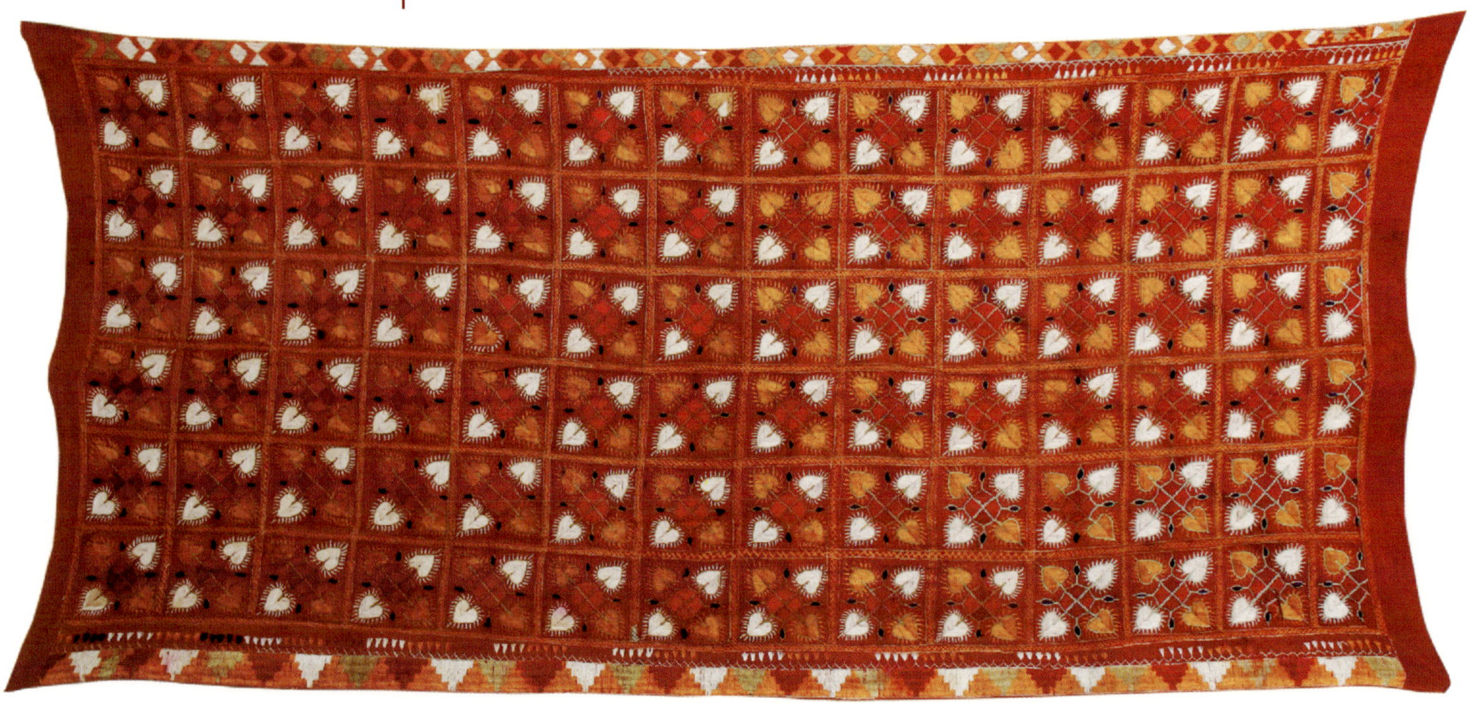

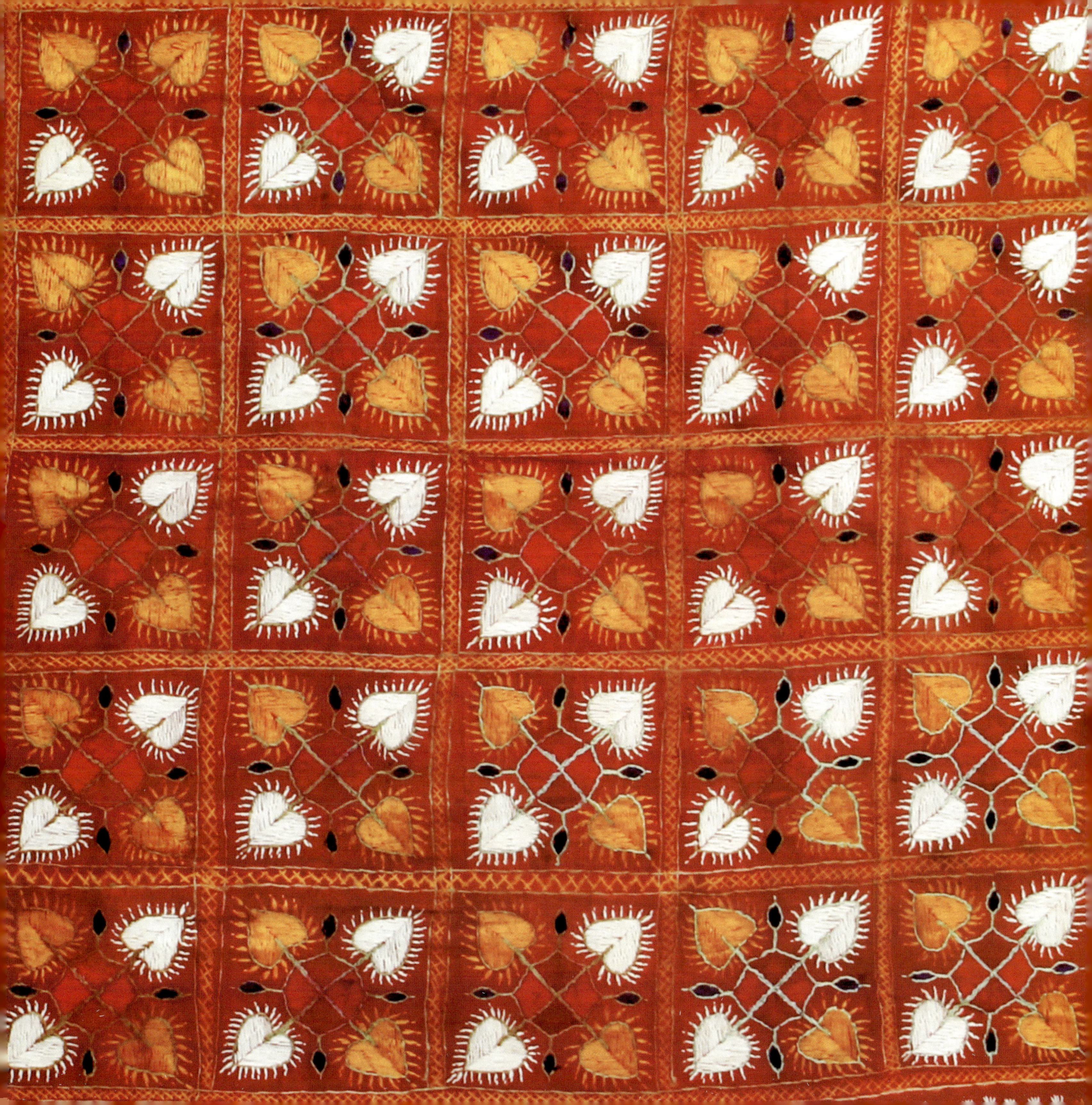

PHULKARI

Acc. No: 99.1.PH-15

Phulkari with geometrical floral borders on two sides. The two end pieces (*pallus*) have stylized lotus pattern arranged in squares. One *pallu* depicts rows of foliage motifs, while the other has floral design. The field is divided into four squares each with a row of peacocks.

Early 20th Century; Haryana

Size: L: 267 cm x W: 130 cm

Base fabric: Maroon khaddar.

Pink, mustard, different shades of green, white and red silk threads are used in the embroidery.

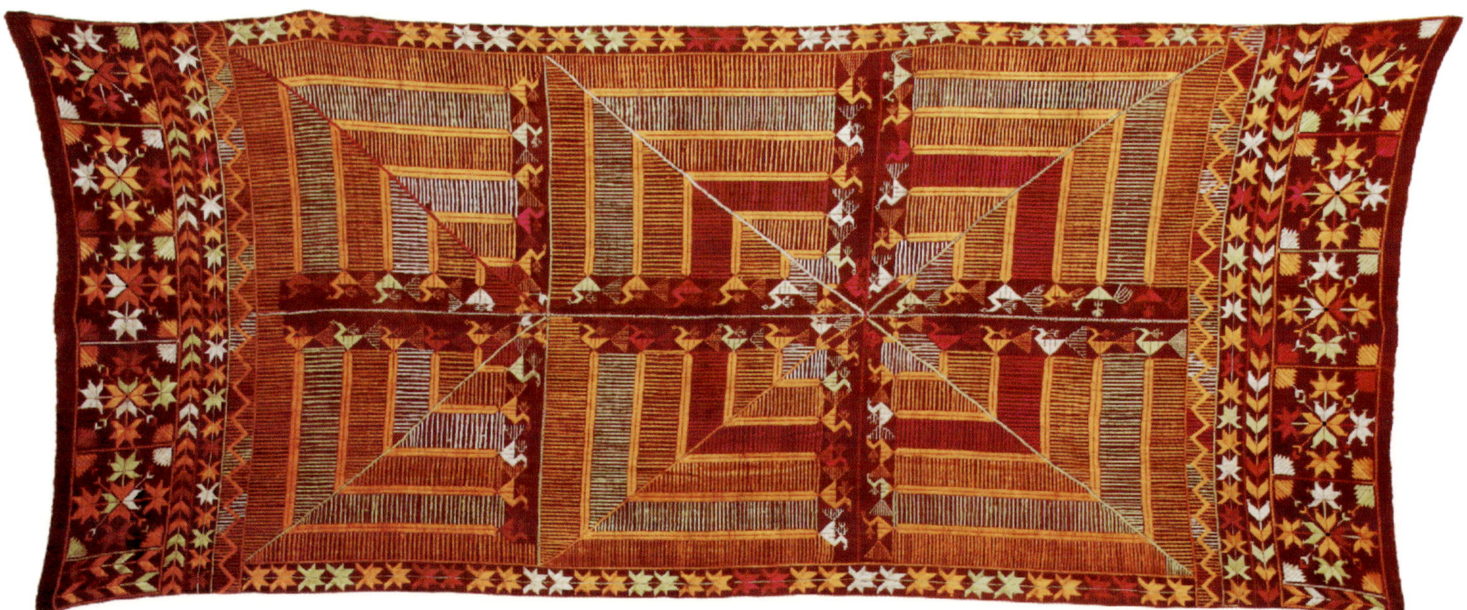

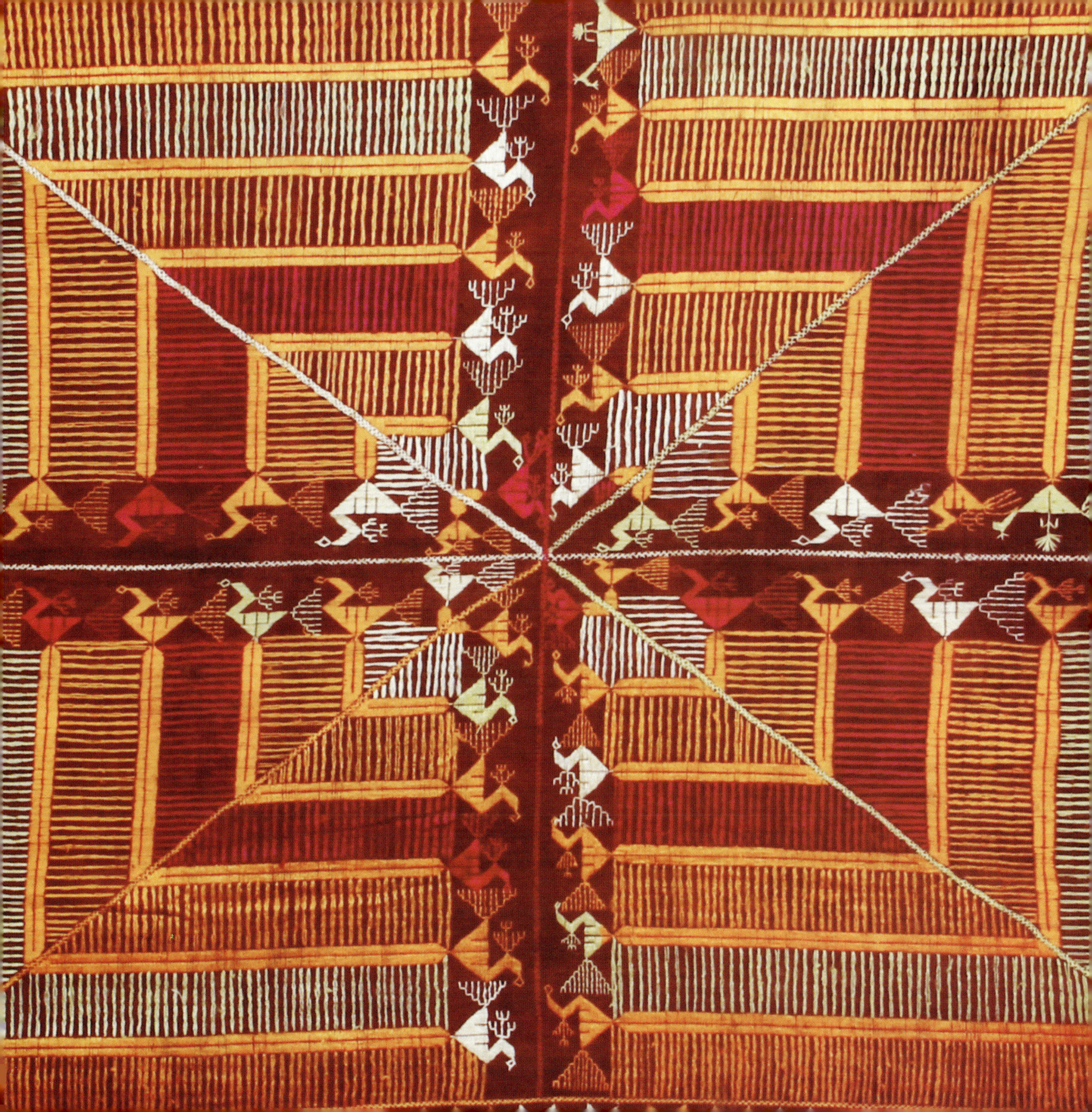

PHULKARI

Acc. No: 99.1.PH-16

Phulkari depicting geometrical floral borders with foliage pattern on the edges. The entire field is divided into rectangles and squares with stylized wheat motifs.

Late 19th Century; Punjab

Size: L: 256 cm x W: 139 cm

Base fabric: Maroon khaddar.

Mustard, light green, white and magenta silk threads are used in the embroidery.

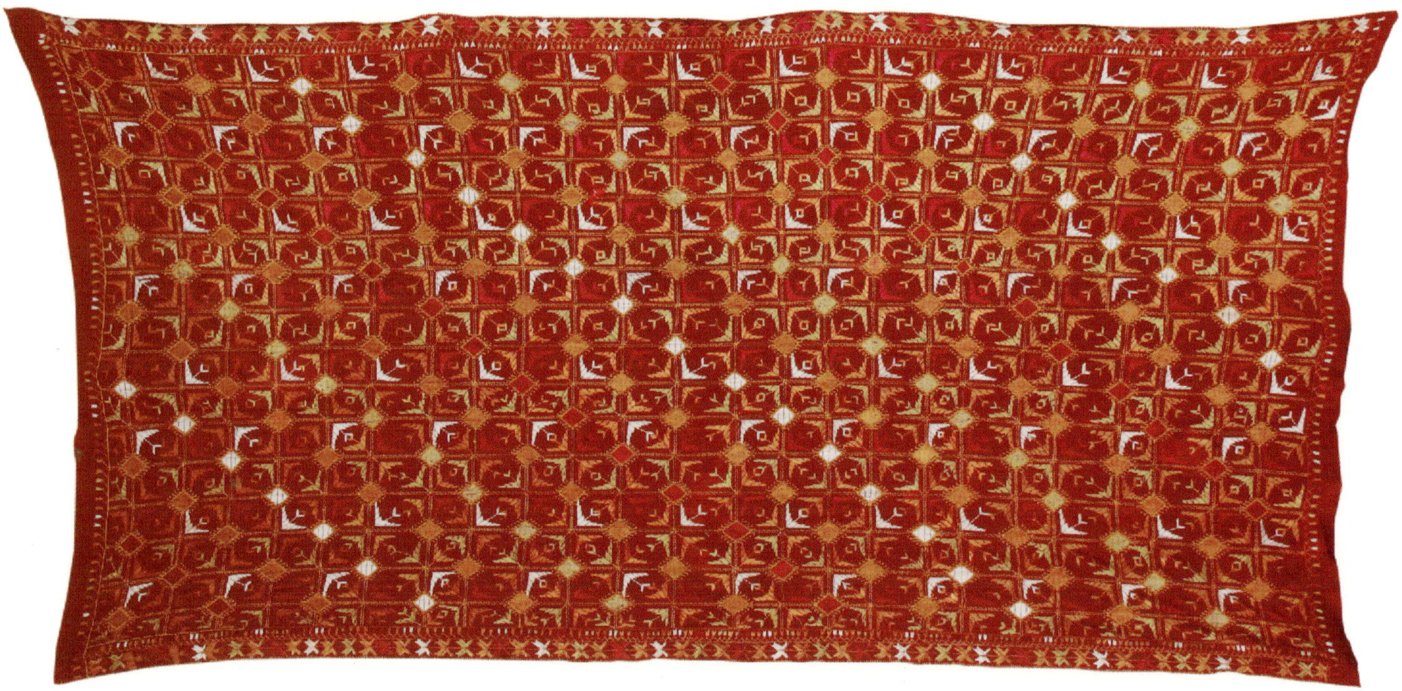

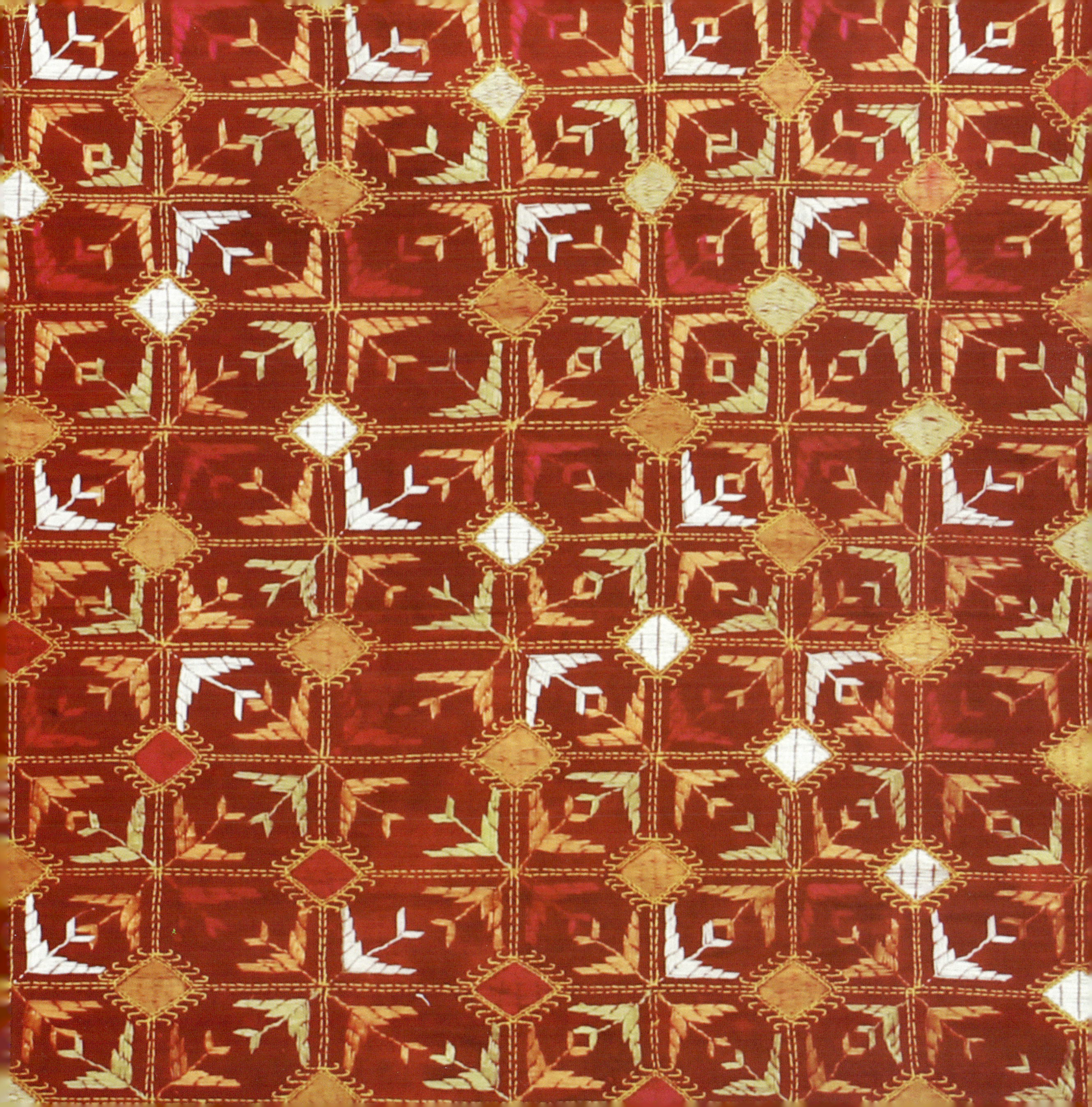

SURAJMUKHI PHULKARI

Acc. No: 99.1.PH-17

Surajmukhi (sunflower) Phulkari with geometrical and floral designs on the two *pallus* in three horizontal lines. The two borders have *nakhoon* (nail) like design arranged in triangles. The entire field is divided into diagonal spaces with Surajmukhi pattern, surrounded by double running stitch, like in Chhope.

Late 19th Century; Haryana

Size: L: 220 cm x W: 142 cm

Base fabric: Maroon khaddar.

Green, white, orange, yellow, magenta and black silk threads are used in the embroidery.

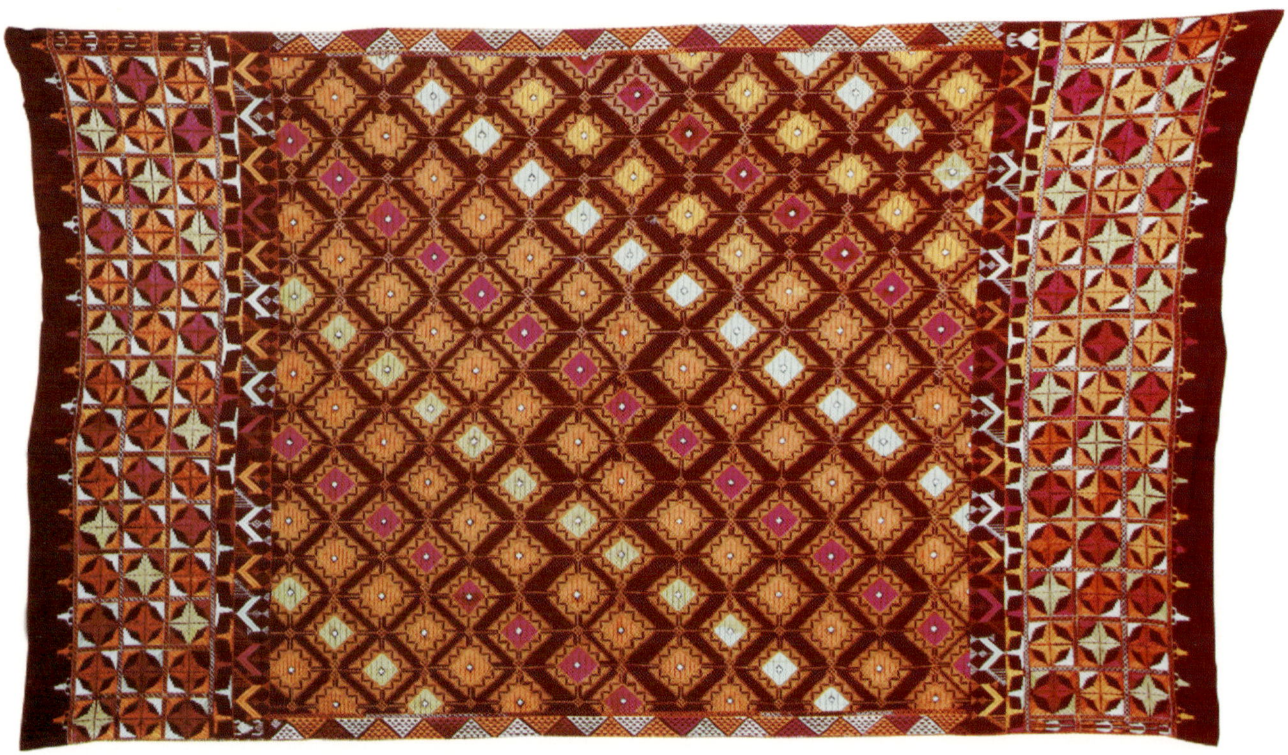

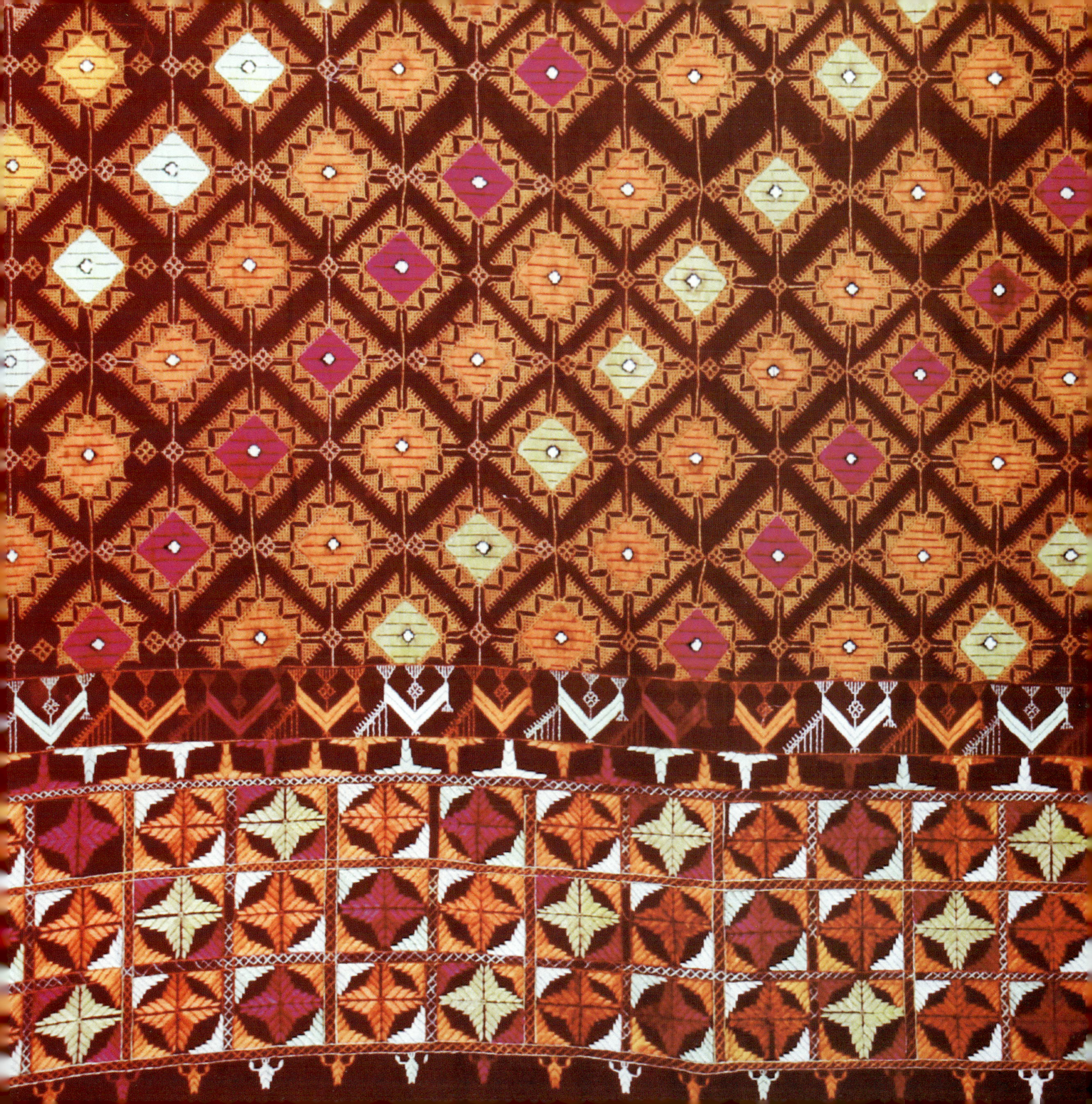

PHULKARI

Acc. No: 99.1.PH-18

Phulkari embroidered with two borders in foliage pattern. The two *pallus* have stylized foliage patterns in squares surrounded by floral and zigzag design. The entire field has long stripes with six-petalled flowers arranged as a garland.

Early 20th Century; Haryana

Size: L: 244 cm x W: 153 cm

Base fabric: Maroon khaddar.

Green, mustard, white, blue and black silk threads are used in the embroidery.

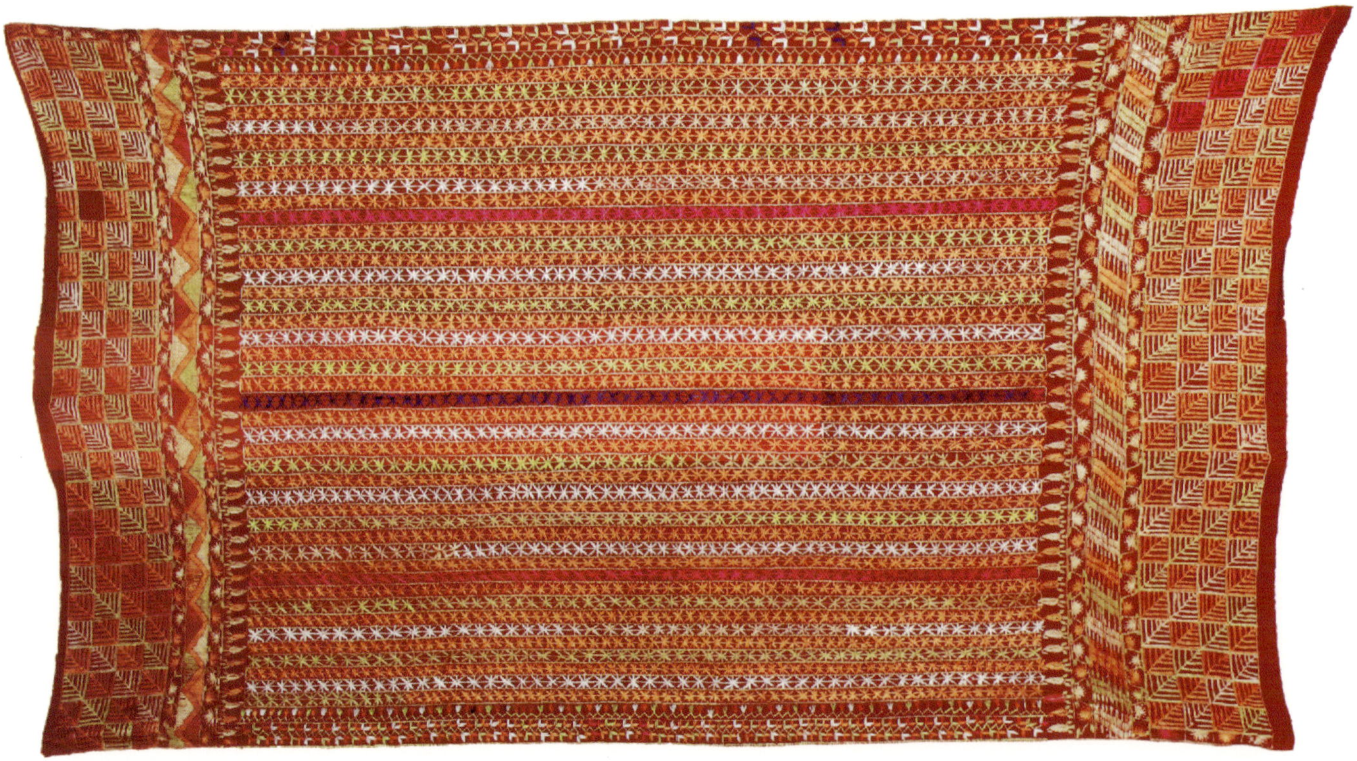

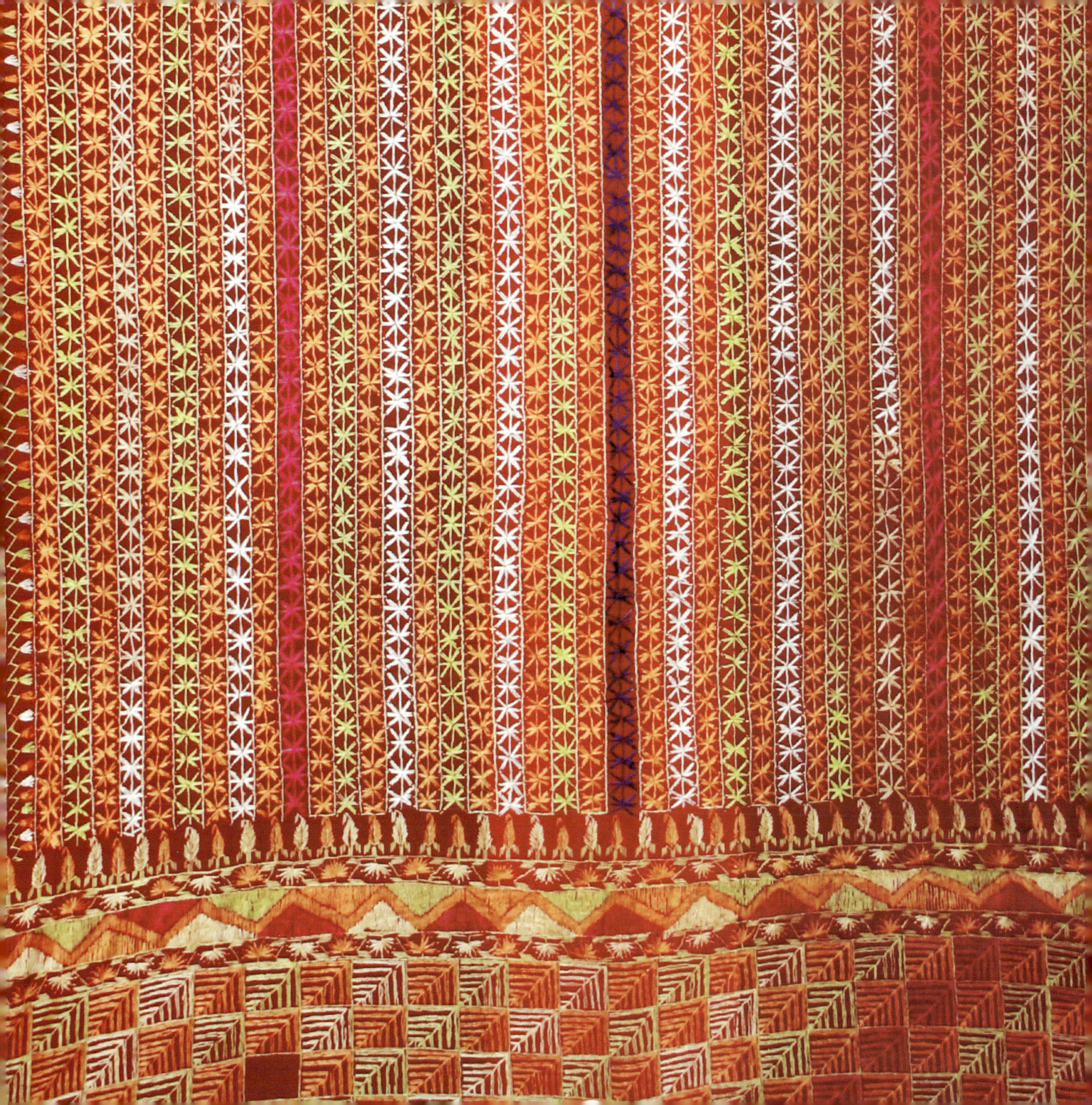

DHOOP CHAWN BAGH CUM PHULKARI

Acc. No: 99.1.PH-19

Dhoop Chawn (sun and shade) Bagh cum Phulkari, with *pallus* and borders embroidered in Vari Da Bagh style. The entire field is covered with geometrical and floral motifs.

Late 19th Century; Punjab

Size: L: 253 cm x W: 145 cm

Base fabric: Maroon khaddar.

Different shades of orange and purple silk threads are used in the embroidery.

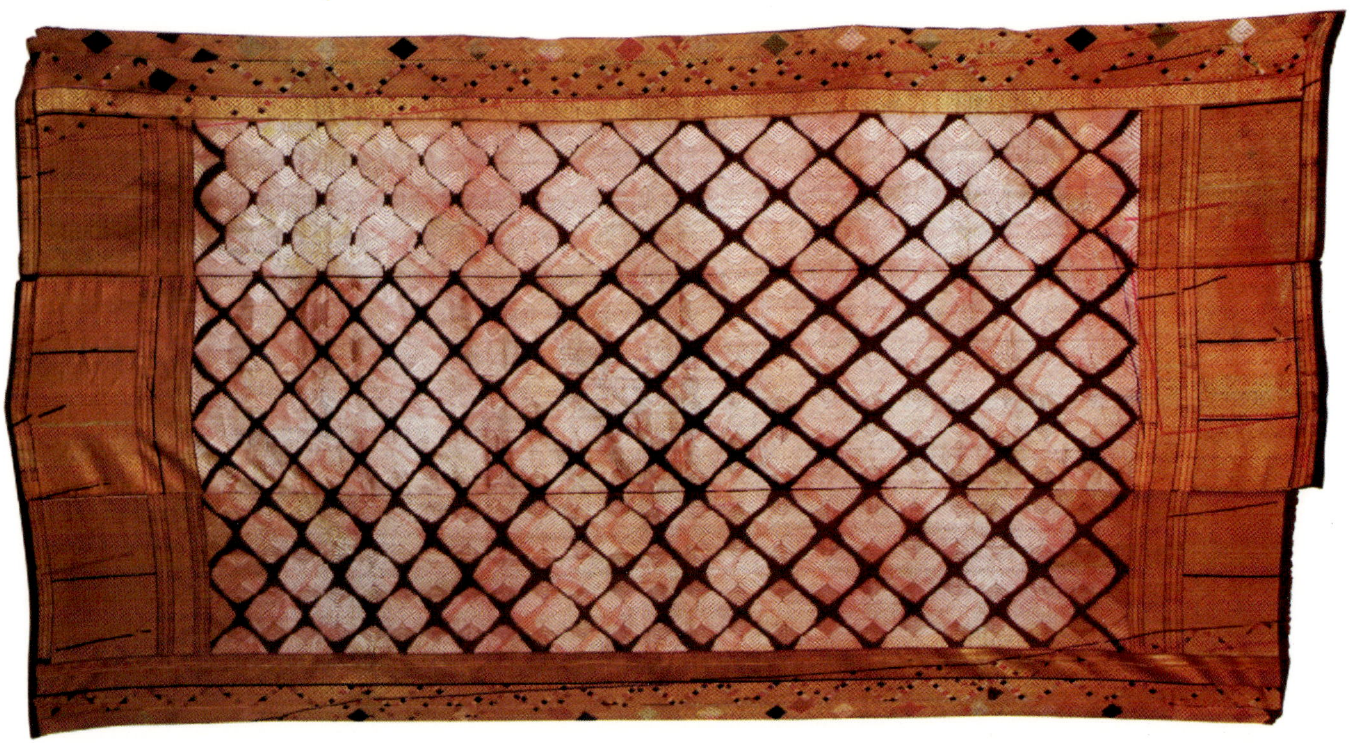

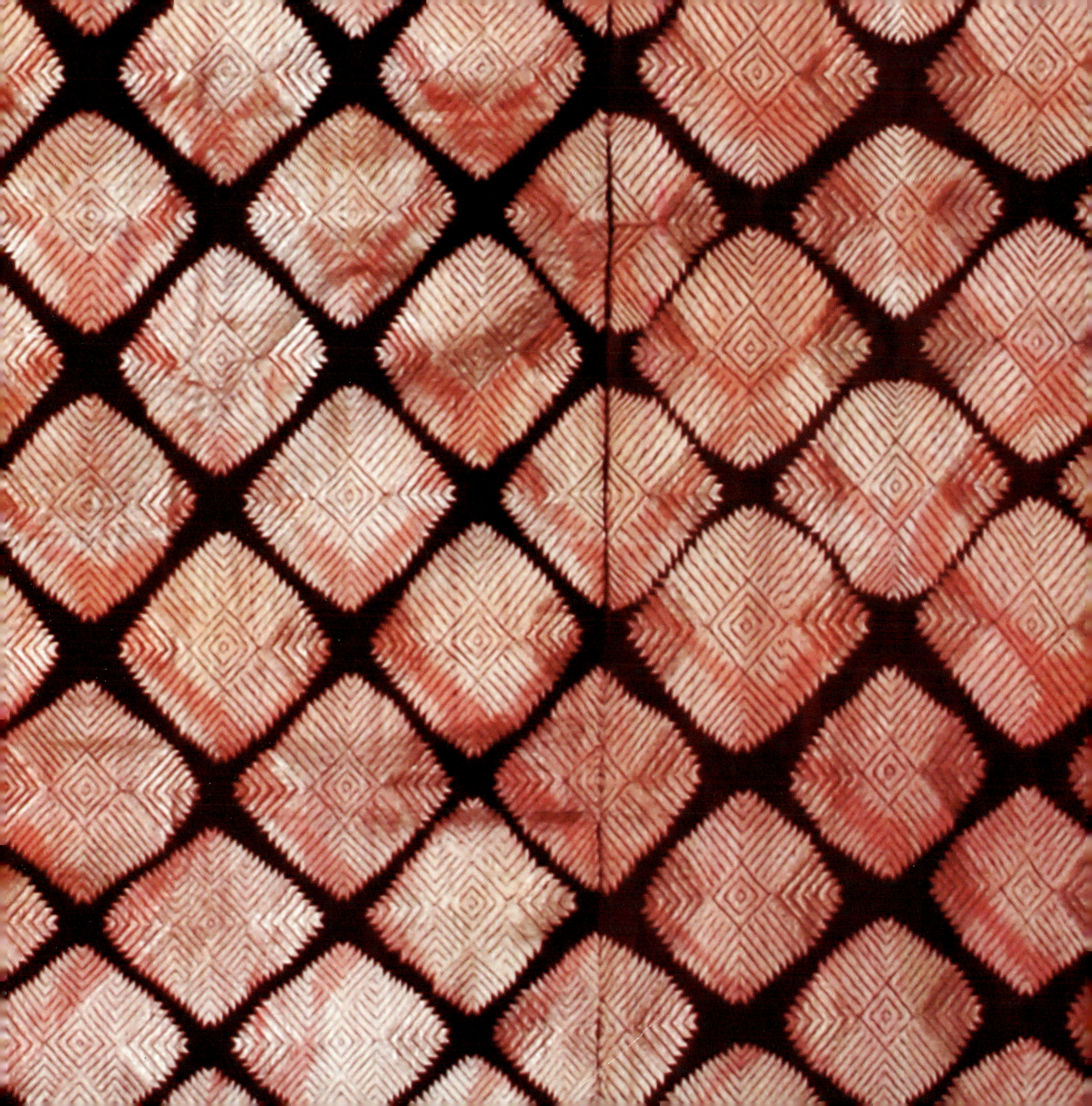

SARPALLU FIGURATIVE PANCHRANGA PHULKARI CUM BAGH

Acc. No: 99.1.PH-20

Rare sarpallu figurative Panchranga Phulkari cum Bagh. The centre panel depict rows of triangles and birds enclosed within wheat like motif in triangles. Multicoloured *patang* (kites) like motifs joined together are embroidered on both the sides. It has borders on four sides with cowrie (conch) pattern surrounded with geometrical designs.

Late 19th Century; Haryana

Size: L: 224 cm x W: 166 cm

Base fabric: Maroon khaddar.

Mustard, green, magenta, red and purple silk threads are used in the embroidery.

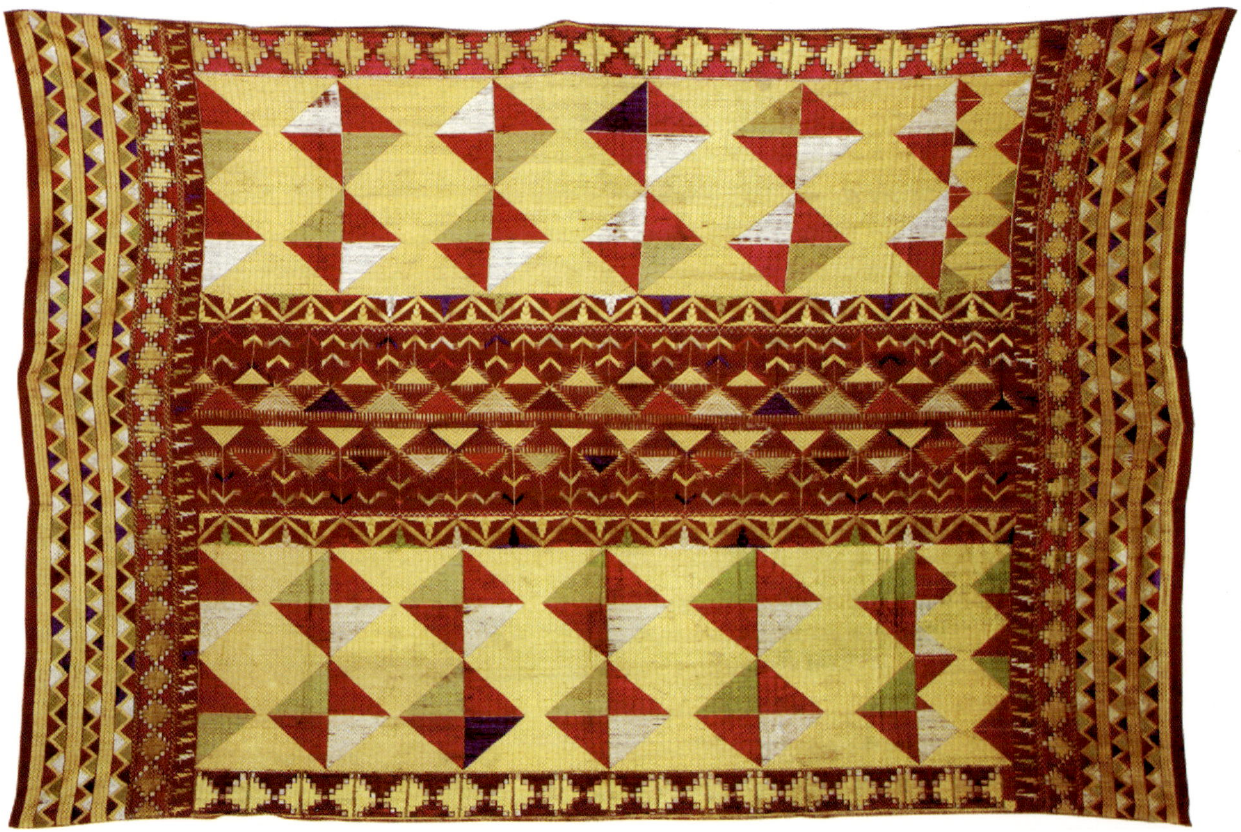

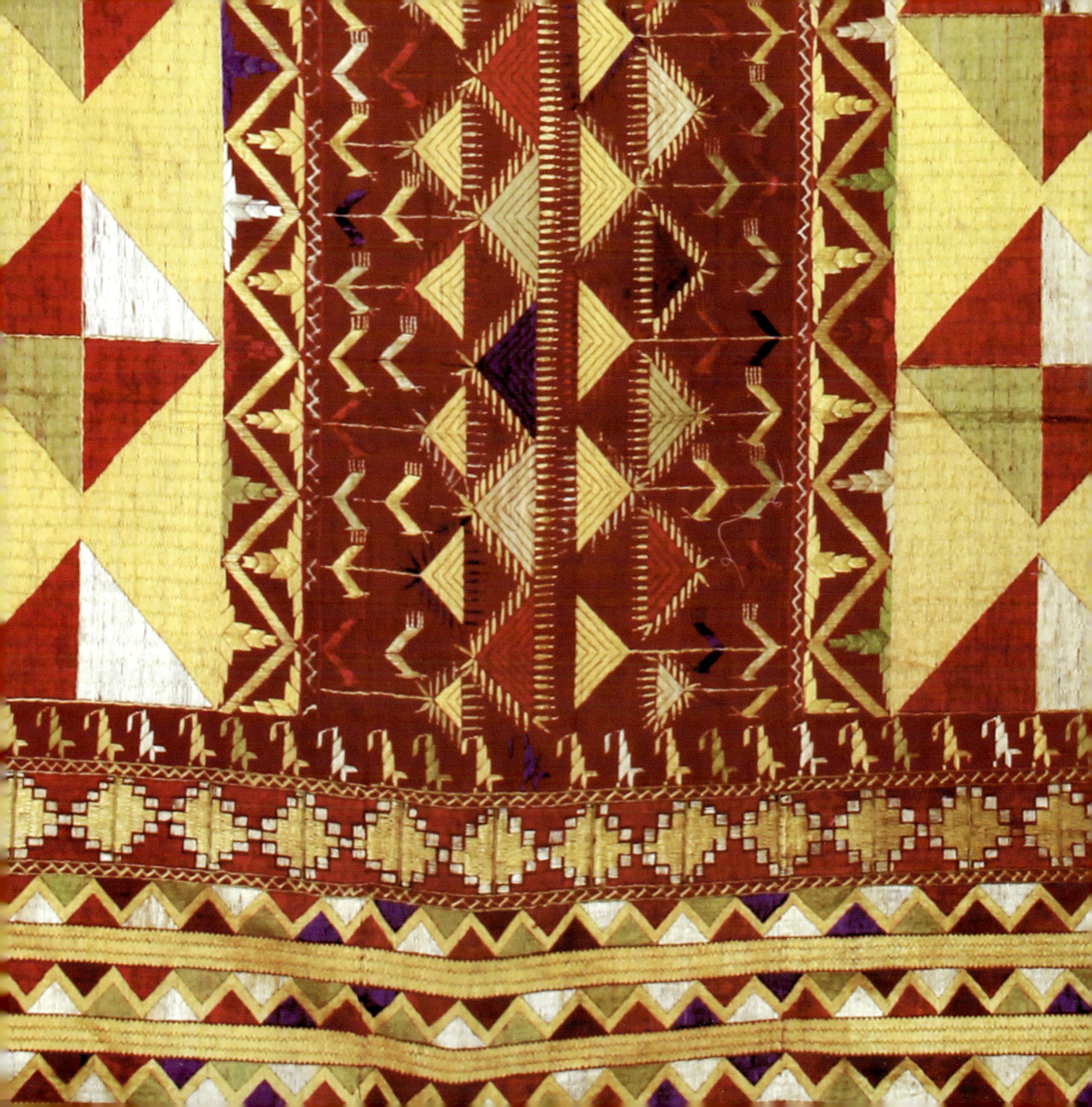

VARI DA BAGH

Acc. No: 99.1.PH-21

Vari Da Bagh in deep mustard colour with borders on two sides. The entire field is embroidered with triangles arranged in diagonal lines. The broad borders have small diagonal squares each with a tiny square inside a large one.

Late 19th Century; Punjab

Size: L: 251 cm x W: 150 cm

Base fabric: Red khaddar.

Orange, green and cream silk threads are used alternatively. In some parts of the central panel, different shades of shaded golden colour is used in the field.

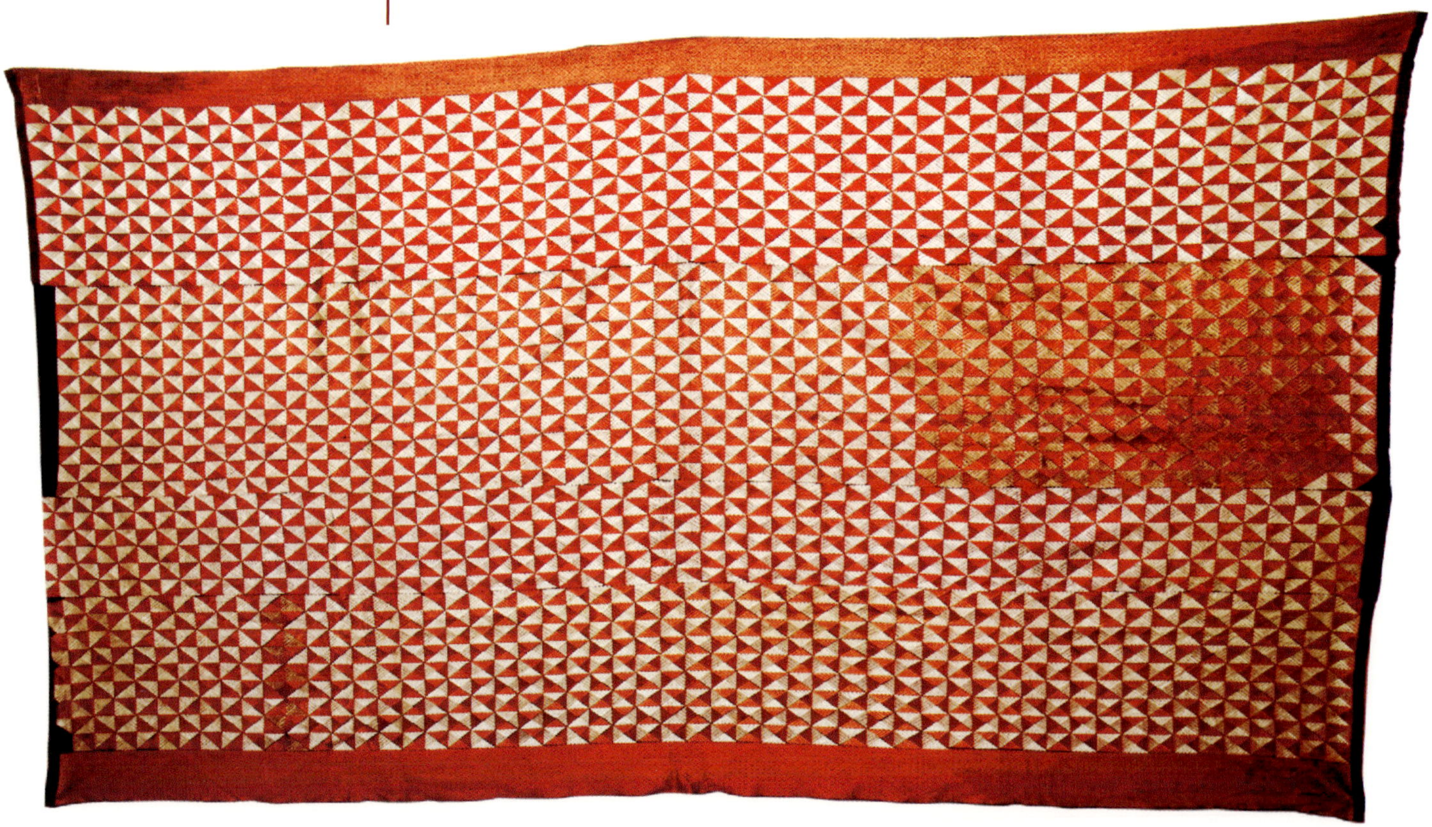

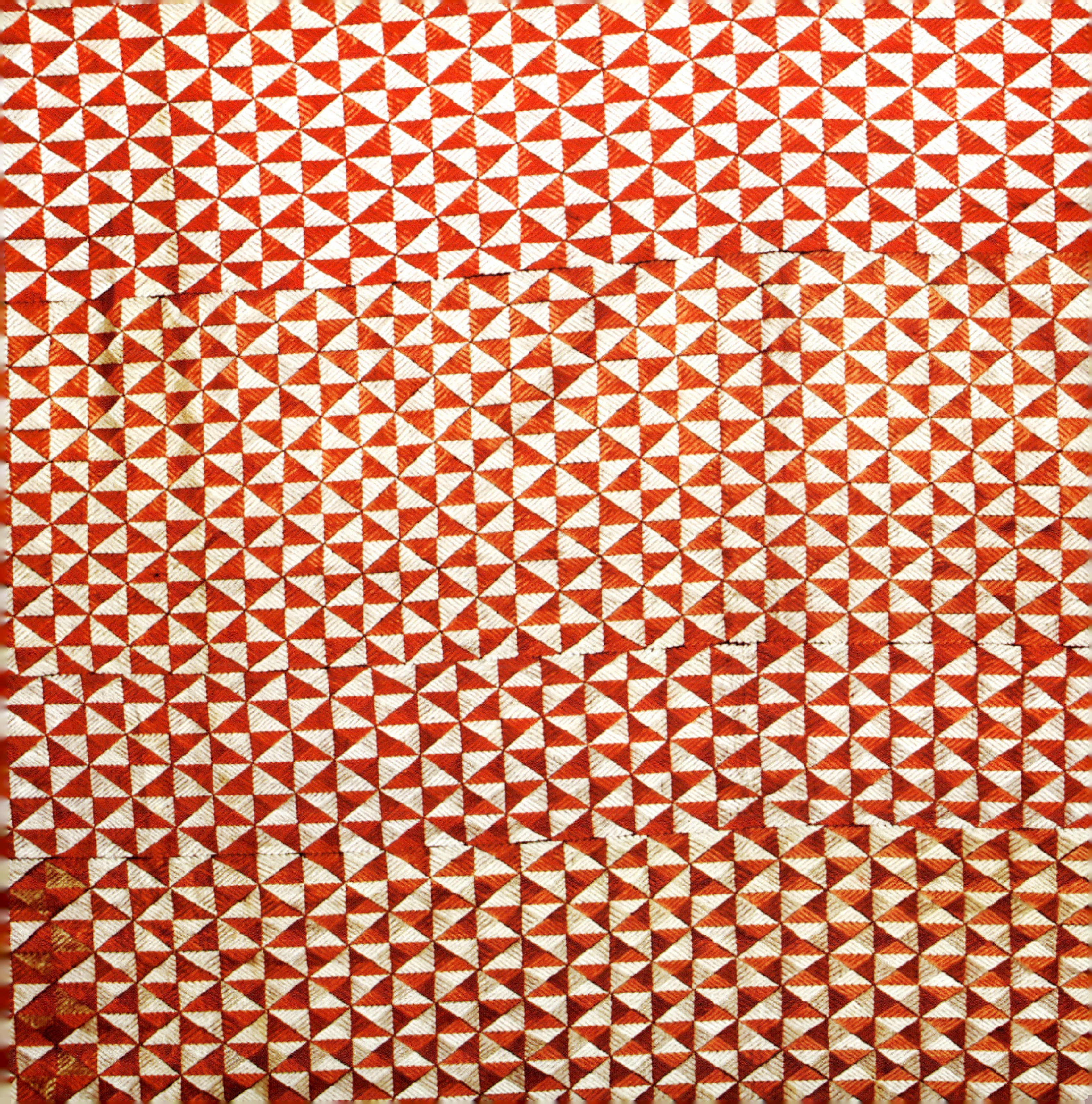

BAGH

Acc. No: 99.1.PH-22

Bagh with multicoloured triangles with cowrie motifs on the borders. Two *pallus* have stylized geometrical floral motifs arranged in diagonal squares. Above the *pallu*, there are two borders, one with small diagonal rows and diamond pattern in between; and the other with *nakhoon* pattern arranged in triangles. The two borders have multi-coloured arrow head design arranged vertically.

Late 20th Century; Haryana

Size: L: 231 cm x W: 139 cm

Base fabric: Maroon khaddar.

Embroidery is in golden mustard, different shades of green, white, black and magenta silk threads.

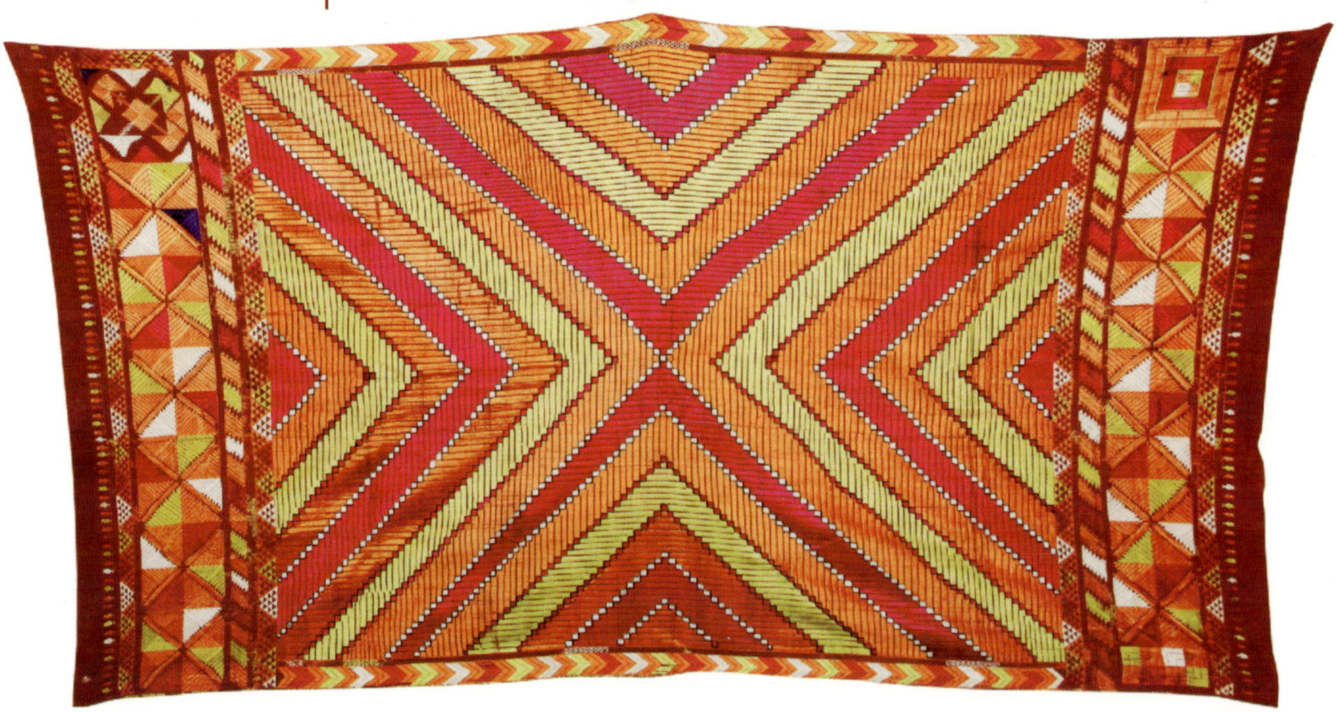

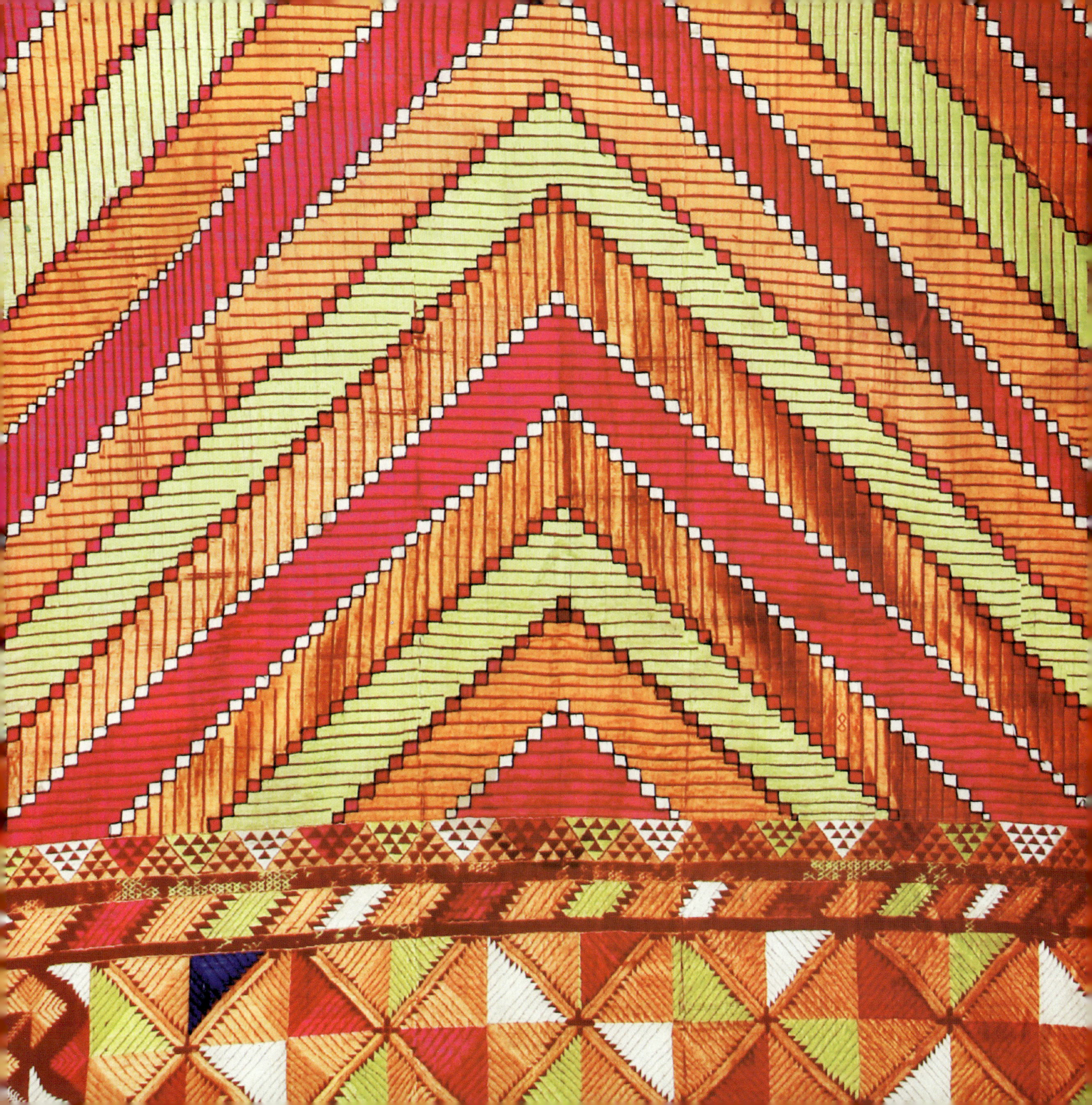

SURAJMUKHI BAGH

Acc. No: 99.1.PH-23

Surajmukhi bagh, richly embroidered in geometrical pattern all over the field. The two borders depict arrow heads arranged vertically with diamonds in between. The two *pallus* with several borders are designed with triangles, diamonds and various geometrical patterns.

20th Century; Punjab

Size: L: 235 cm x W: 135 cm

Base fabric: Maroon khaddar.

Different shades of green, gold, mustard, red, magenta and black silk threads are used at places.

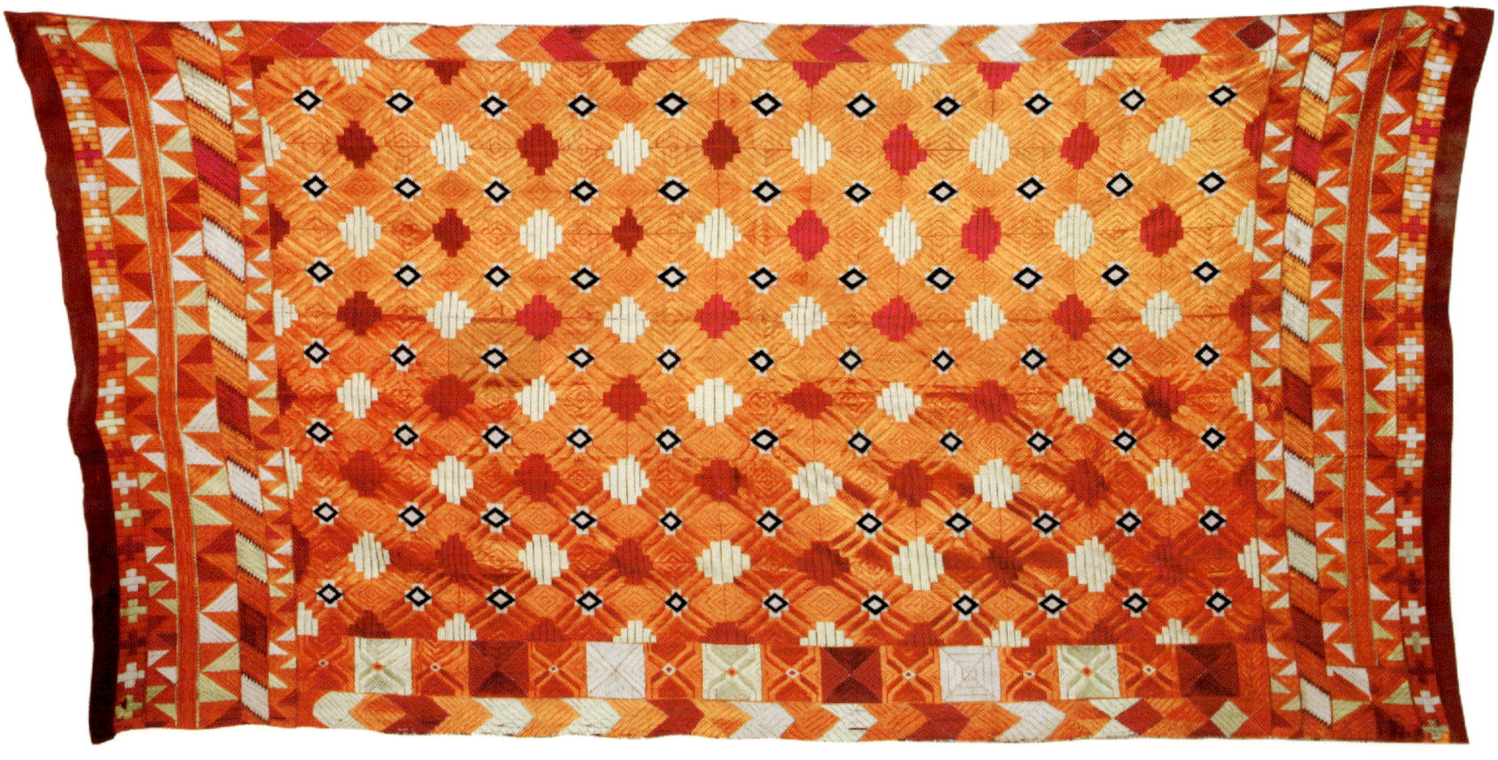

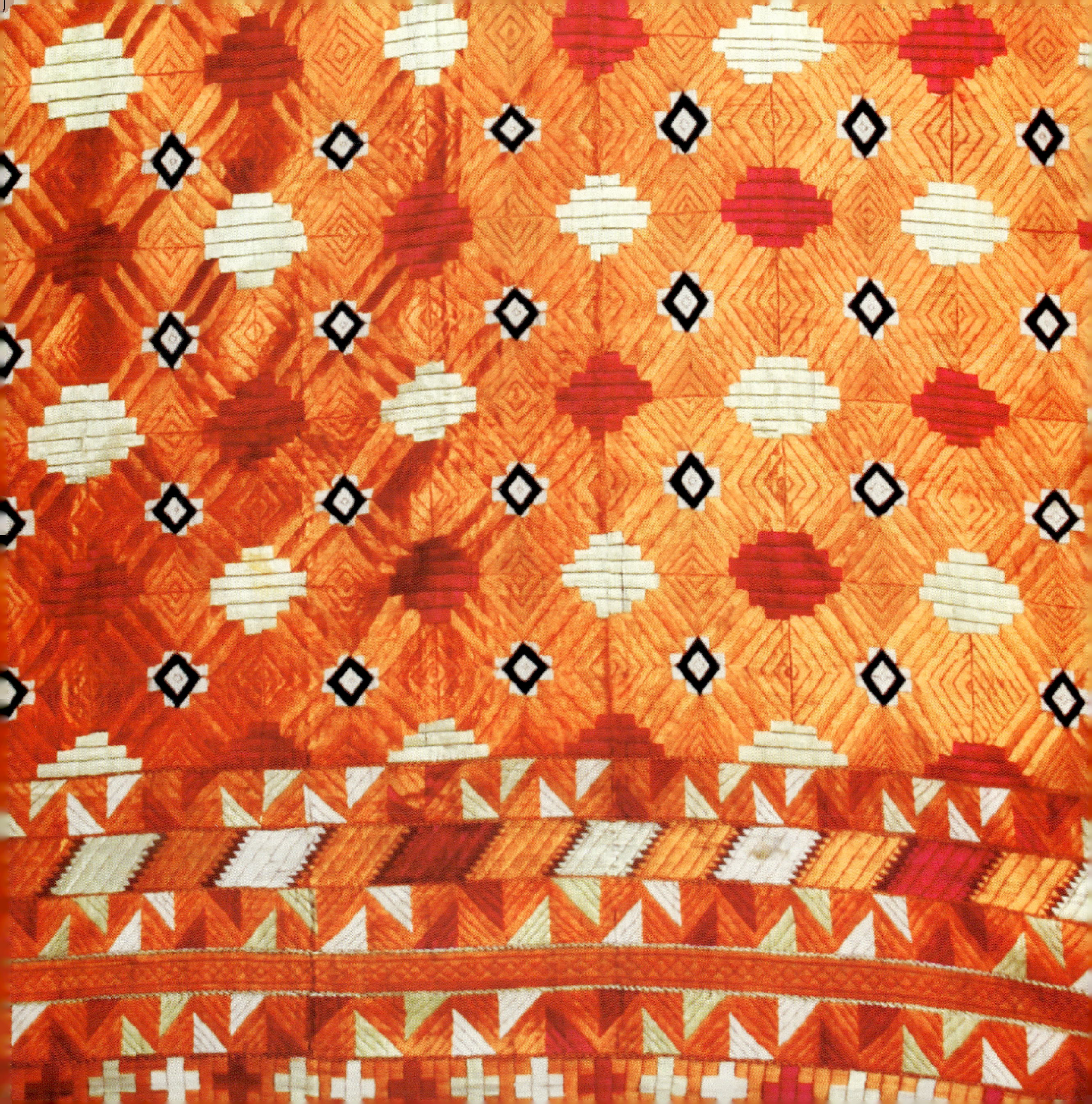

BELAN BAGH

Acc. No: 99.1.PH-24

Belan Bagh (Rolling pin) depicting multicoloured belans on the field. The borders are embroidered with diamond pattern, the two pallus have diagonal broad lines in geometrical pattern embroidered in Vari-Da-Bagh style, enclosed in triangles. The *pallus* in four rows are embroidered with cross stitch.

Early 20th Century; Haryana

Size: L: 257 cm x W: 139 cm

Base fabric: Maroon khaddar.

White, gold, orange, mustard, different shades of green, magenta and red silk threads are used in the embroidery.

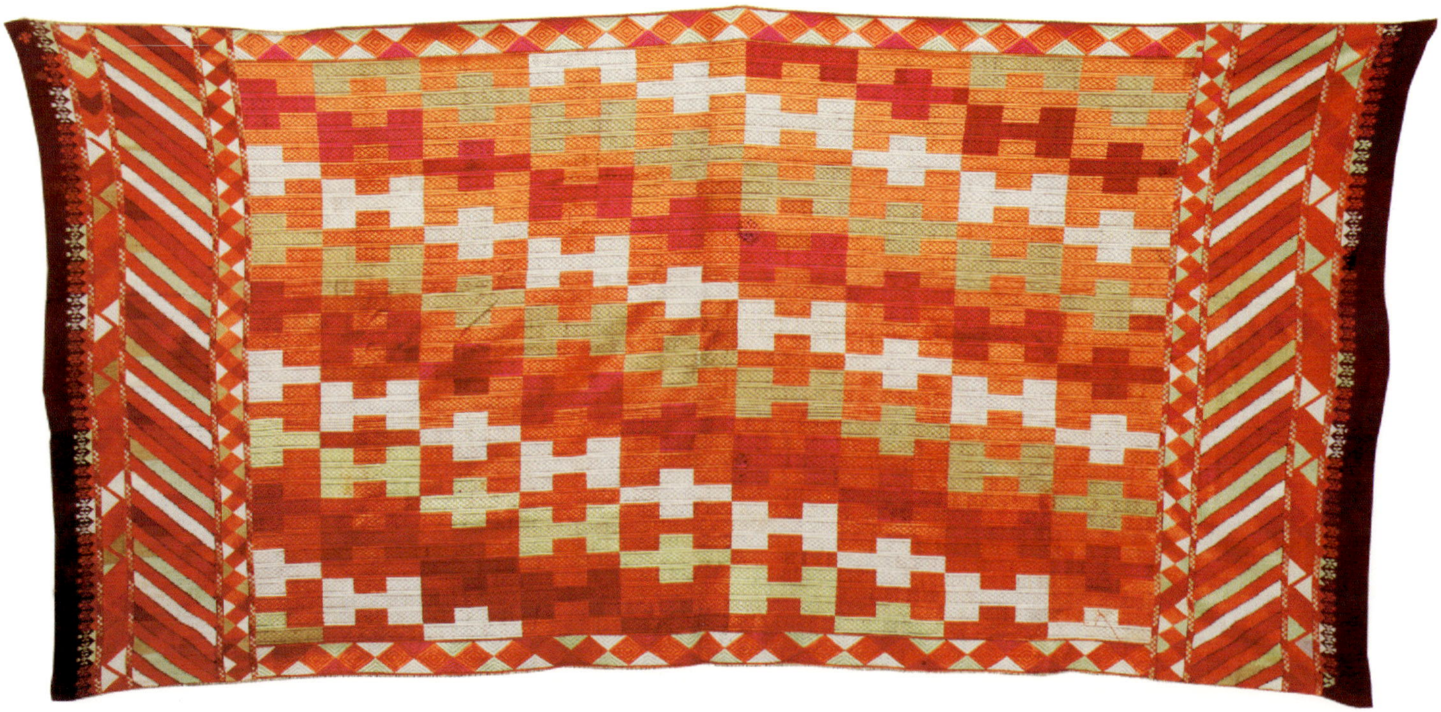

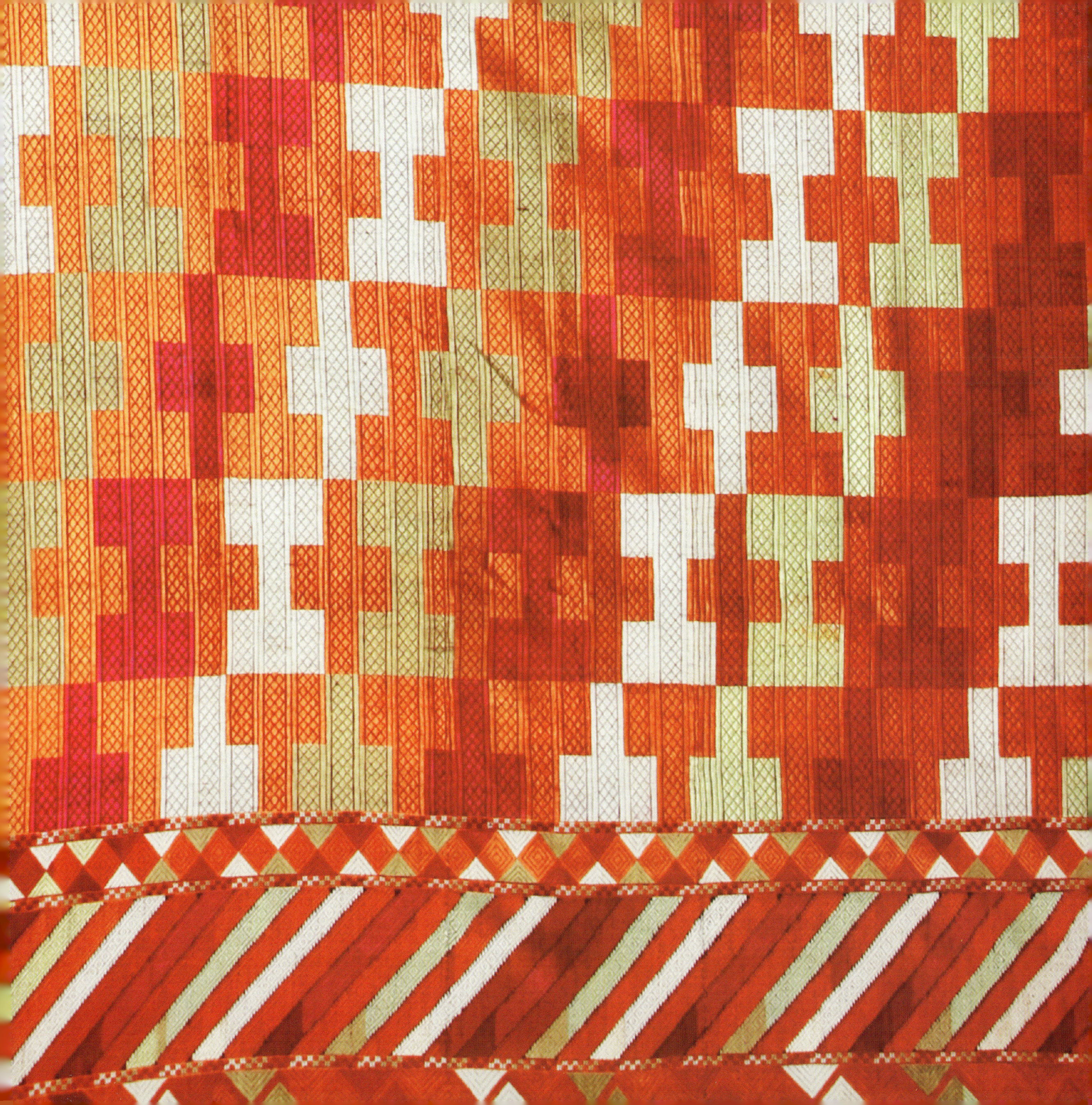

PHULKARI

Acc. No: 99.1.PH-25

Phulkari cum bagh with *Nakhoon*, arranged in triangles on the borders and stylized geometrical trefoil pattern on the two *pallus*. The entire field is embroidered with diagonal squares.

Mid 20th Century; Haryana

Size: L: 227 cm x W: 129 cm

Base fabric: Maroon khaddar.

Embroidery is in magenta, mustard, green and white silk threads .

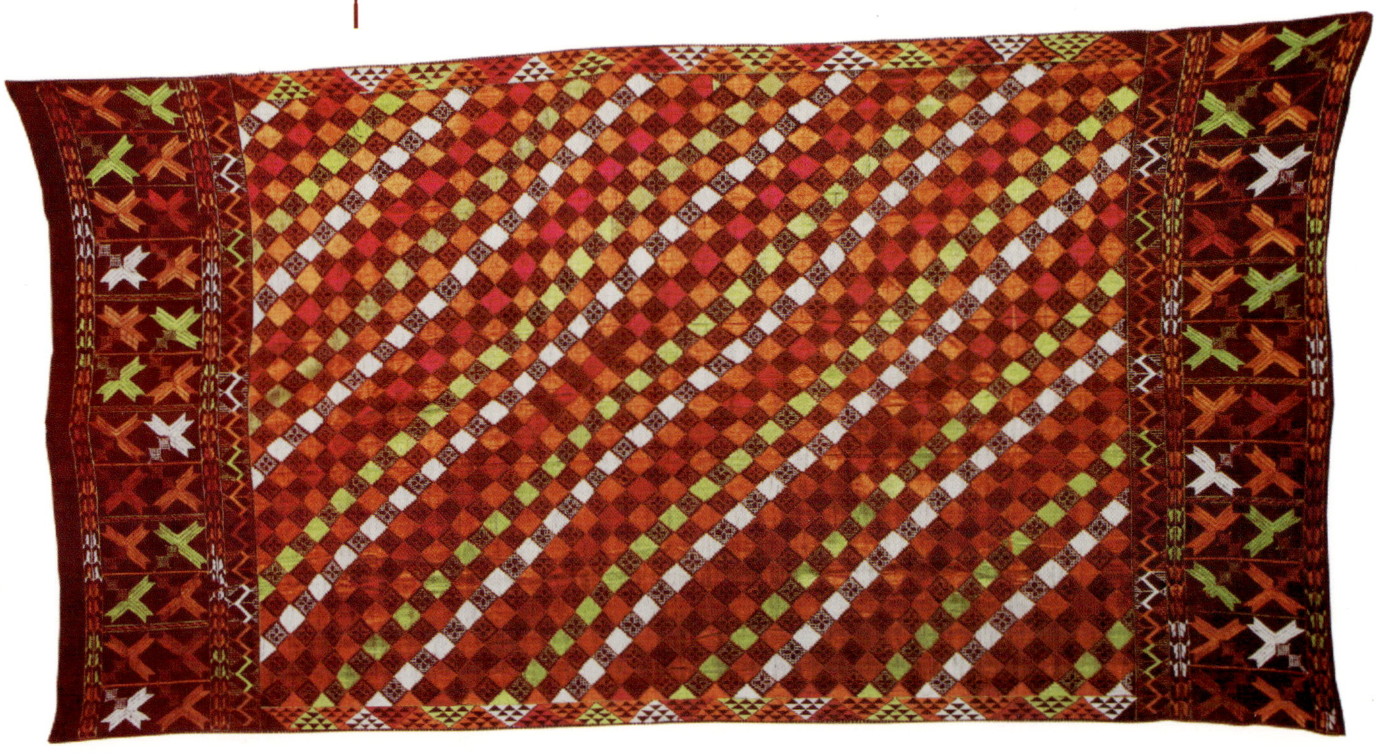

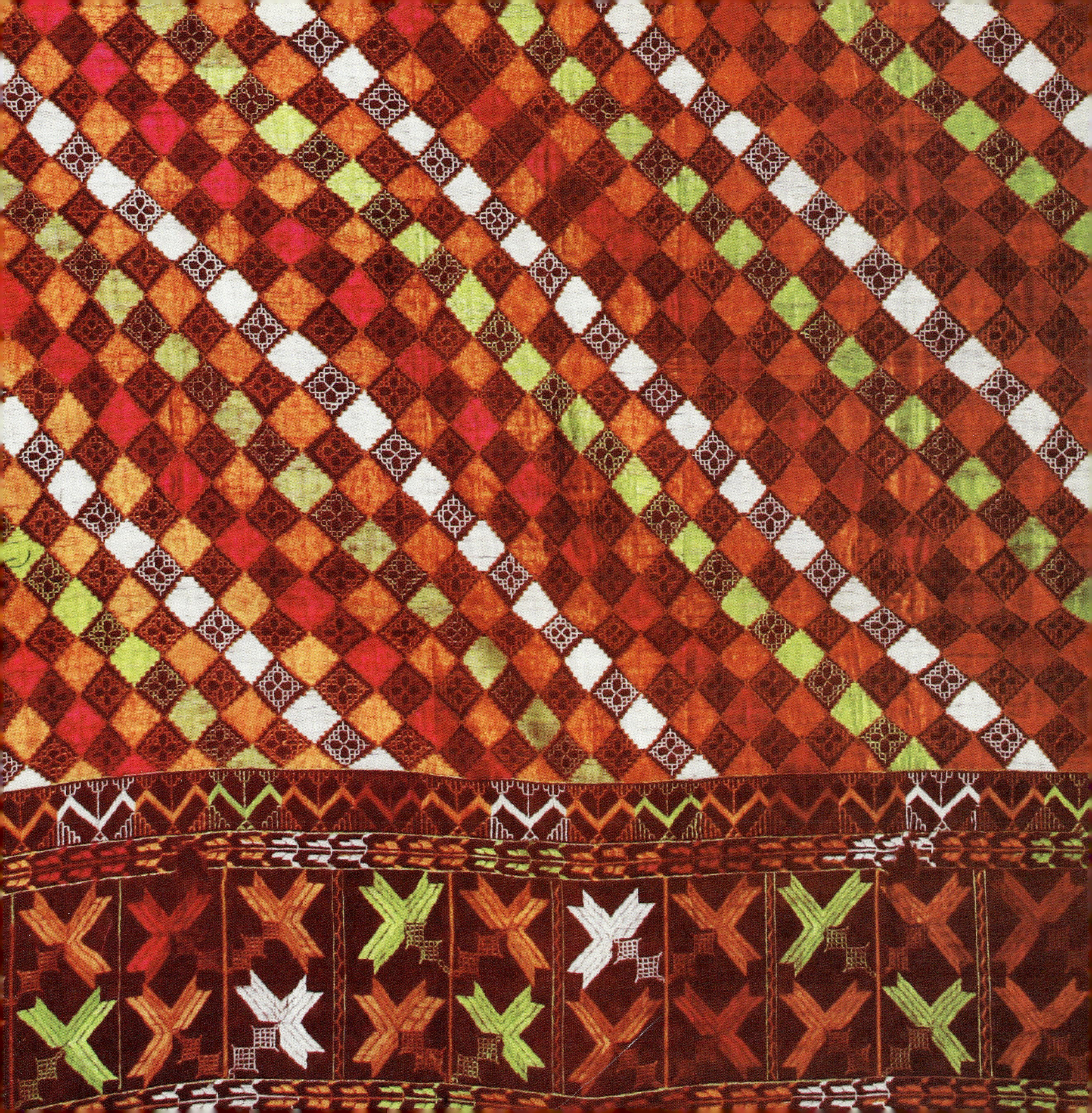

BAGH

Acc. No: 99.1.PH-26

Bagh with *pallu* and border embroidered with cowrie motifs. The entire field is covered with multicoloured squares with borders in *dhania* (corriander) stitch.

Late 19th Century; Punjab

Size: L: 233 cm x W: 139 cm

Base fabric: Maroon khaddar.

Magenta, mustard, white, navy blue, green, and pink silk threads are used in the embroidery.

The centre has black outline.

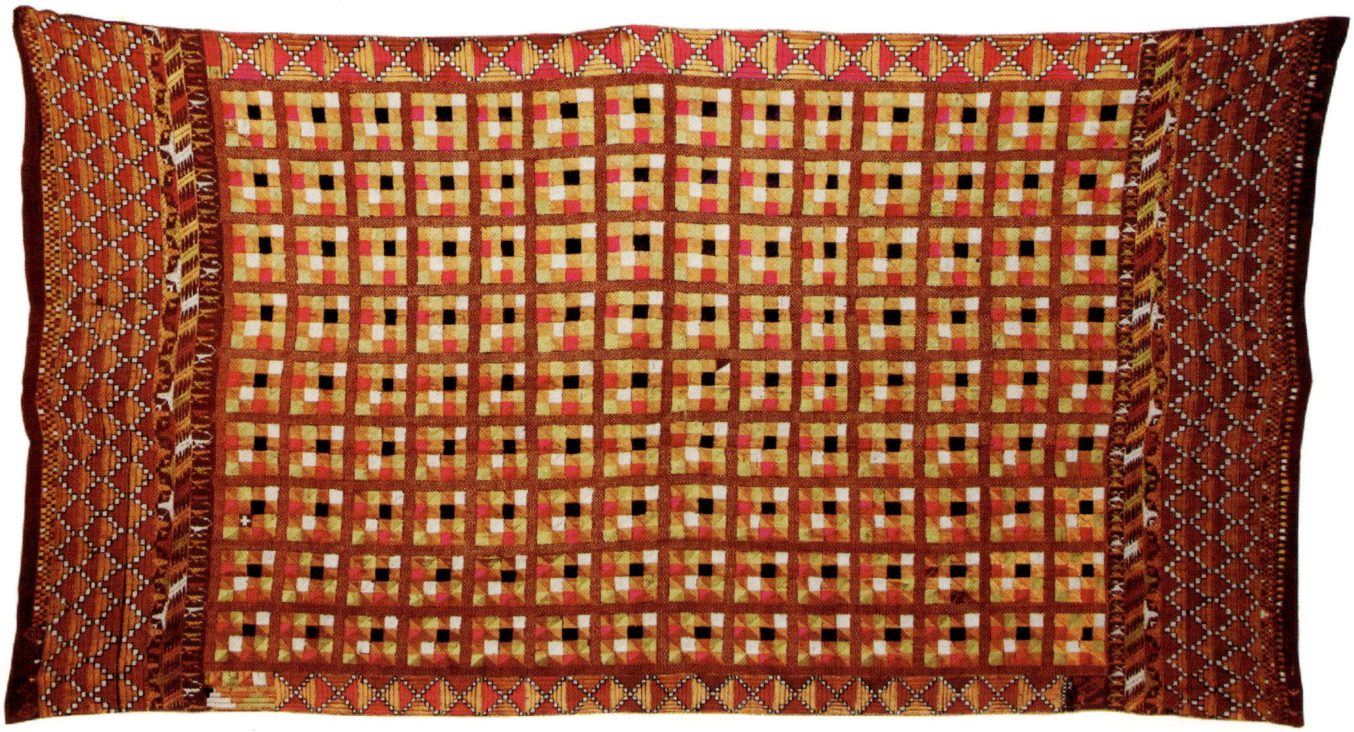

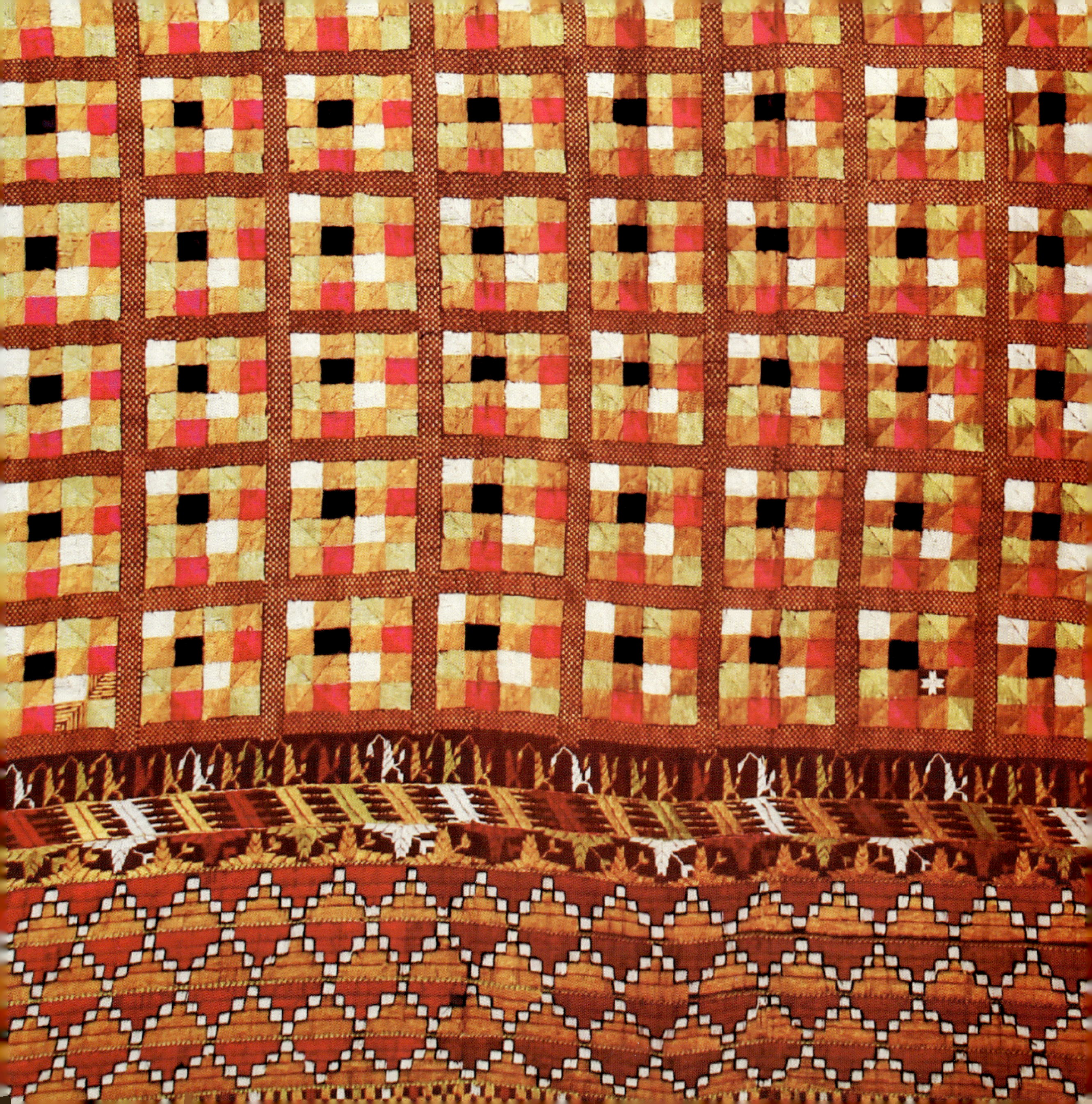

CHAR BAGH

Acc. No: 99.1.PH-27

Char Bagh (four) with multicoloured diagonal lines in cross stitch. The *pallus* are embroidered with *belan* pattern enclosed in triangles. The border is embroidered with arrow head pattern with diamonds in between.

20th Century; Punjab

Size: L: 246 cm x W: 144 cm

Base fabric: Maroon khaddar.

Mustard yellow, magenta, light green, white and dark blue silk threads are used in the embroidery.

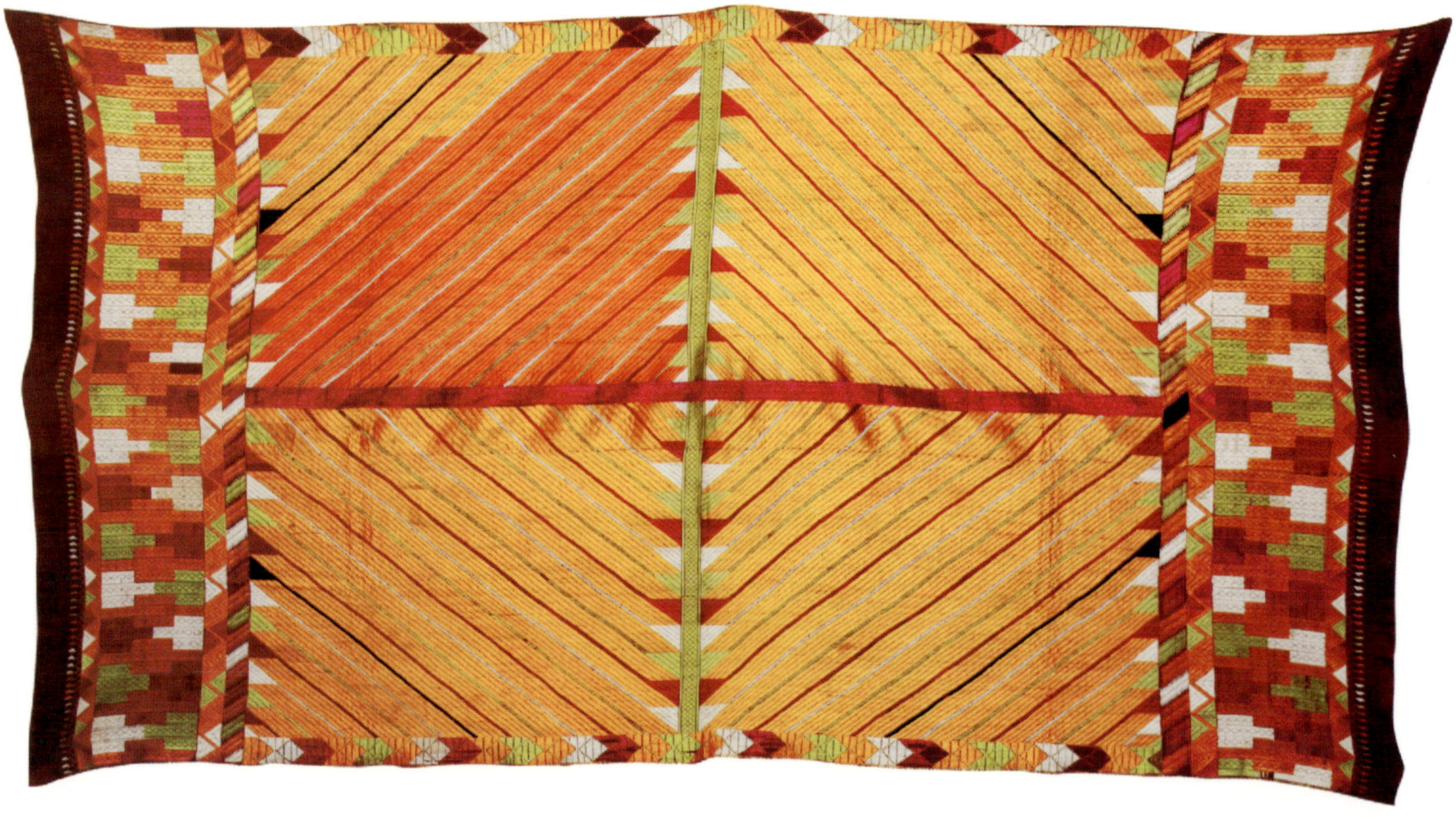

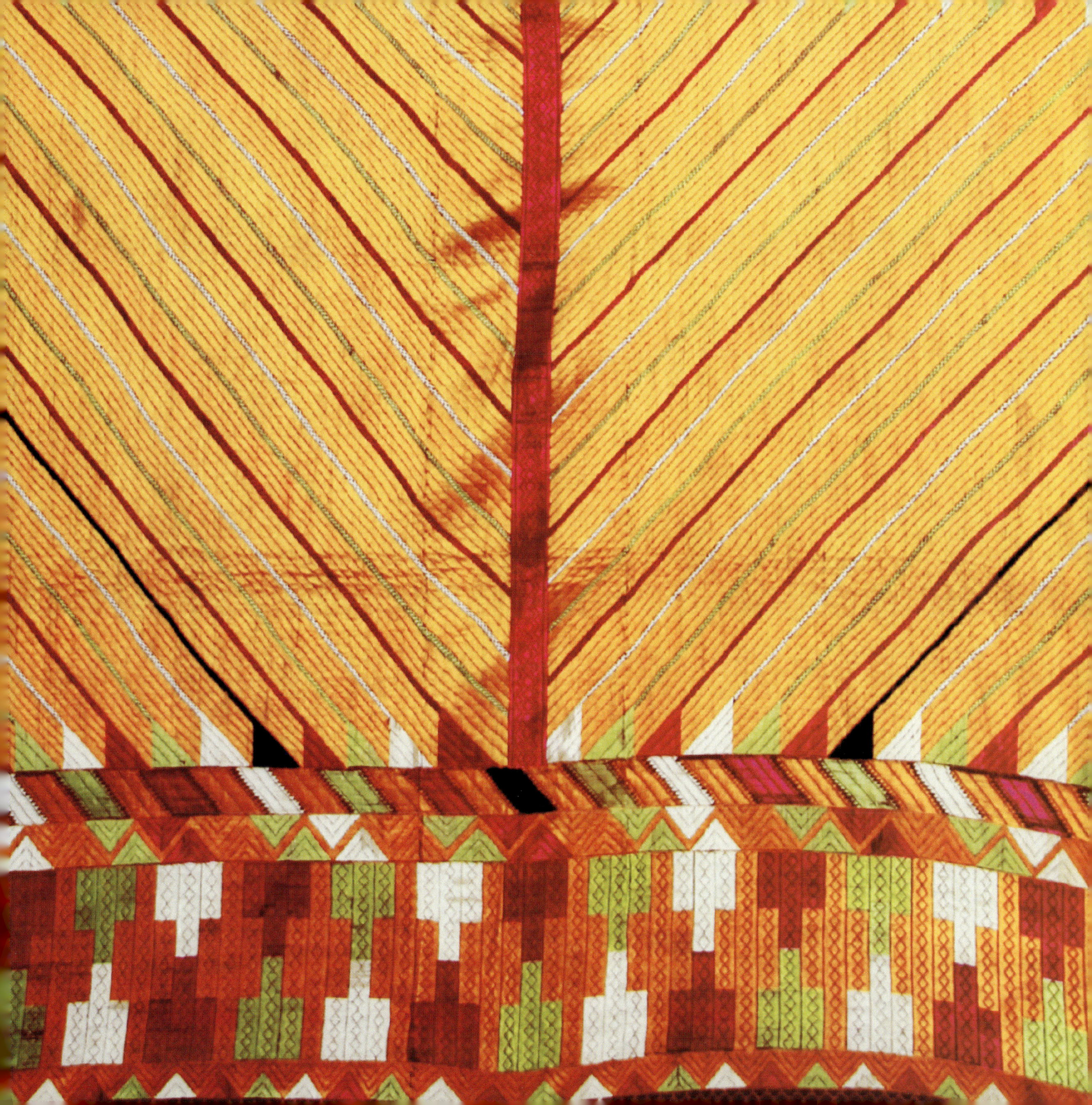

SARPALLU BAGH-CUM-PHULKARI

Acc. No: 99.1.PH-28

Sarpallu Bagh-cum-Phulkari. Two borders have diamond motifs on yellow background. The two *pallus* are embroidered with triangular motifs on top, arranged horizontally with rows of cross stitch in between the field. The two borders (broad) depict geometrical and wheat patterns while the centre panel is plain.

Late 19th Century; Punjab

Size: L: 232 cm x W: 146 cm

Base fabric: Red khaddar.

Embroidery is in yellow, mustard, different shades of green, maroon, red, black and turquoise blue silk threads with plain central panel.

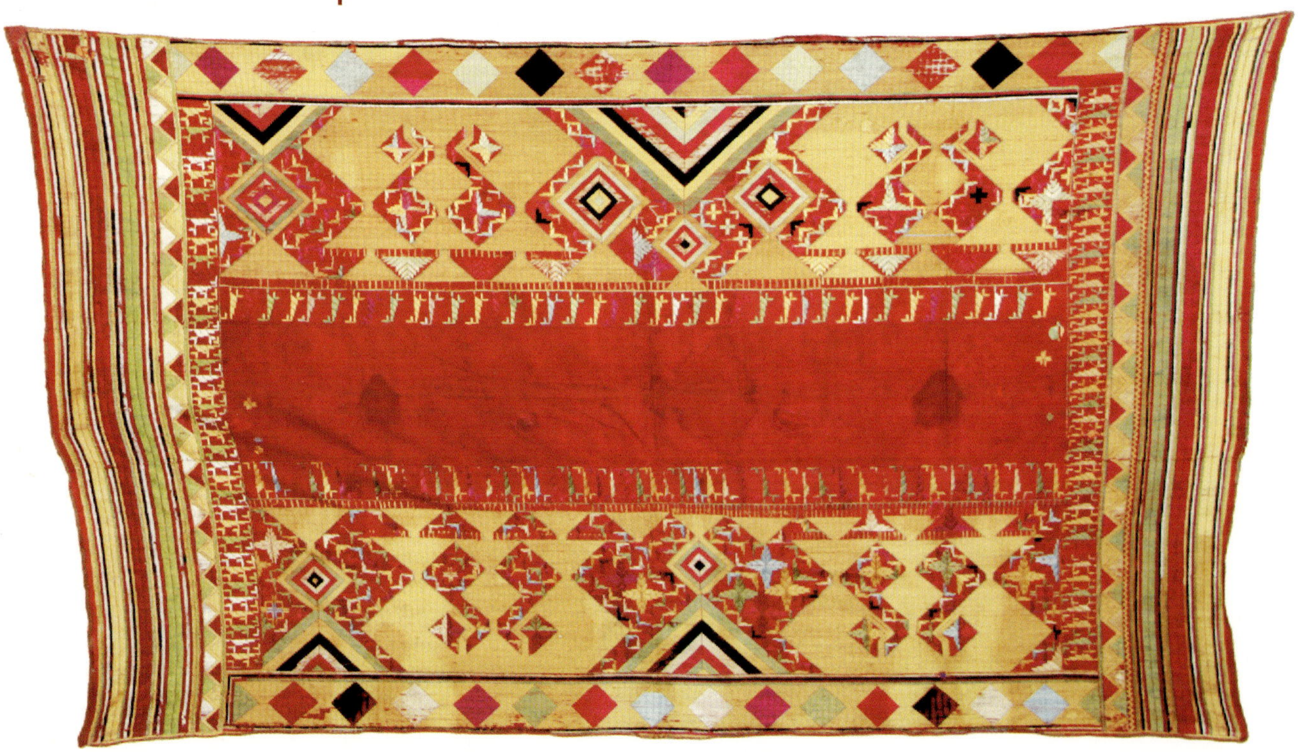

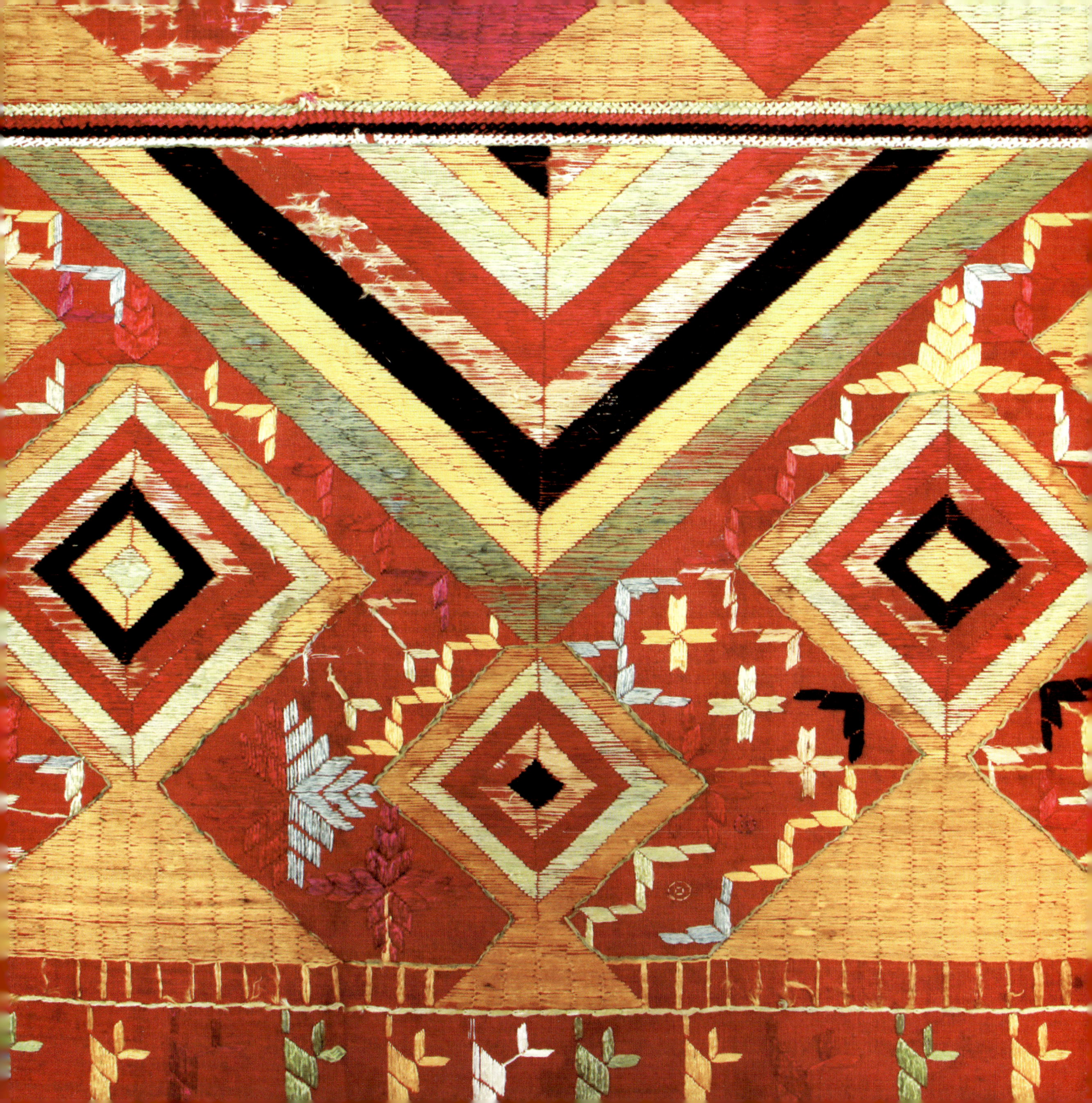

BAGH

Acc. No: 99.1.PH-29

Bagh arranged with rectangular motifs, each outlined with cross stitch. Borders are embroidered with diamond motifs, the *pallu* has several borders with stylized triangular arrow heads and flowers arranged in squares outlined by cowrie patterns.

20th Century; Punjab

Size: L: 229 cm x W: 150 cm

Base fabric: Red khaddar.

Different shades of green, white, mustard, orange, magenta and black silk threads are used in the embroidery.

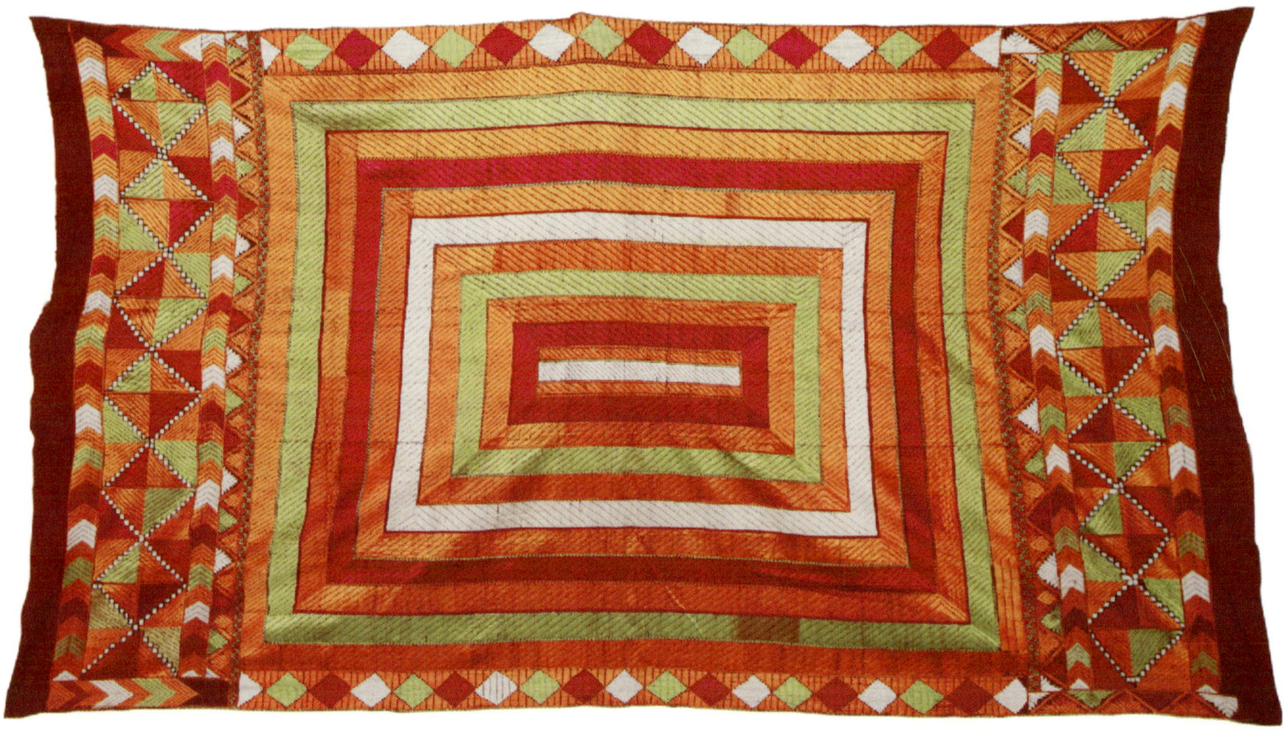

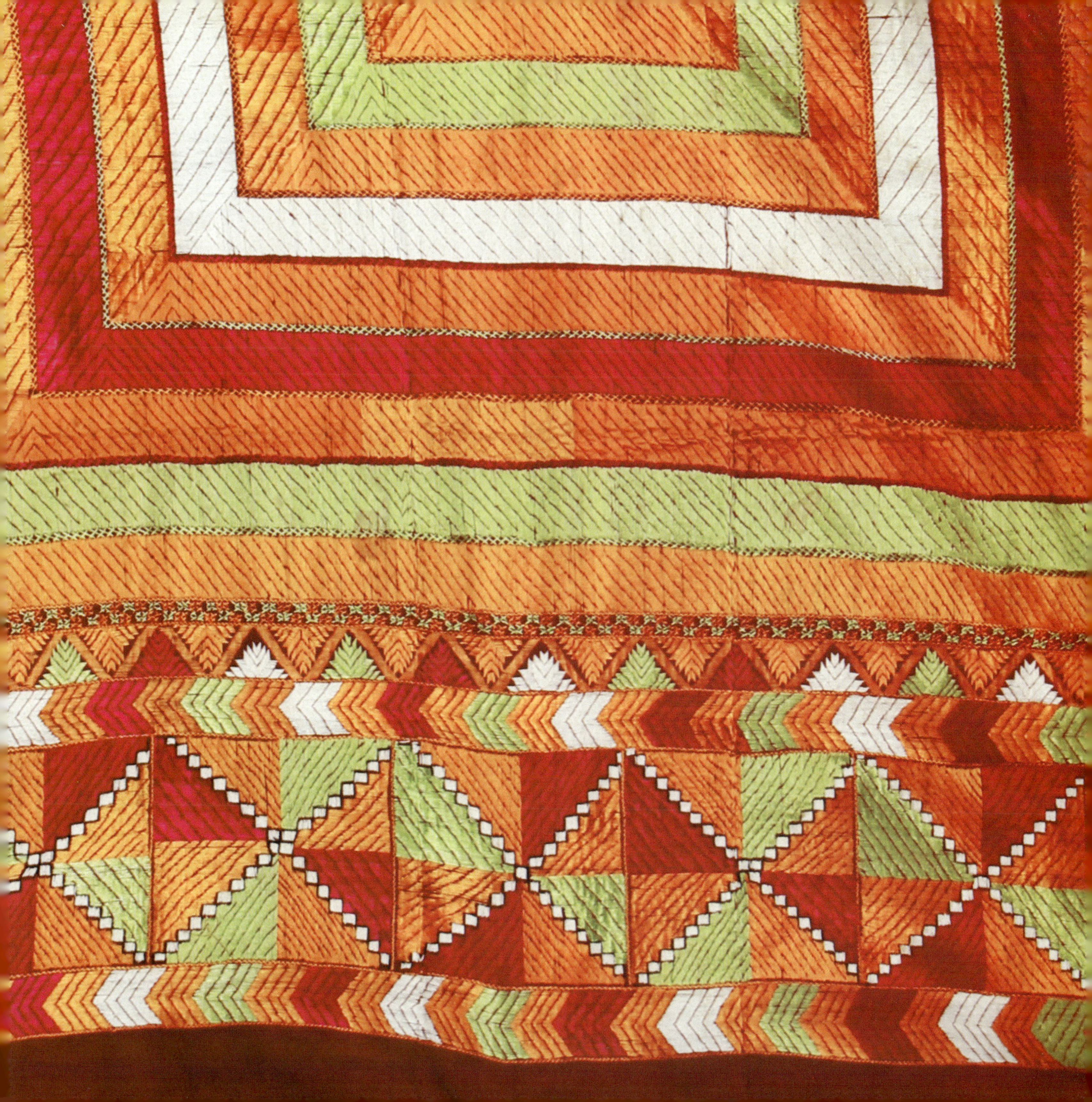

PHULKARI

Acc. No: 99.1.PH-30

Phulkari with two *pallus* divided into three parts. The lower part has stylized multi-coloured creeper pattern. The central part has floral cum geometrical motifs while a small part has diagonal lines with zigzag motifs on the edges. Both the borders are embroidered with two rows of cross stitch arranged in three lines. The upper part has a row of peacocks. The two borders have diagonal lines with serrated edges. Entire field has squares outlined with cross stitch and stylized motifs.

Early 20th Century; Haryana

Size: L: 247 cm x W: 147 cm

Base fabric: Maroon khaddar.

Embroidered with silk threads of different shades of green, mustard, orange, white, and maroon.

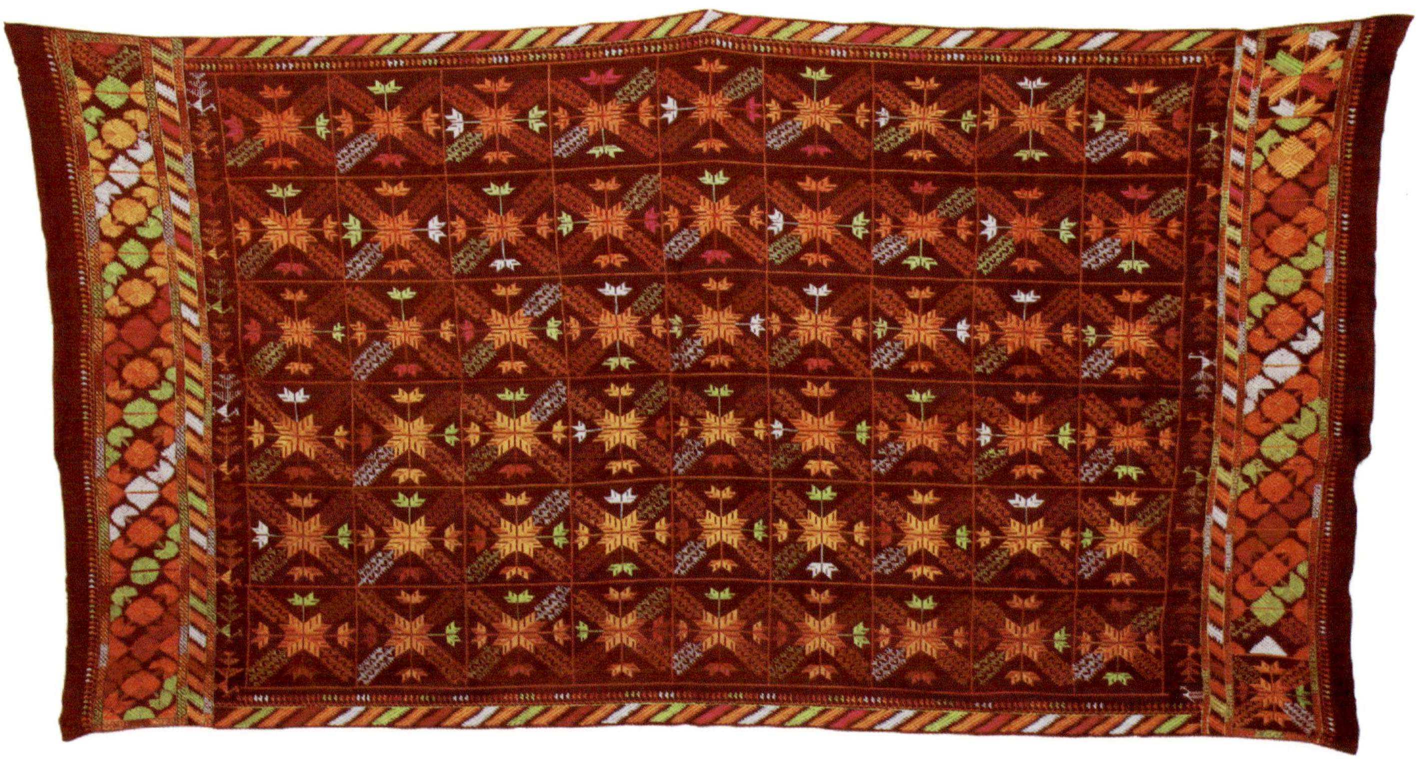

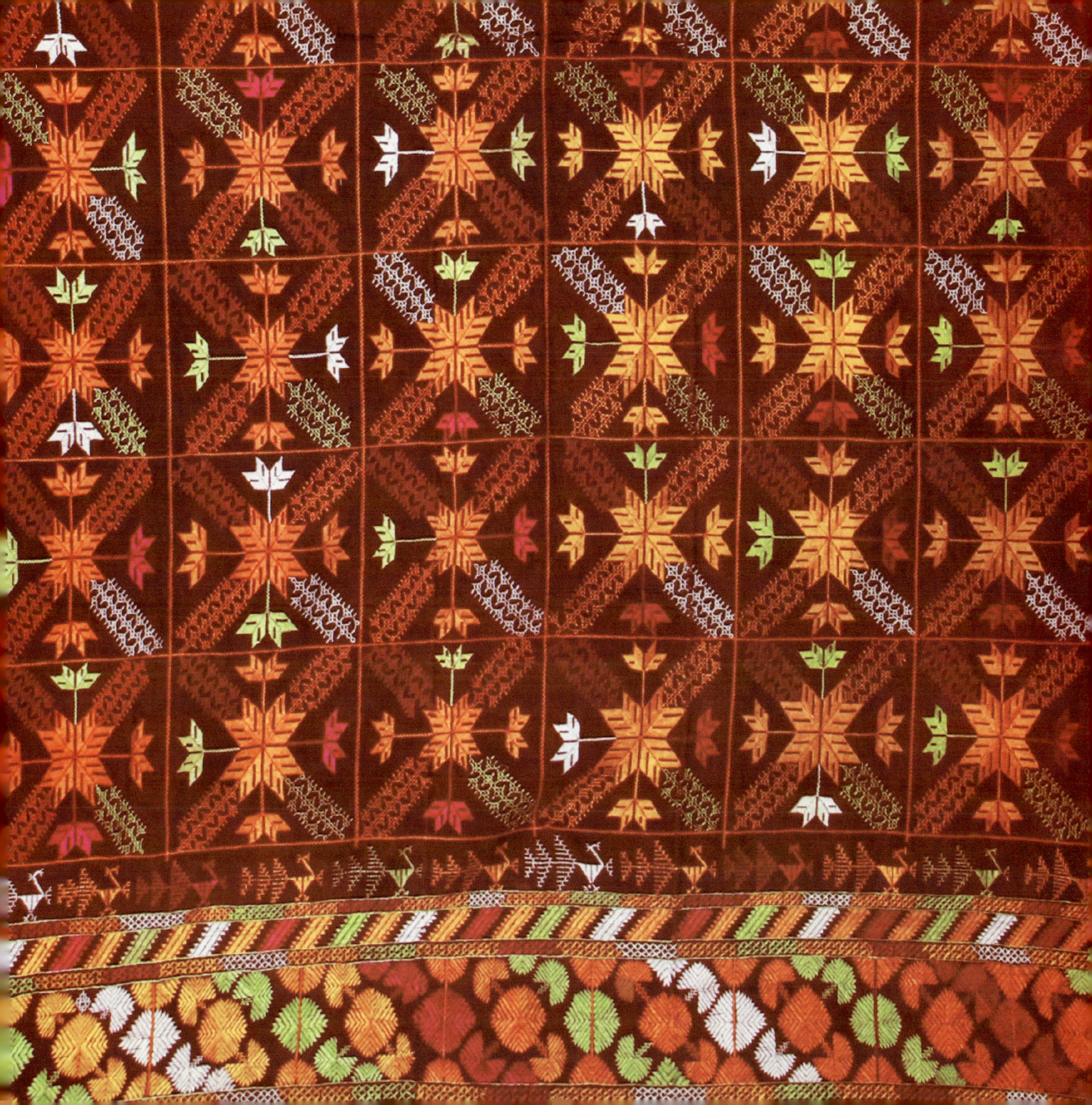

PATANGI PHULKARI

Acc. No: 99.1.PH-31

Patangi (kite) Phulkari with two *pallus* embroidered with stylized floral pattern surrounded by a row of pecocks. The borders are embroidered with stylized geometrical pattern. Entire field is in multicoloured stylized kite pattern arranged in vertical rows.

Early 20th Century; Punjab

Size: L: 208 cm x W: 137 cm

Base fabric: Red khaddar.

Embroidered with mustard, light green, red and magenta silk threads.

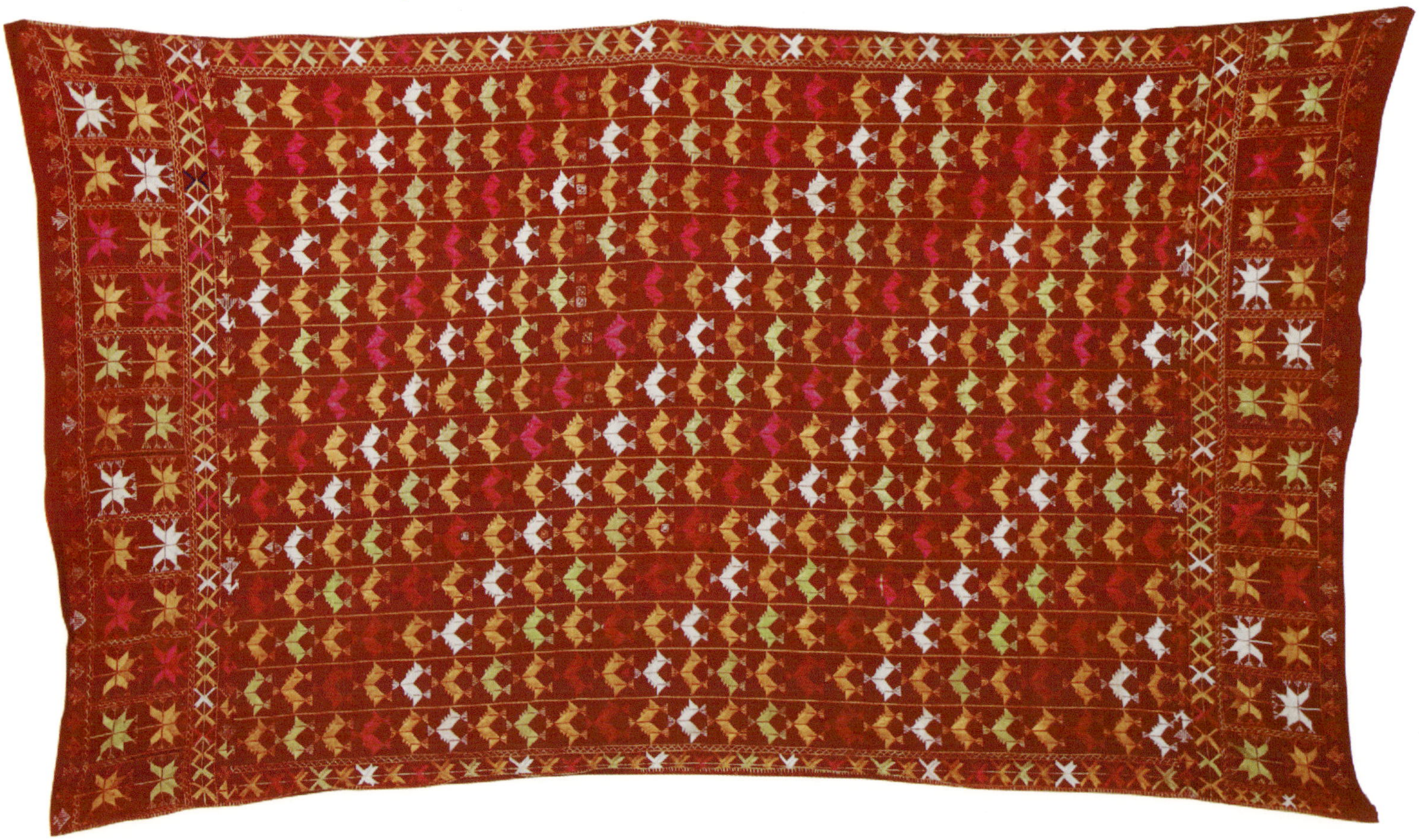

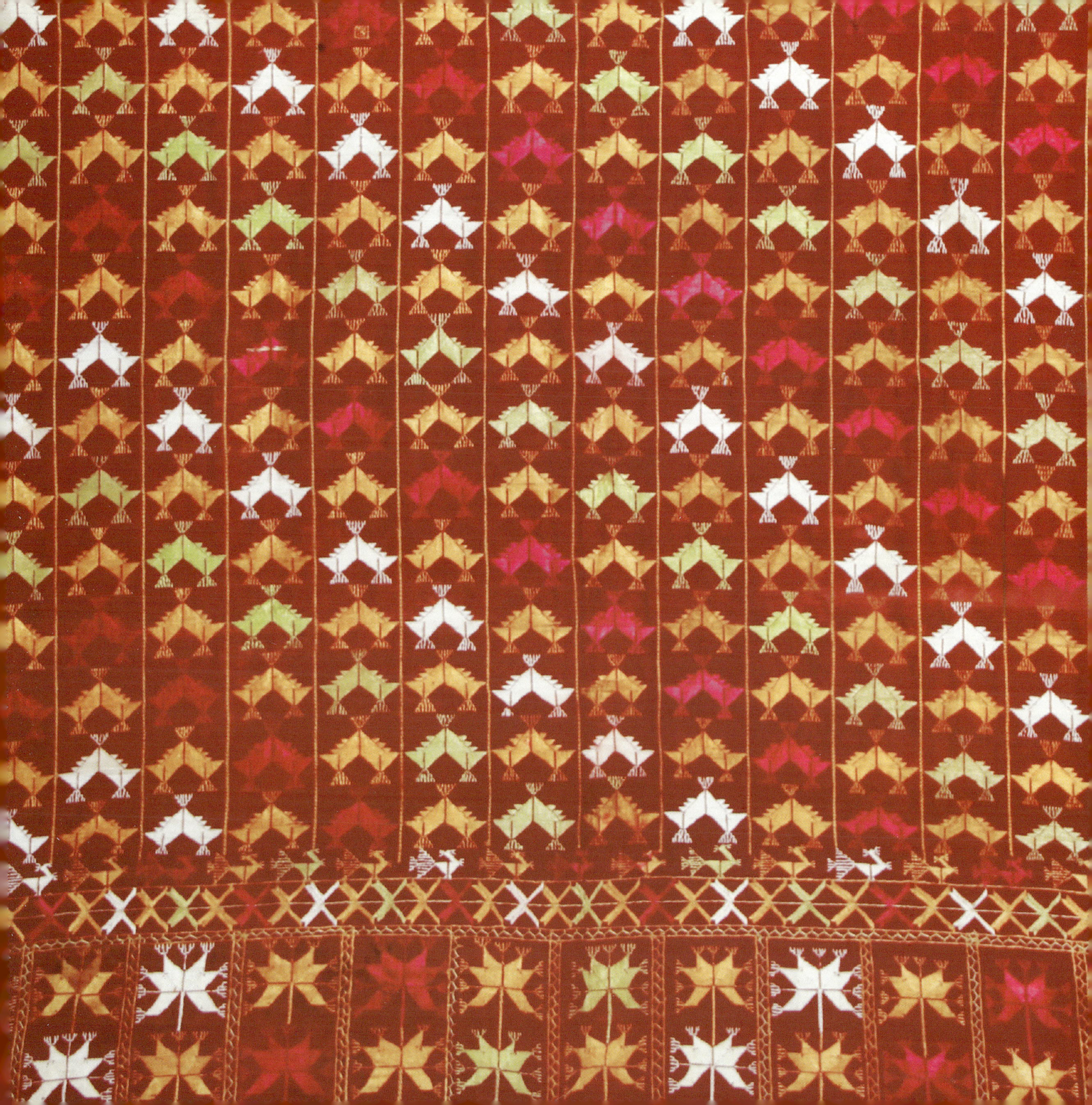

GHUNGHAT BAGH CUM PHULKARI

Acc. No: 99.1.PH-32

Ghunghat bagh cum Phulkari with two broad borders on two sides, each depicting multi coloured diamond and architectural motifs with a *kalash* (pitcher) in between, alternating with wheat and triangular motifs. The *ghunghat* (veil) part has an auspicious motif in the centre surrounded by floral and architectural designs with *kalash*. Rest of the field has floral branches.

Early 20th Century; Haryana

Size: L: 254 cm x W: 130 cm

Base fabric: Maroon khaddar.

Mustard, navy blue, orange, white, light green and magenta silk threads are used in the embroidery.

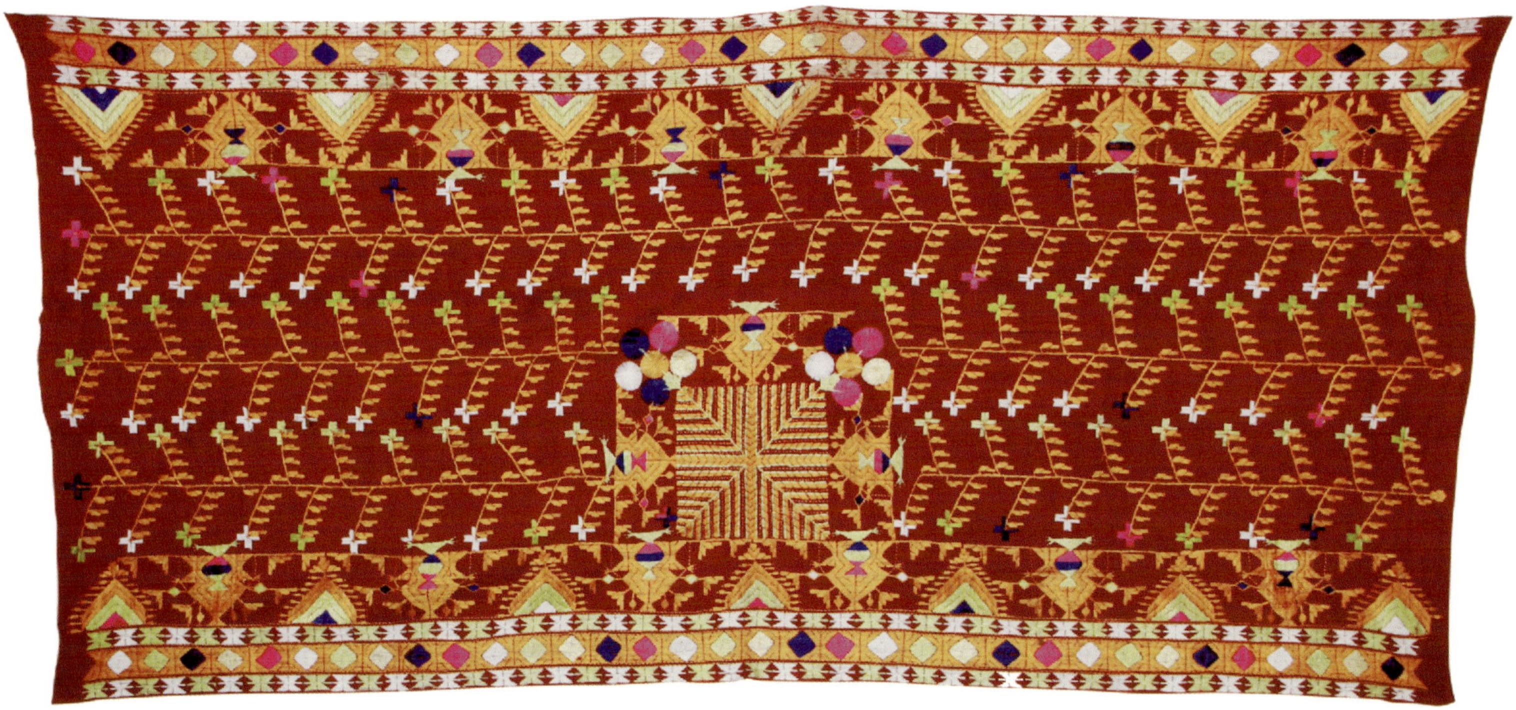

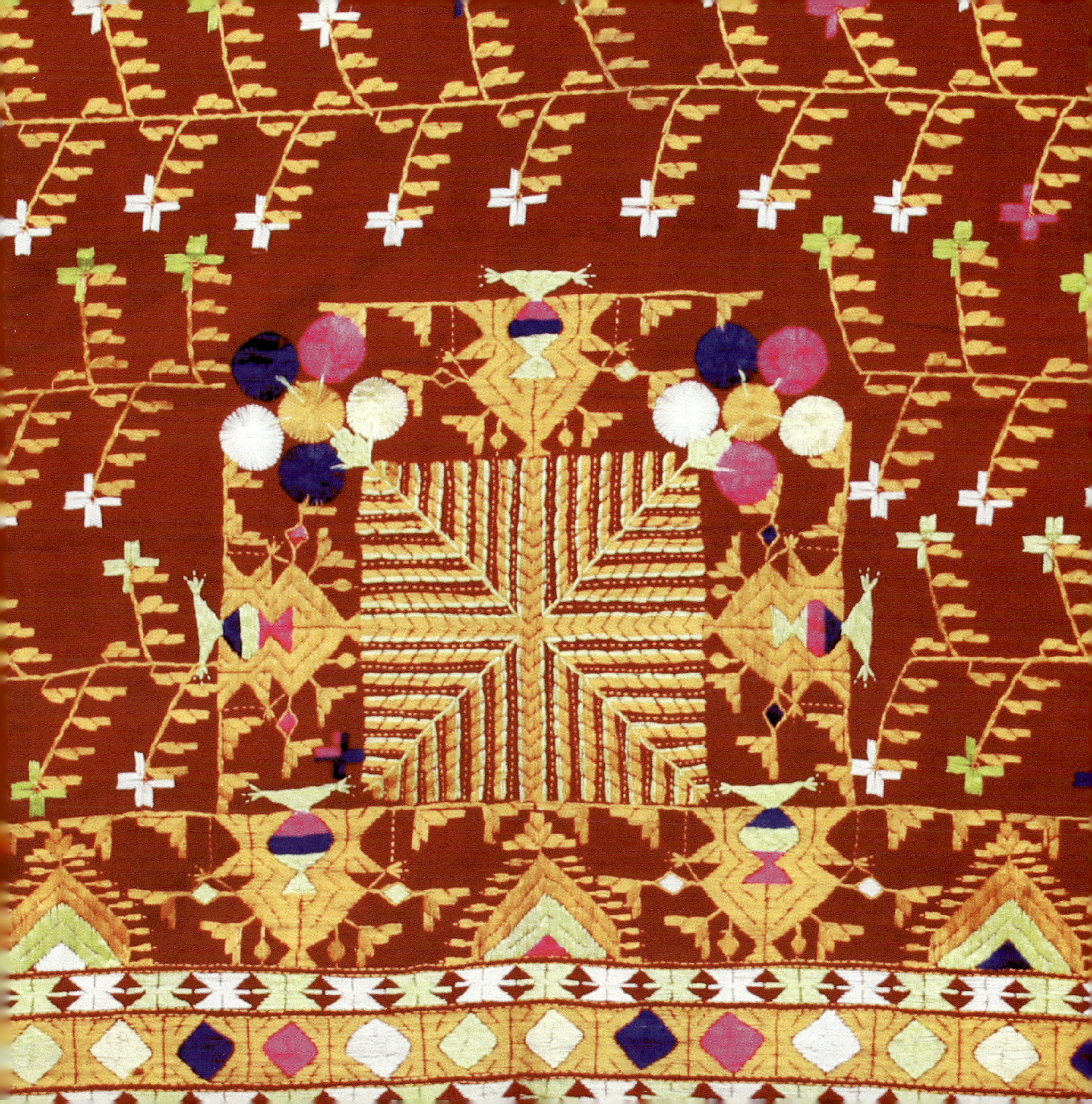

PHULKARI

Acc. No: 99.1.PH-33

Phulkari with *pallu* embroidered with stylized floral pattern arranged in rows. The borders have stylized wheat pattern. The entire field is divided into squares, each with a stylized geometrical floral pattern.

Early 20th Century; Haryana

Size: L: 244 cm x W: 142 cm

Base fabric: Maroon khaddar.

Mainly mustard, green, white and magenta silk threads are used in the embroidery.

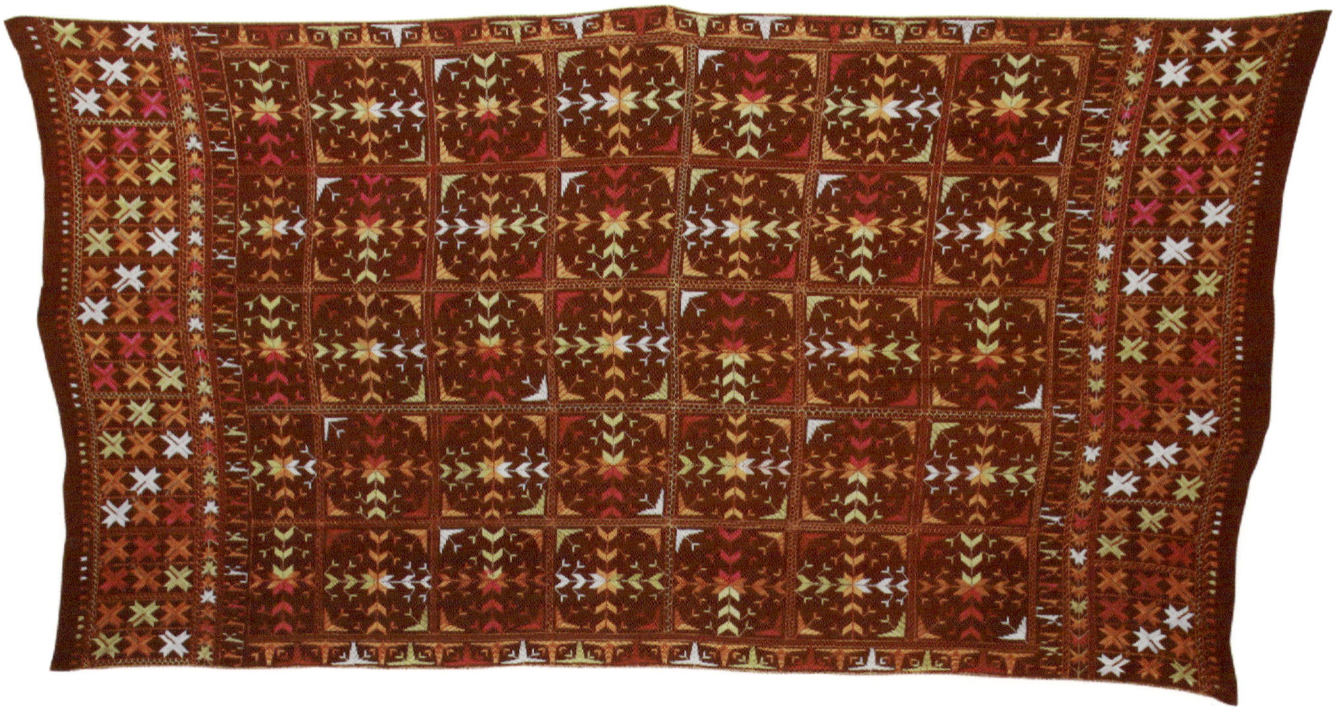

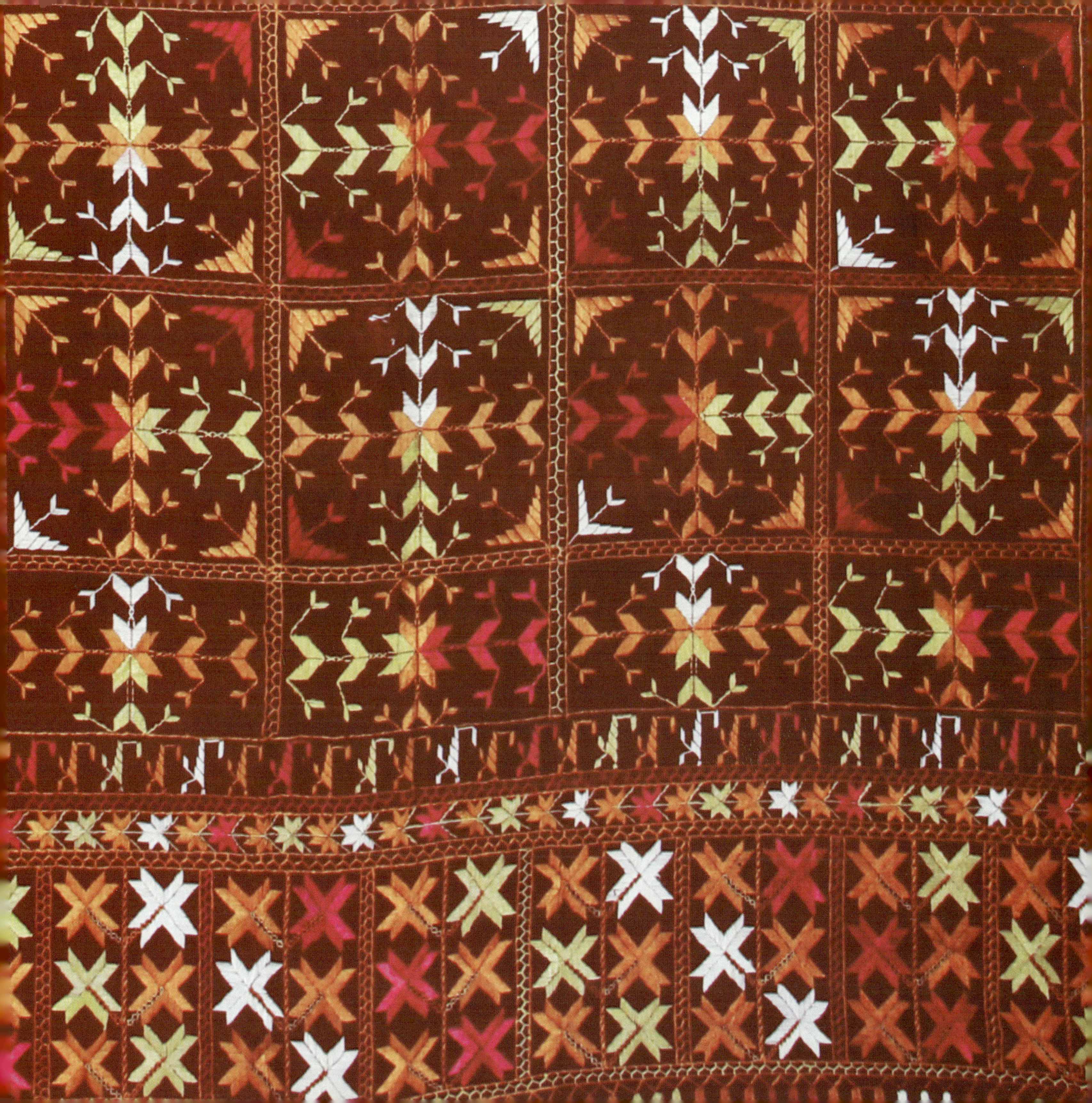

Acc. No: 99.1.PH-34

Phulkari with two *pallus* embroidered with floral branches in zigzag and trefoil pattern; borders are embroidered with stylized floral pattern. The entire field is embroidered with foliage arranged in horizontal rows, each with cross stitch in between.

Late 20th Century; Haryana

Size: L: 255 cm x W: 154 cm

Base fabric: Maroon khaddar.

Orange, white and light green silk threads are used in the field.

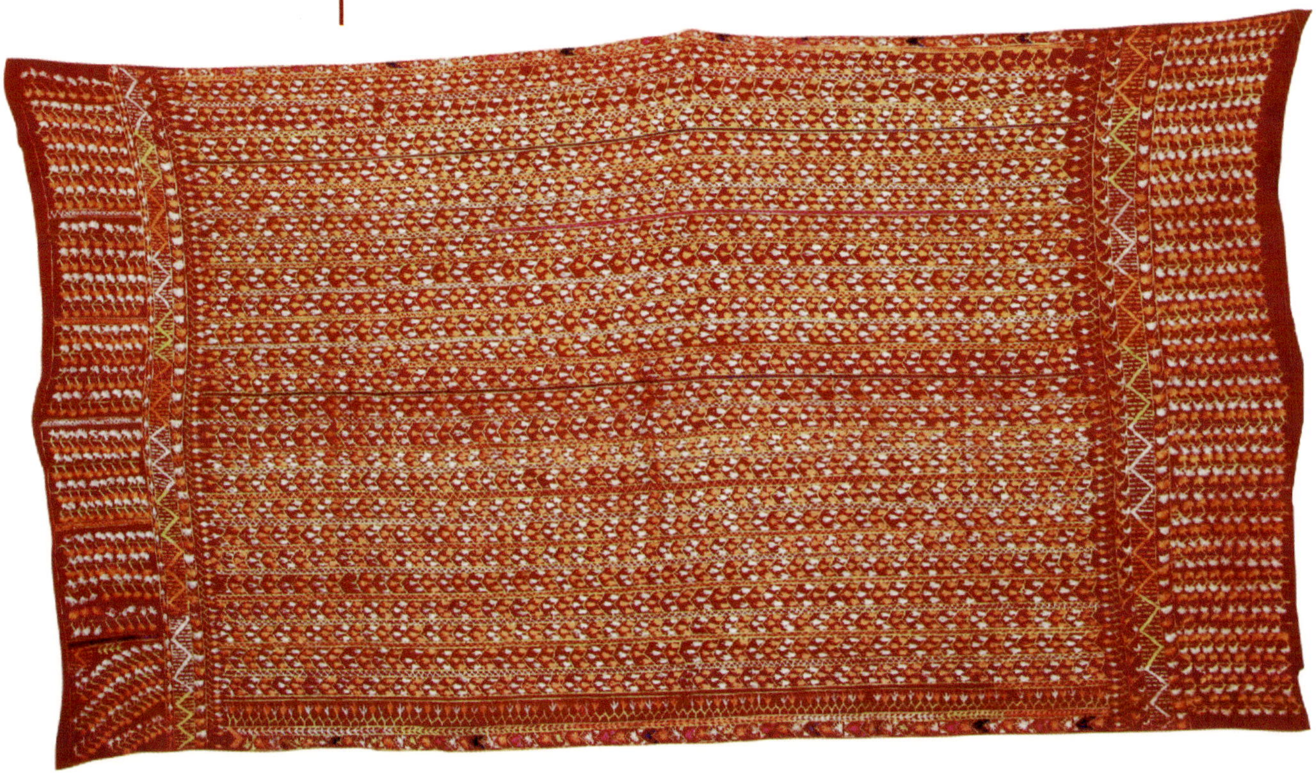

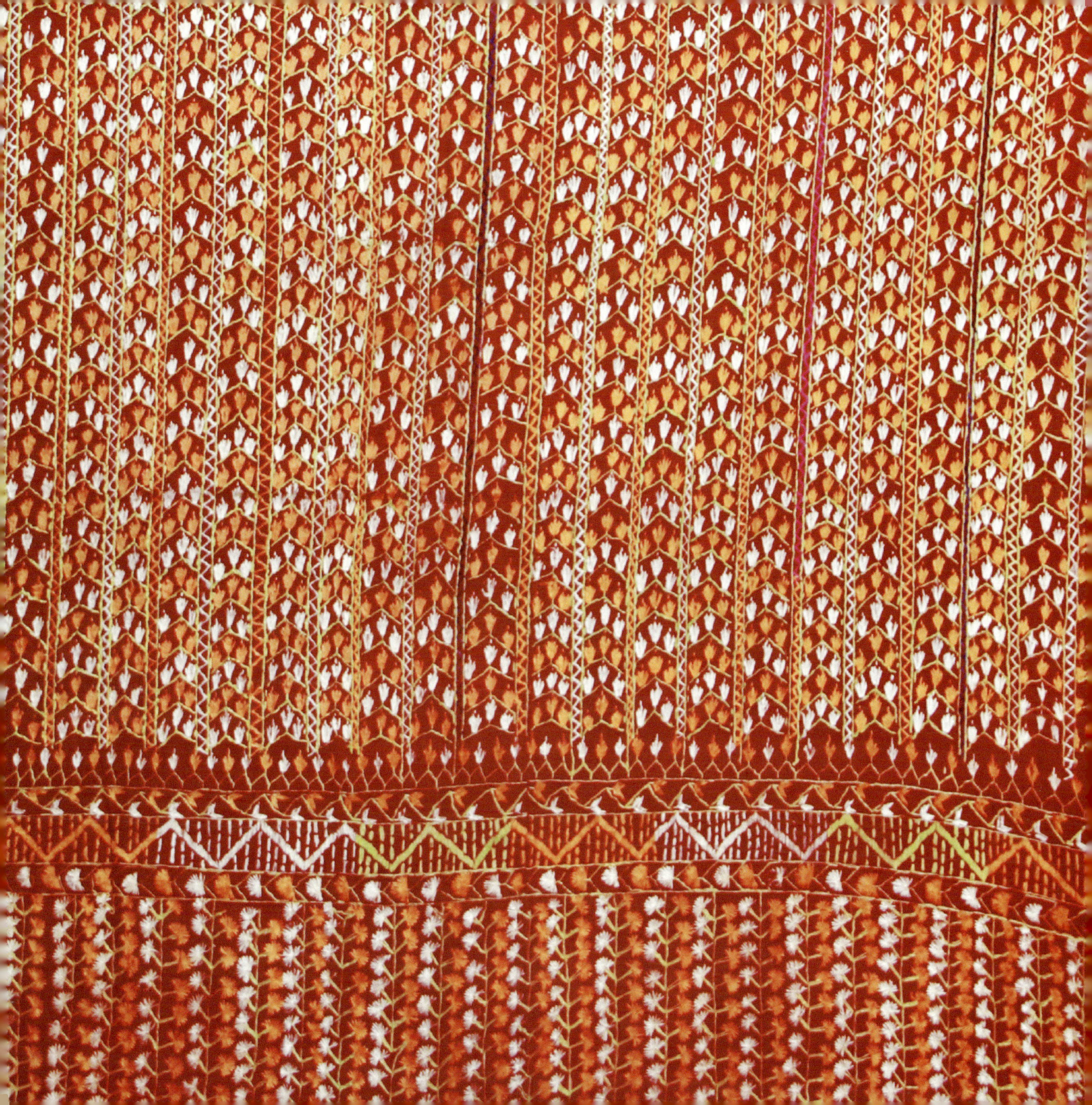

BAGH

Acc. No: 99.1.PH-35

Bagh with two *pallus* embroidered in *belan* motif enclosed in triangles in diagonal lines. The entire field has horizontal lines with triangles on the borders and stylized geometrical pattern in between, arranged in rows. Each row is outlined with *nakhoon* (nail) motif.

Late 19th Century; Punjab

Size: L: 220 cm x W: 155 cm

Base fabric: Maroon khaddar.

Richly embroidered with orange, light green, magenta, white and blue silk threads.

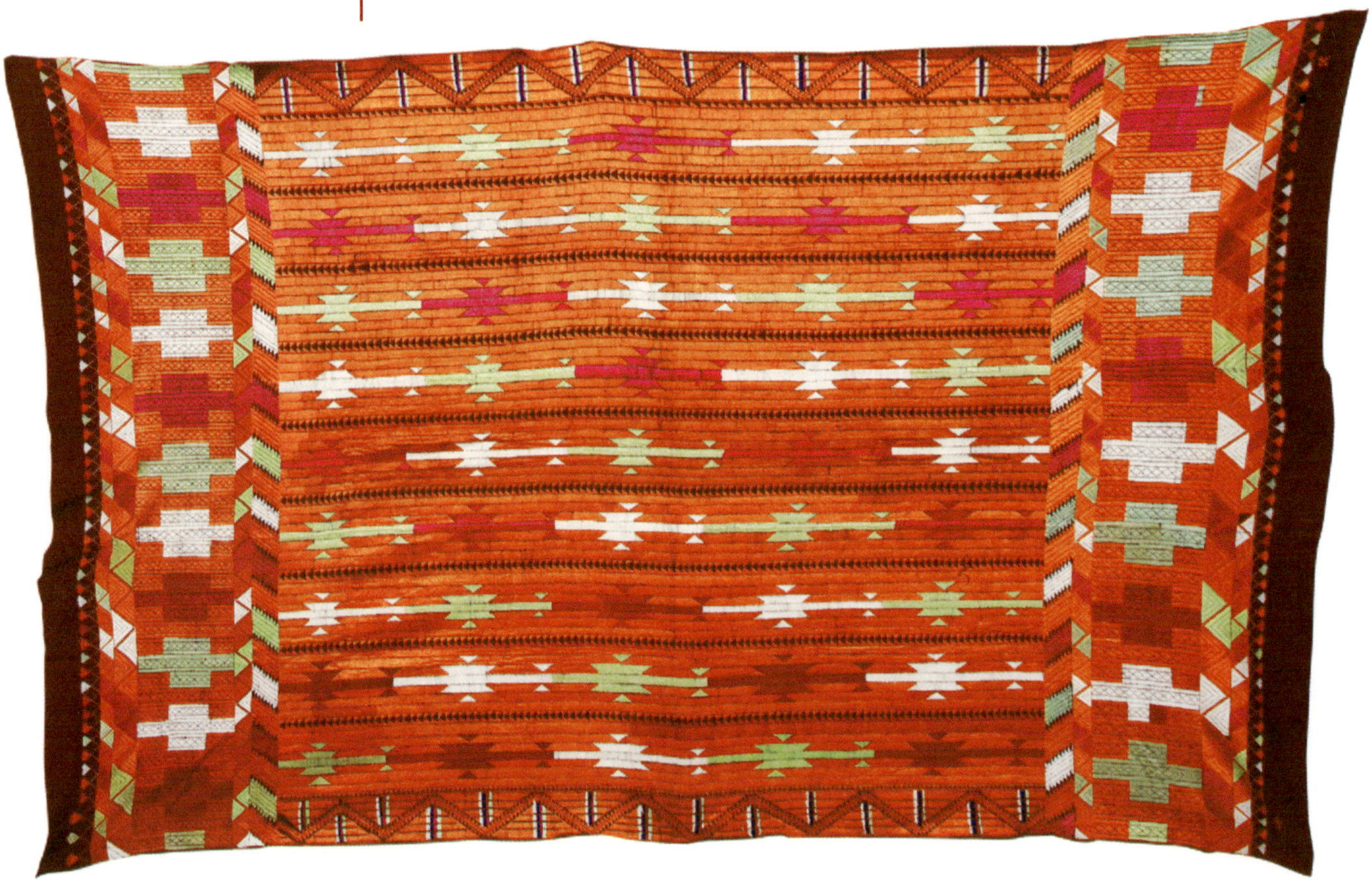

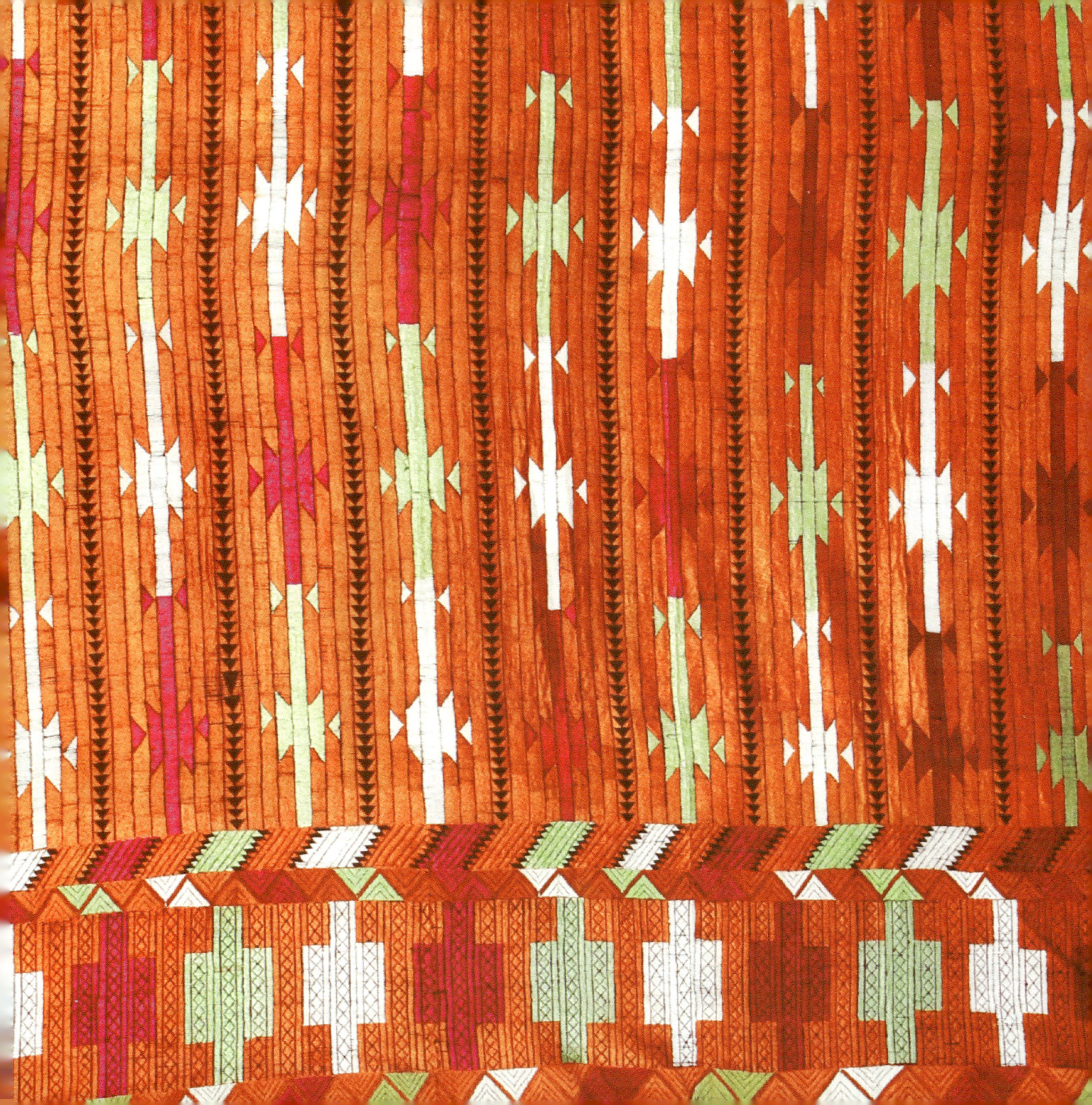

DHARSHAN DWAR PHULKARI

Acc. No: 99.1.PH-36

Dharshan Dwar phulkari with borders and two *pallus* consisting of zigzag, linear and diagonal lines with a row of wheat pattern. The field has two borders and several pavilions on two sides embroidered in diamond shapes. The centre and side panels have female figures and birds outlined in cross stitch. Rest of the field is covered with human figures, kites, surajmukhi flowers, animals, peacocks and floral pattern. Double line stitch is used at different places.

Early 20th Century; Haryana

Size: L: 224 cm x W: 132 cm

Base fabric: Maroon khaddar.

Orange, mustard, white, pink, green, violet, and red silk threads are used in the embroidery.

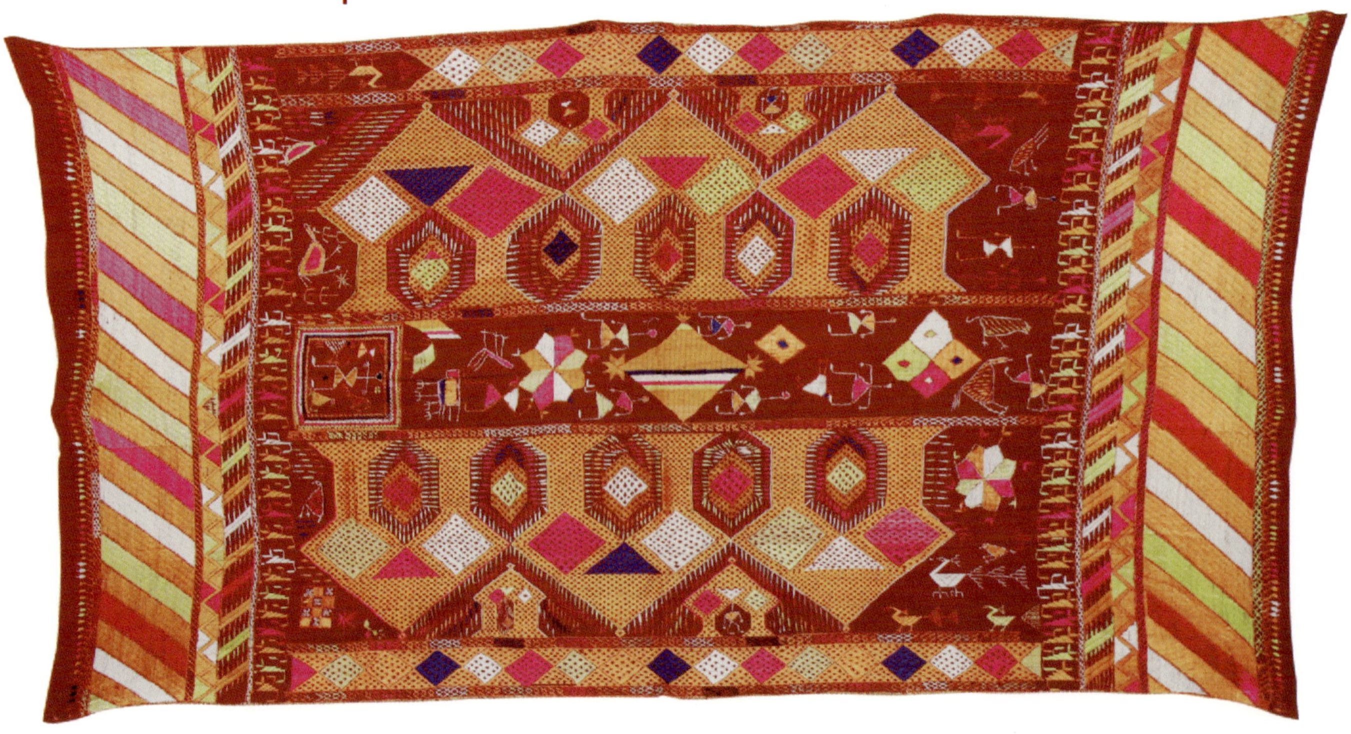

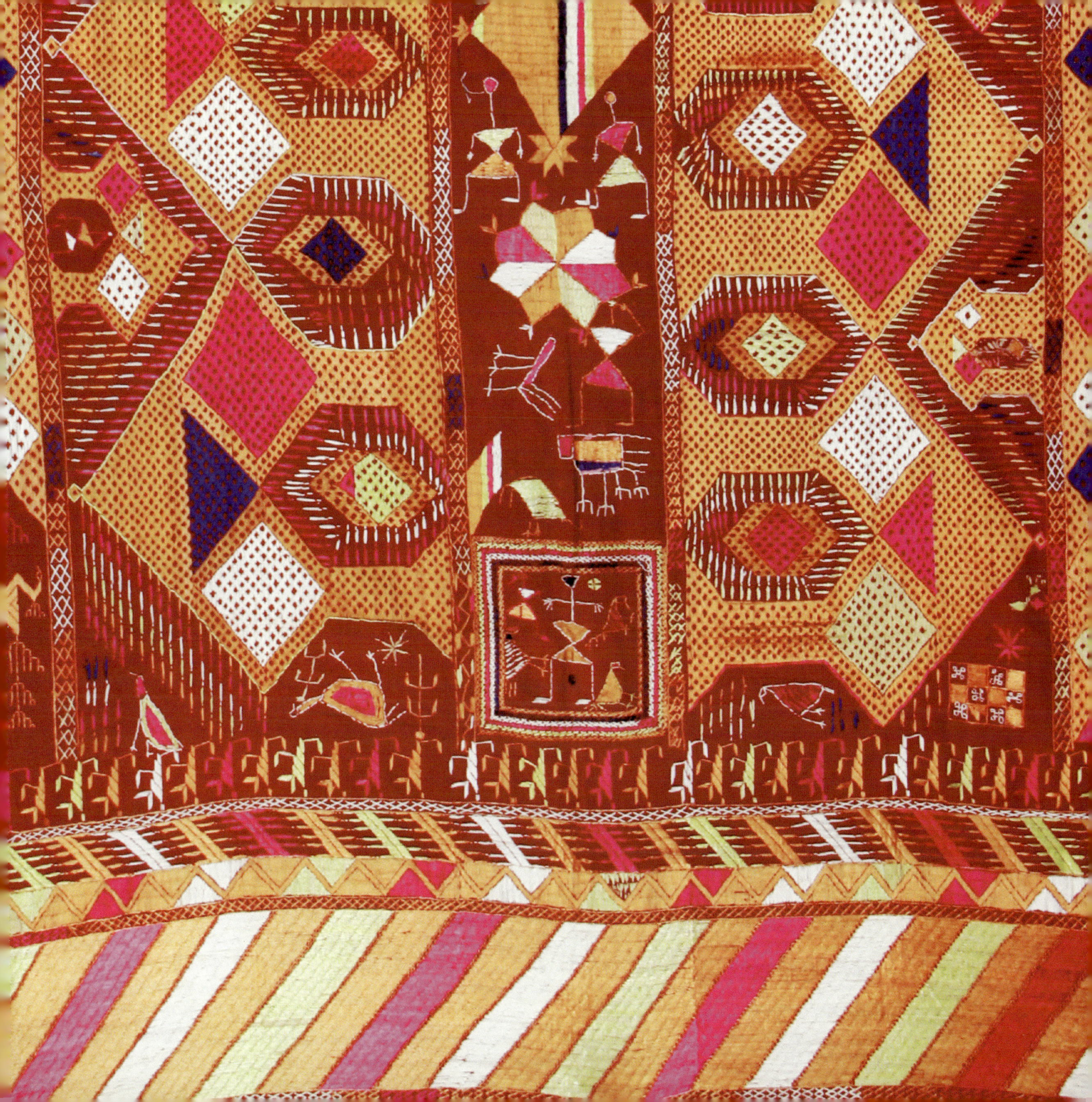

BAGH CUM PHULKARI

Acc. No: 99.1.PH-37

Bagh cum Phulkari with two *pallus* in char bagh style. The borders depict *nakhoon* pattern; the field has horizontal lines with stylized uniform foliage pattern in between.

Early 20th Century; Punjab

Size: L: 214 cm x W: 132 cm

Base fabric: Maroon khaddar.

Mustard, magenta, light green, white and navy blue silk threads are used in the embroidery.

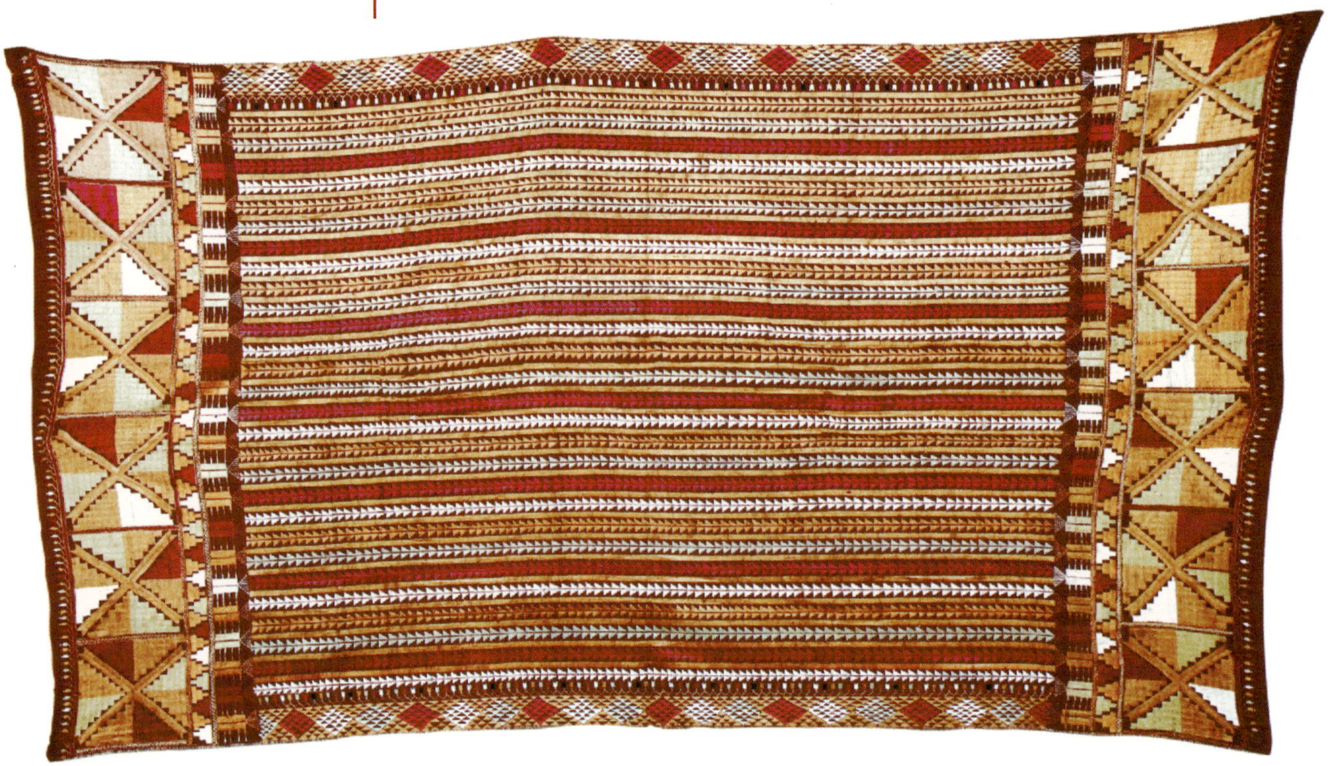

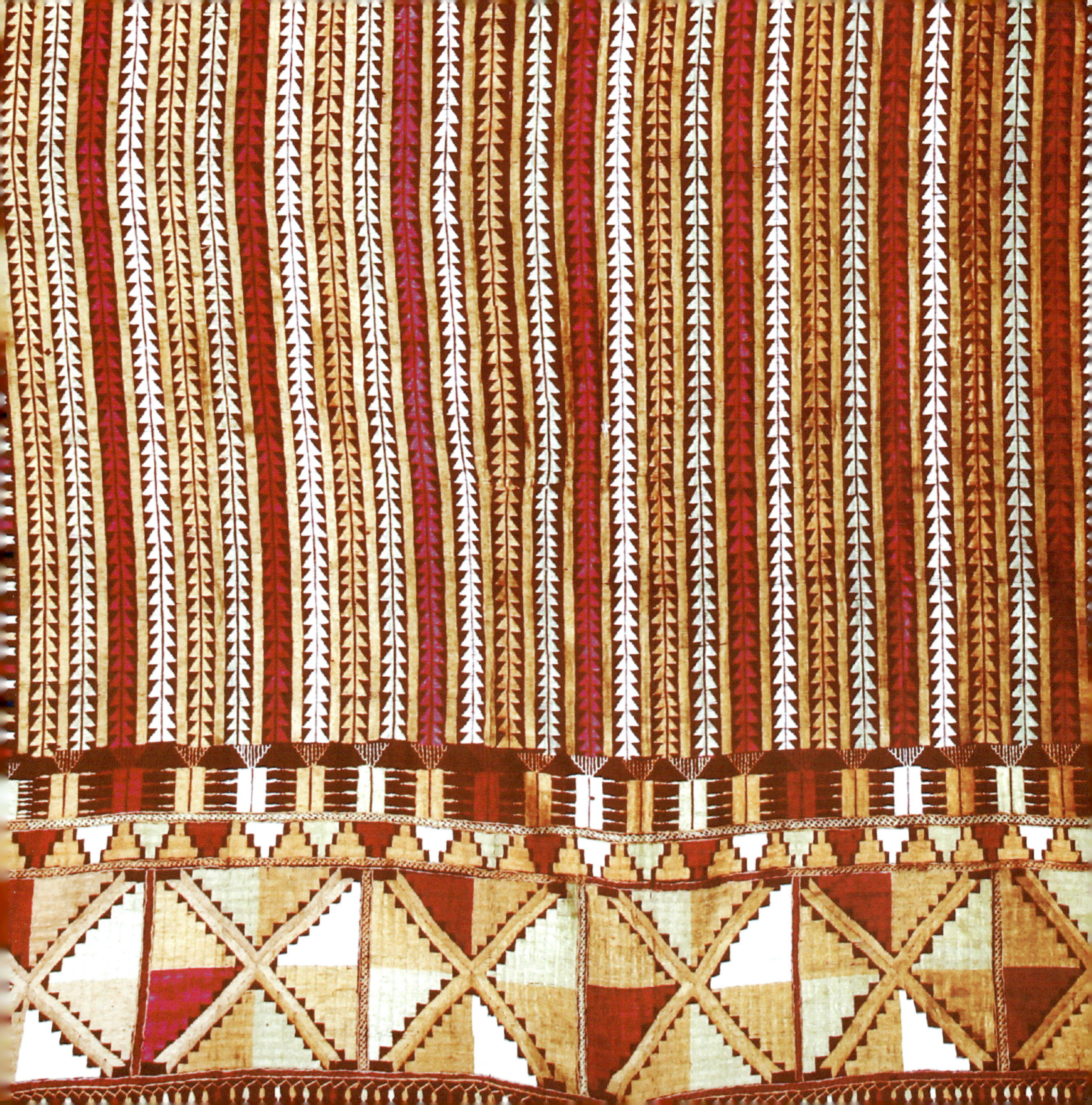

BAGH

Acc. No: 99.1.PH-38

Bagh with two *pallus* richly embroidered in horizontal lines in a triangle. Stylized floral edges surrounded by stylized wheat pattern. The entire field is covered with a cluster of multicoloured diamonds with surajhmukhi pattern. The borders depict pyramids. Each cluster has space around it which is embroidered in two line stitch, like in chhope.

Late 19th Century; Punjab

Size: L: 229 cm x W: 130 cm

Base fabric: Maroon khaddar.

Orange, mustard, magenta, white, green and brown silk threads are used in the embroidery.

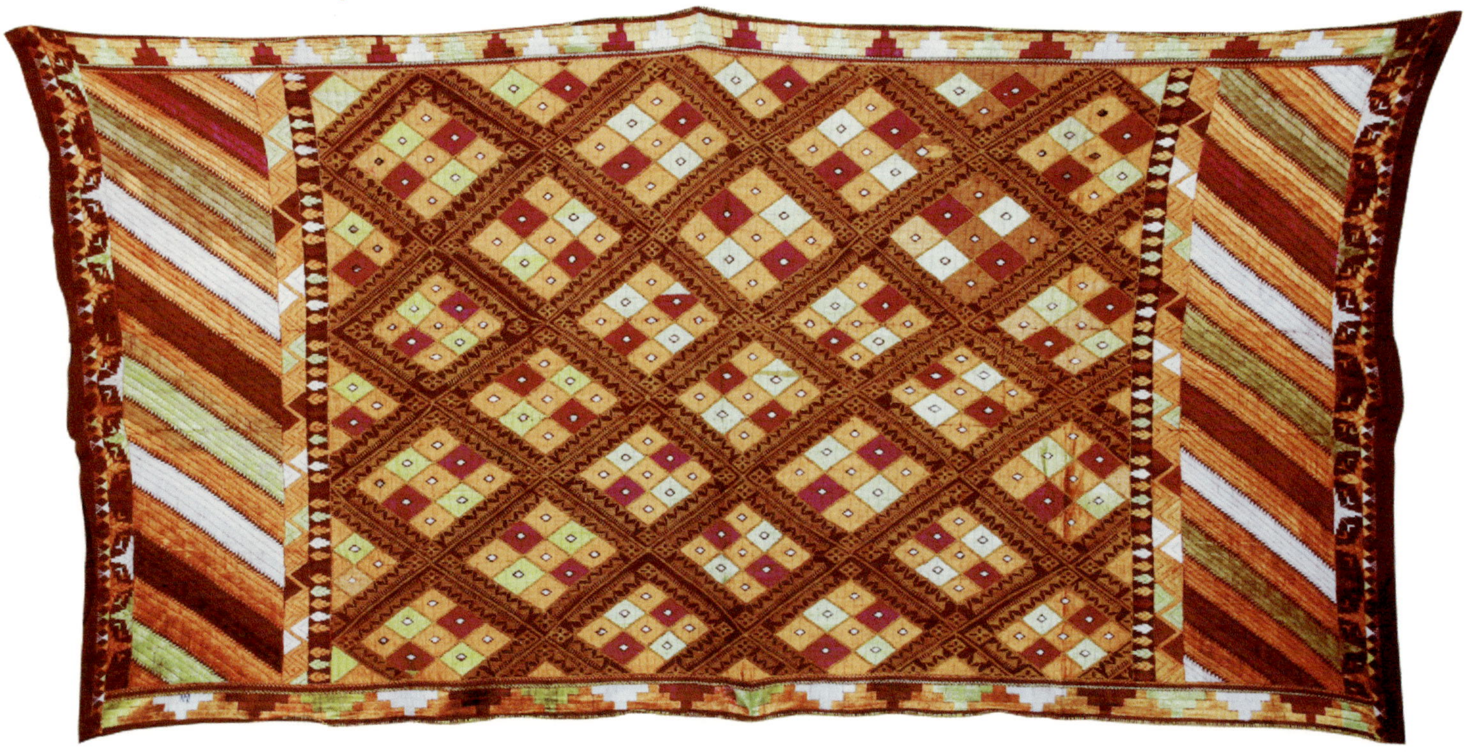

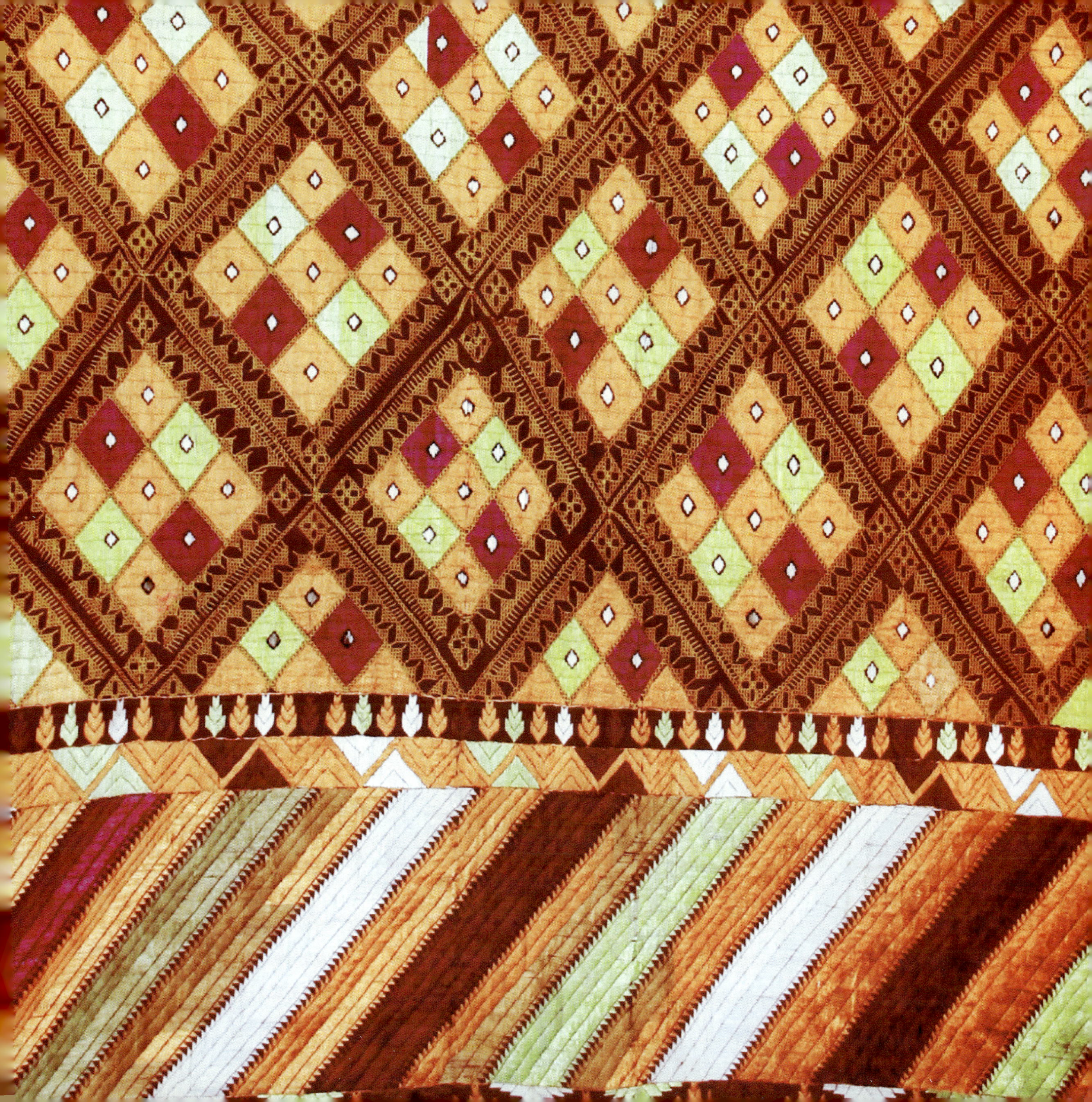

PATANGI BAGH

Acc. No: 99.1.PH-39

Patangi bagh with *pallus* in five rows, each with different geometrical, zigzag, triangles and horizontal lines. The two borders are embroidered with diamond motifs. The entire field is embroidered with kites and vertical lines in between.

Early 20th Century; Punjab

Size: L: 248 cm x W: 140 cm

Base fabric: Maroon khaddar.

Deep mustard, purple, orange, magenta and white silk threads are used in the embroidery.

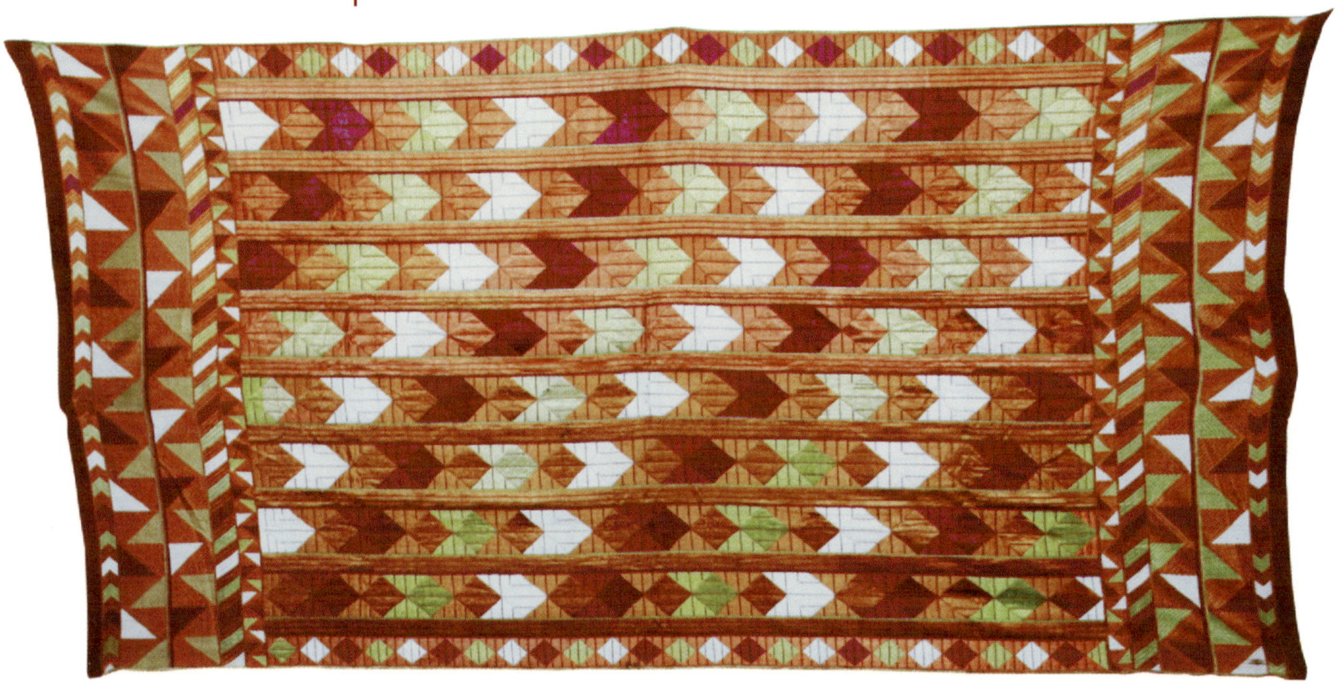

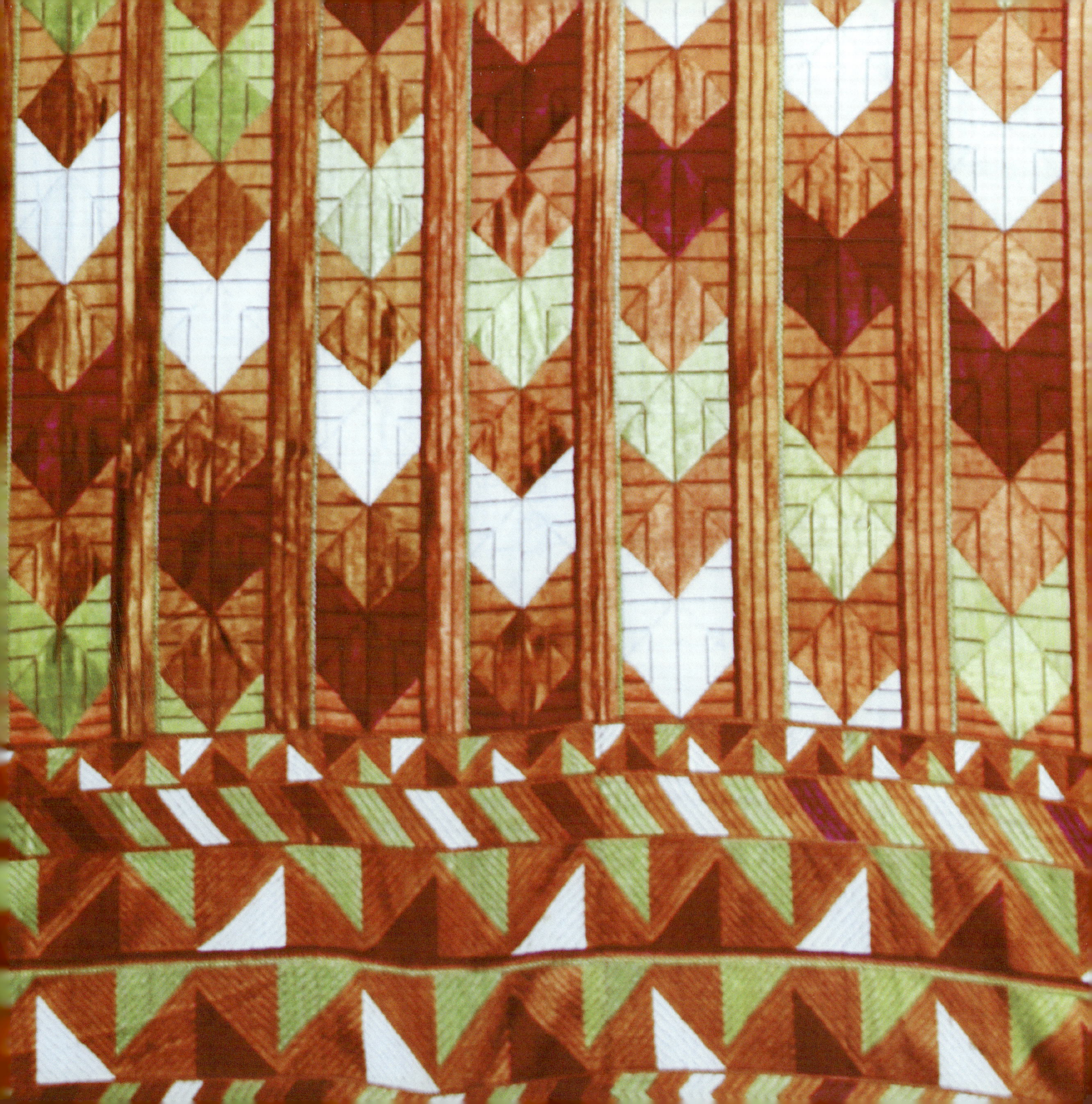

PANCHRANGI PHULKARI

Acc. No: 99.1.PH-40

Panchranga patangi bagh with five rows of geometrical pattern on the two *pallus*. The entire field is embroidered with stylized kite motifs arranged in vertical broad lines. Borders are in multicoloured diamond pattern.

Mid 20th Century; Punjab

Size: L: 235 cm x W: 150 cm

Base fabric: Maroon khaddar.

Different shades of green, mustard, orange, magenta and white silk threads are used in embroidery.

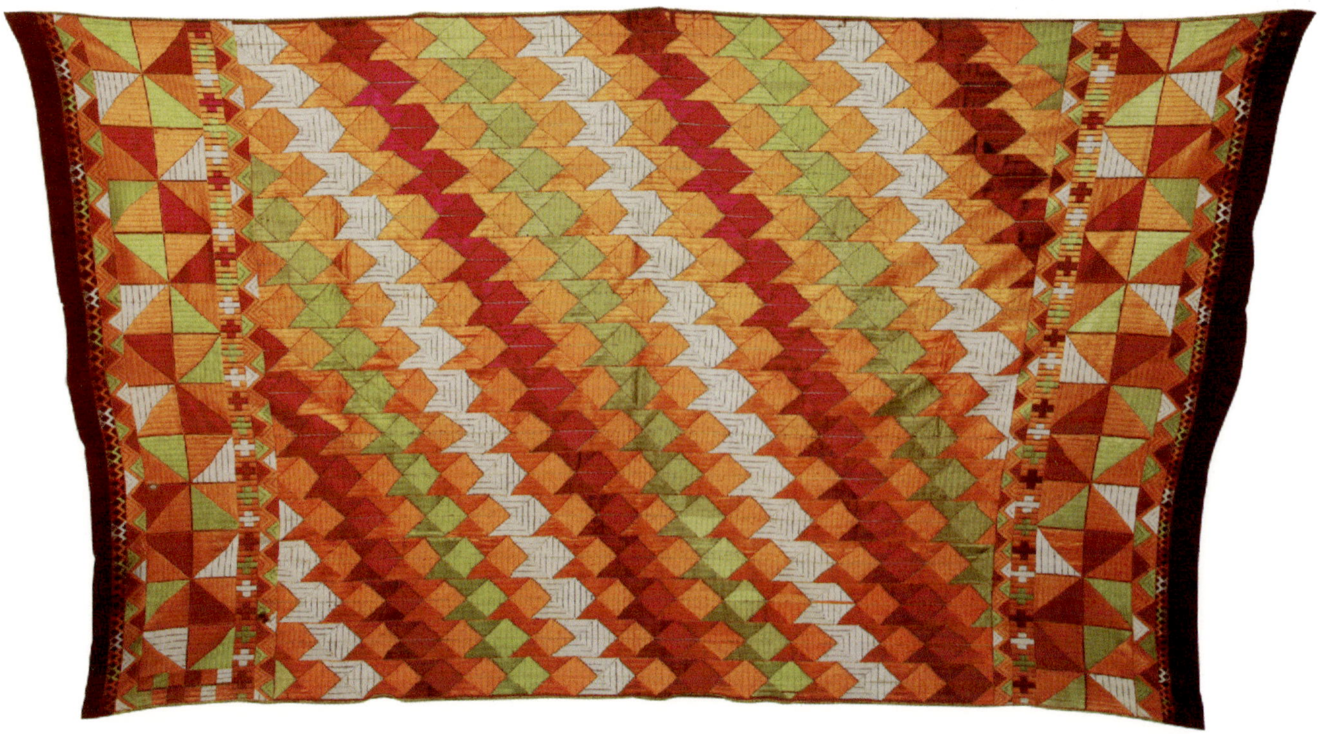

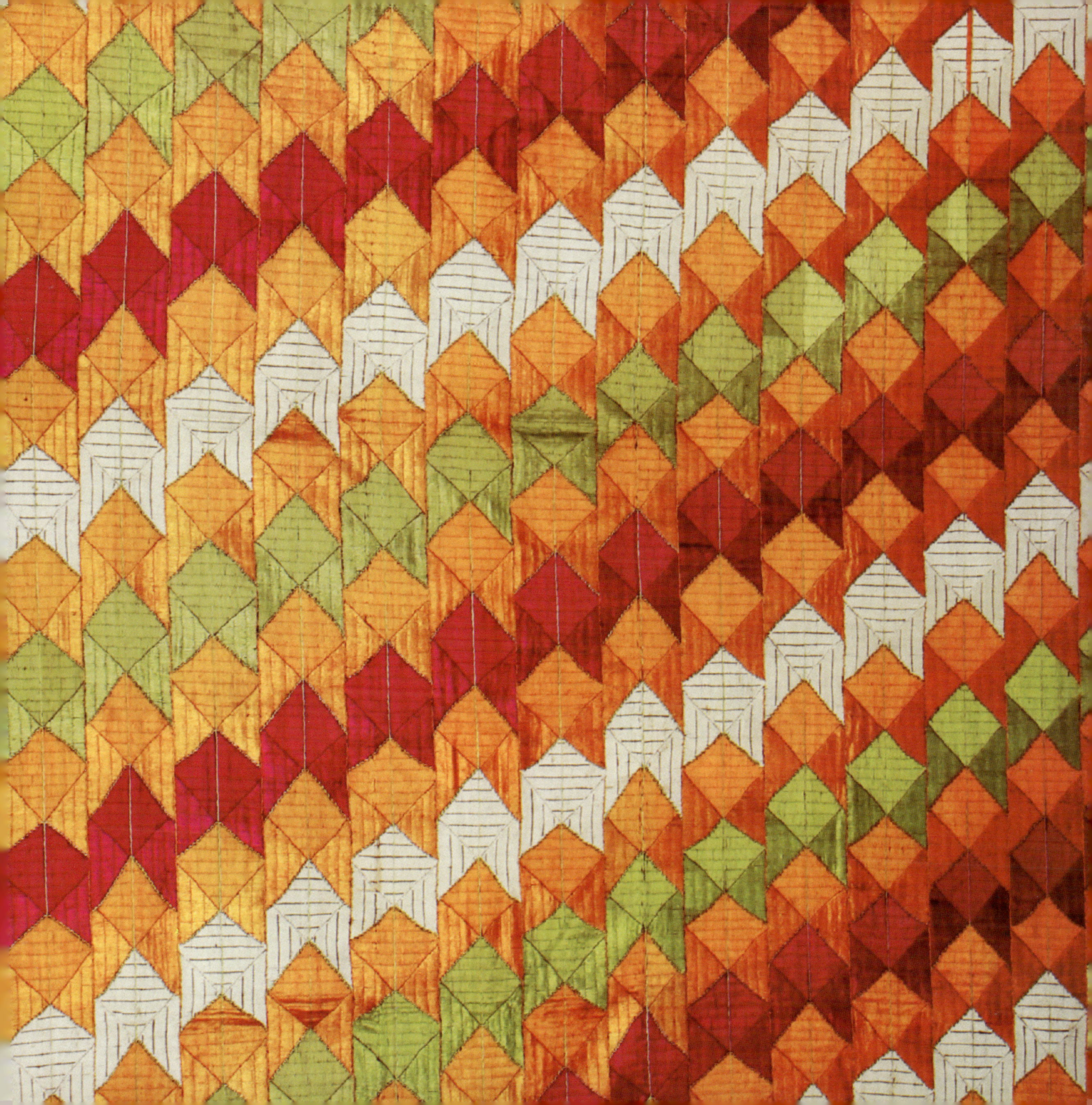

BAGH

Acc. No: 99.1.PH-41

Bagh with four rows of stylized geometrical, pyramid and floral patterns on the two *pallus*. The borders have horizontal motifs in Vari da Bagh style. The entire field has small multicoloured diagonal squares depicting arrow heads and kite like motifs.

Early 20th Century; Punjab

Size: L: 220 cm x W: 147 cm

Base fabric: Maroon khaddar.

The entire embroidery is in different shades of green, mustard, magenta, orange, red and pastel silk threads.

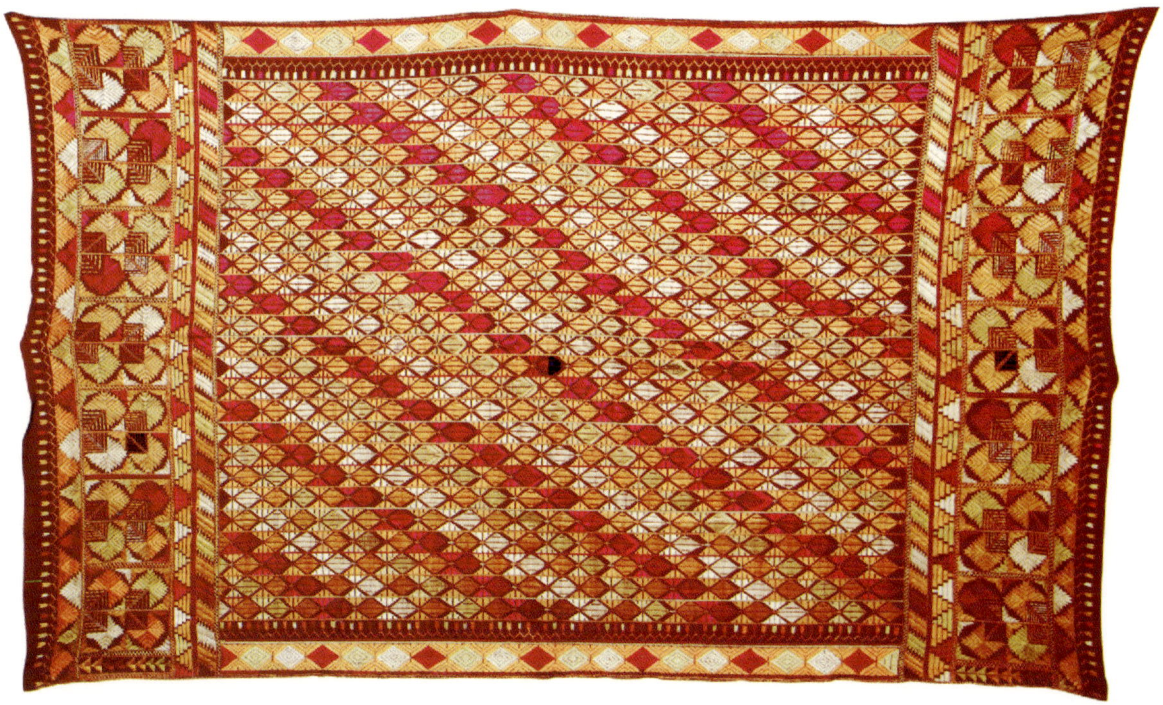

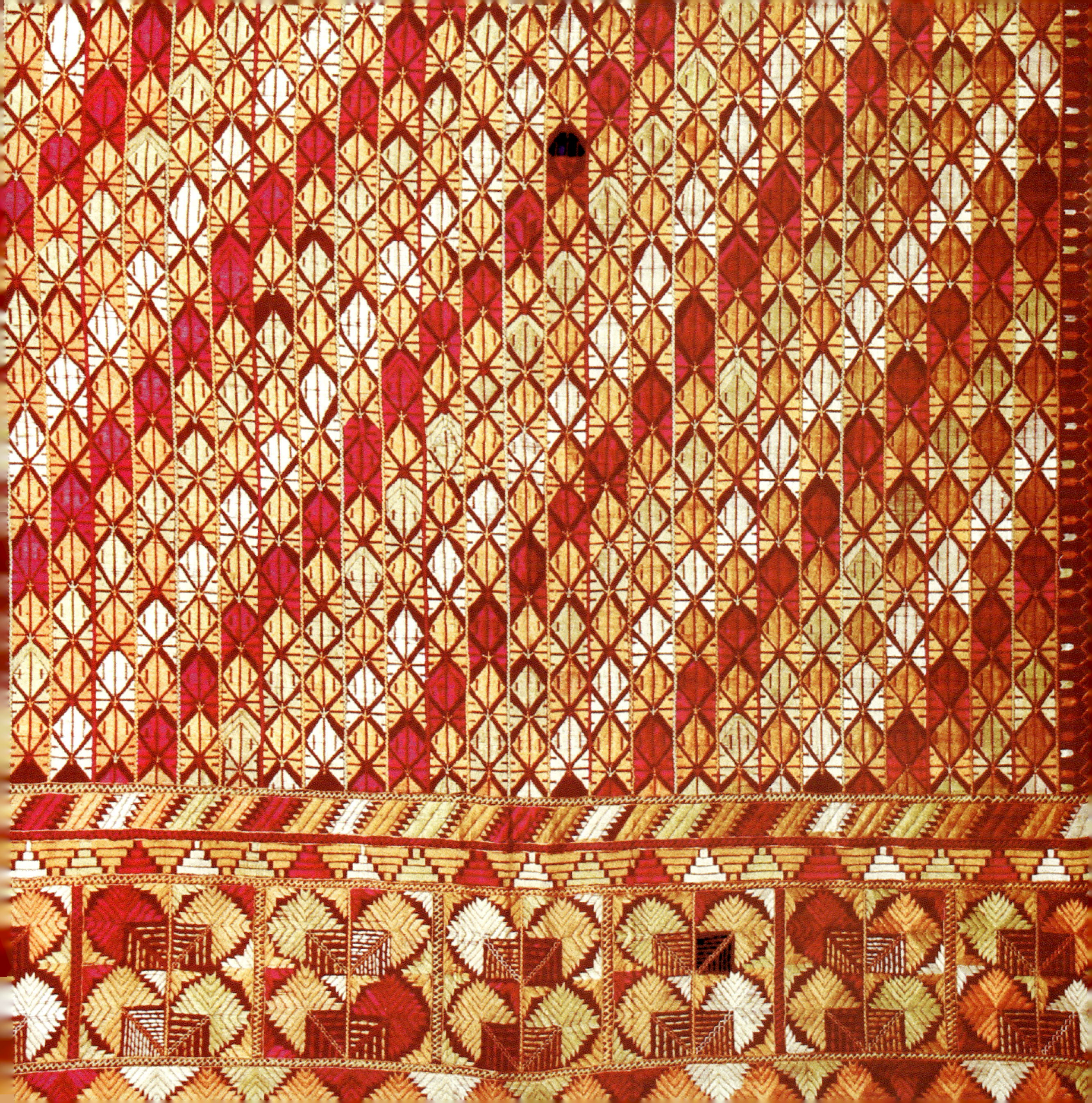

BAGH

Acc. No: 99.1.PH-42

Bagh with six borders on two *pallus* embroidered with foliage, triangles, zigzag multi-coloured squares, pyramids with cowrie, diagonal lines and stylized wheat patterns. The entire field has multicoloured horizontal lines with variety of geometrical motifs embroidered in between. The two borders have diamond patterns.

Early 20th Century; Punjab

Size: L: 234 cm x W: 133 cm

Base fabric: Maroon khaddar.

Mustard, orange, white, green, purple and black silk threads are used in embroidery.

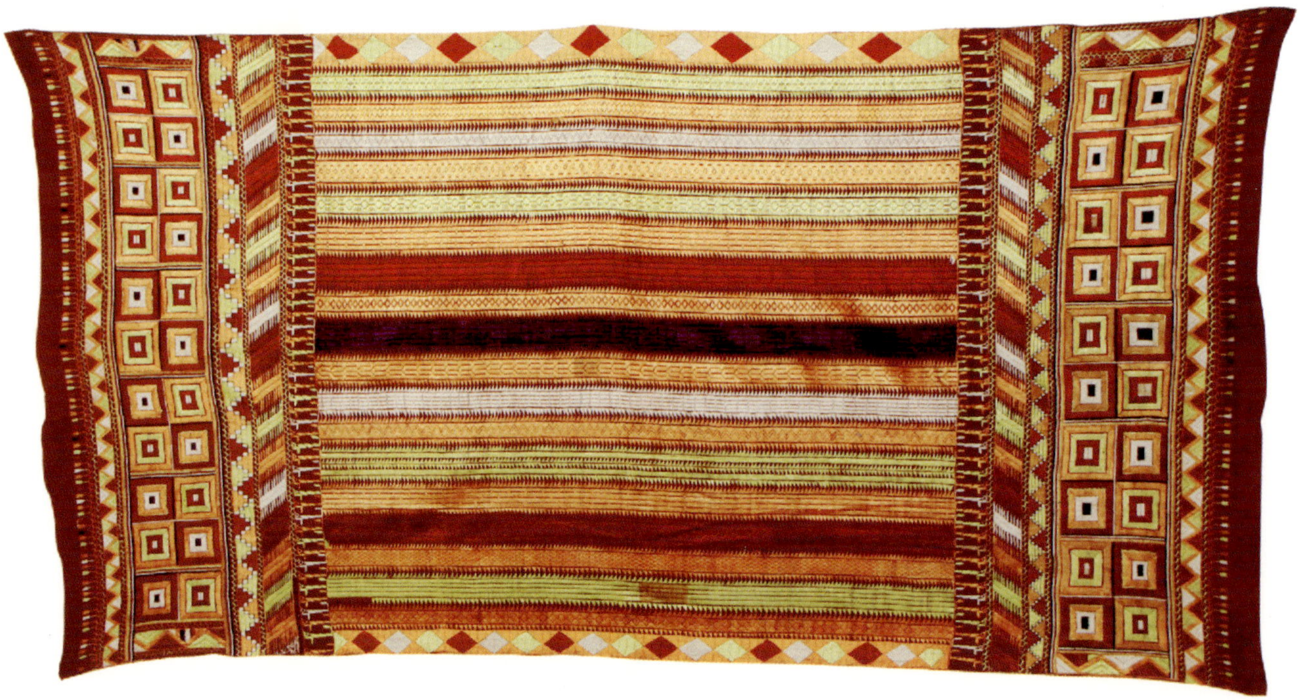

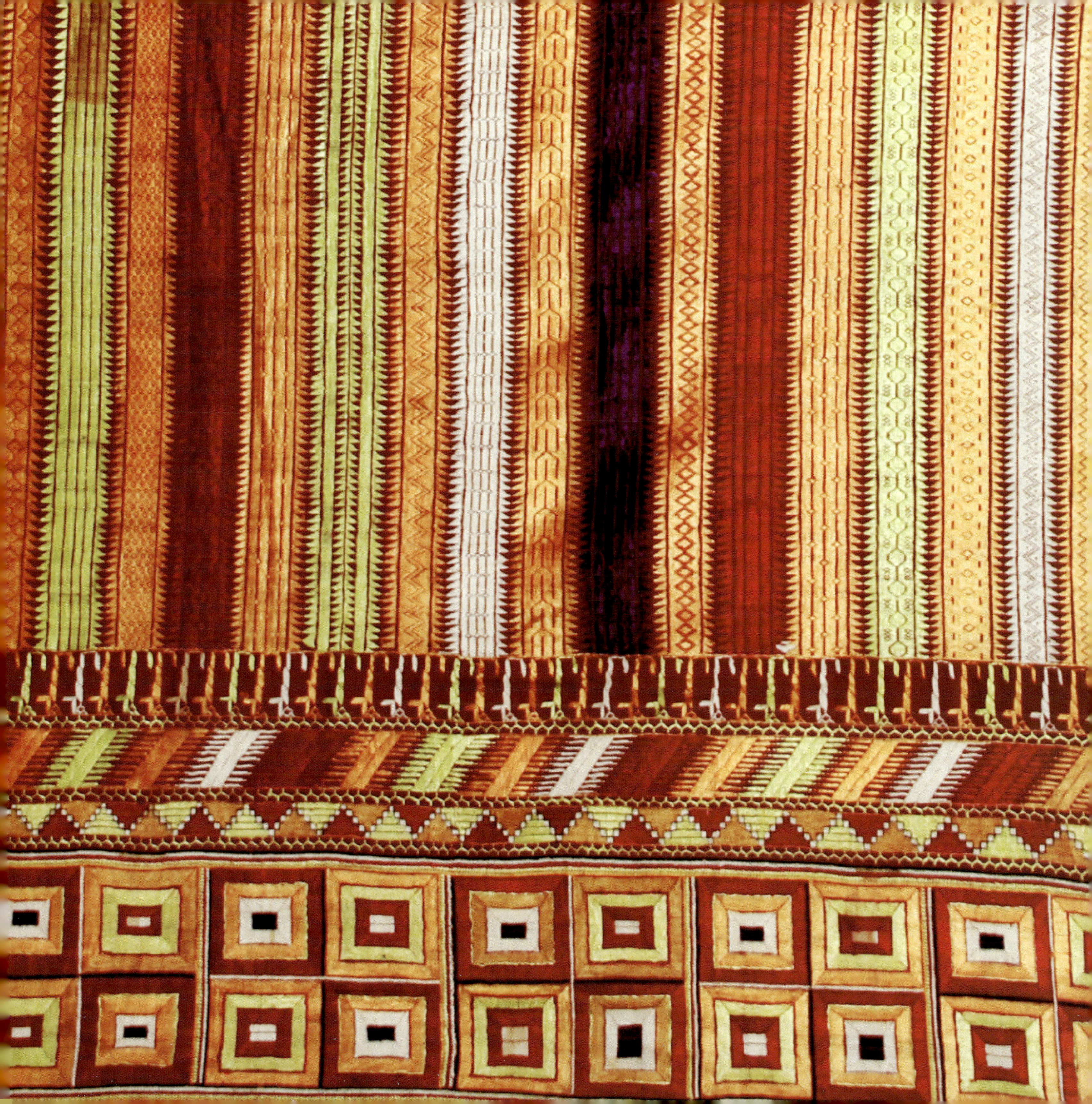

DARSHAN DWAR PHULKARI

Acc. No: 99.1.PH-43

Darshan Dwar Phulkari depicting tall gates with conical tops, with the base of the gates facing each other. The central field consists of human figures, animals, birds, flowers and plants. Gates are embroidered with human figures in standing position. Birds, animals, jewellery, elephant riders and Shrawan Kumar carrying his parents, are embroidered in between the gates on the both sides. The *pallus* have stylized floral motifs and acrobats on horses.

These type of phulkaris are used as an offering to the temples after one's wish is fulfilled. Motif of gates seem to inspire the arched verandas built around the temple for *parikrama*. Hence the name Darshan Dwar (the gate from which one can have darshan of the deity).

Early 20th Century; Haryana

Size: L: 253 cm x W: 134 cm

Base fabric: Maroon khaddar.

Mustard, green, white, red and purple silk threads are used in the embroidery.

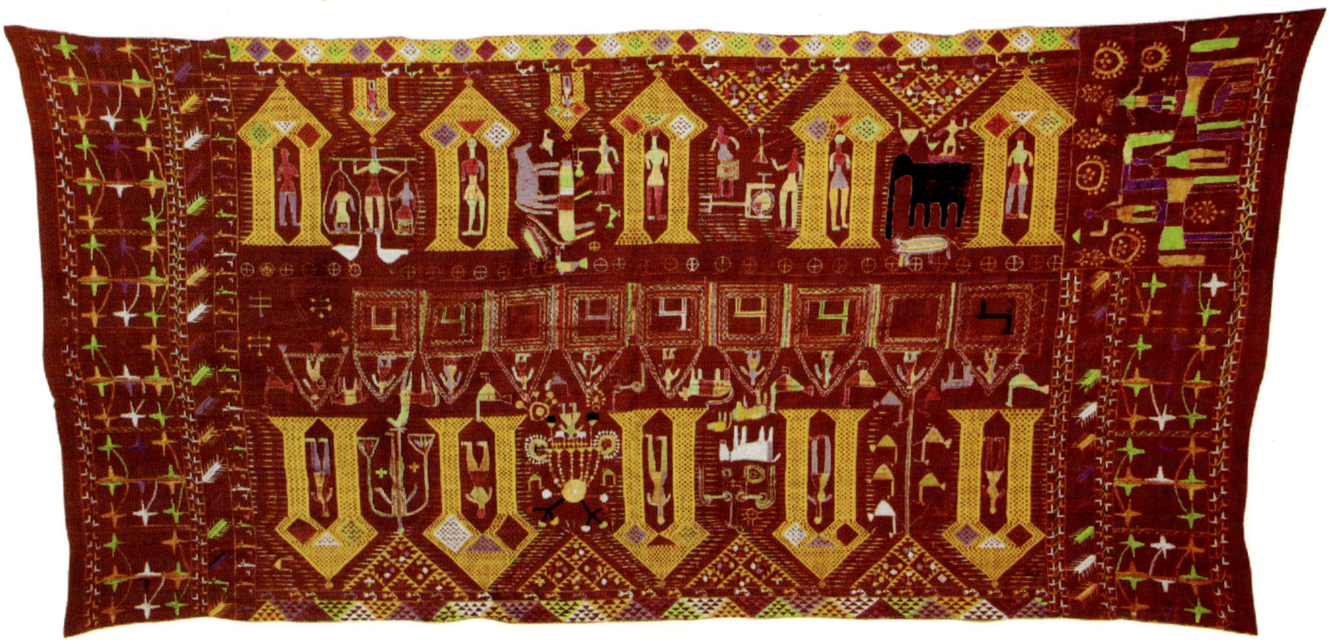

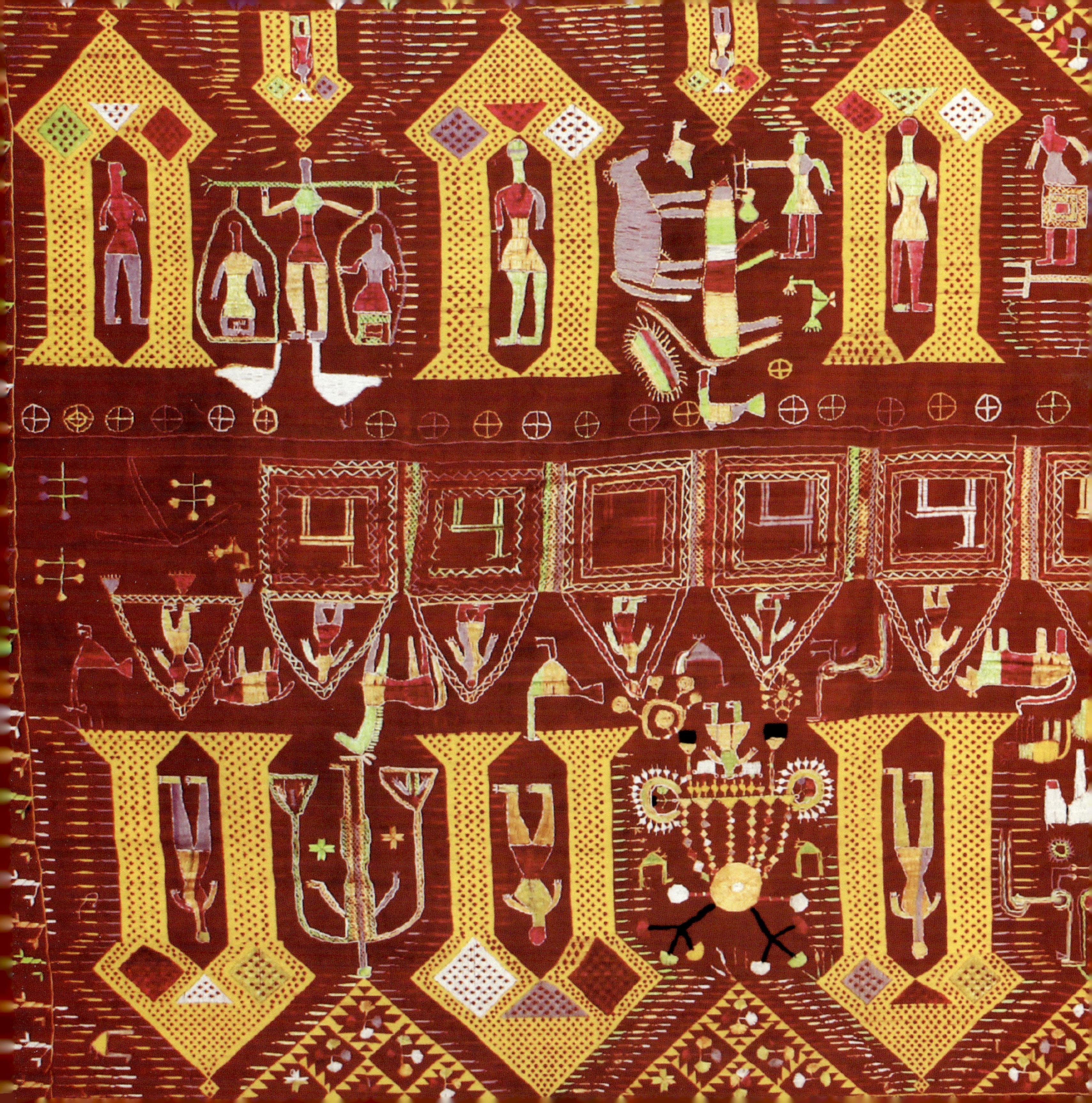

BAGH

Acc. No: 99.1.PH-44

Bagh with two *pallus* embroidered in multicoloured geometrical pattern. The borders have stylized triangles. The field is divided into four panels, each with multicoloured cluster of triangles.

Late 19th Century; Punjab

Size: L: 204 cm x W: 129 cm

Base fabric: Maroon khaddar.

The entire field is embroidered with bright magenta, green, mustard, white, orange and beige silk threads.

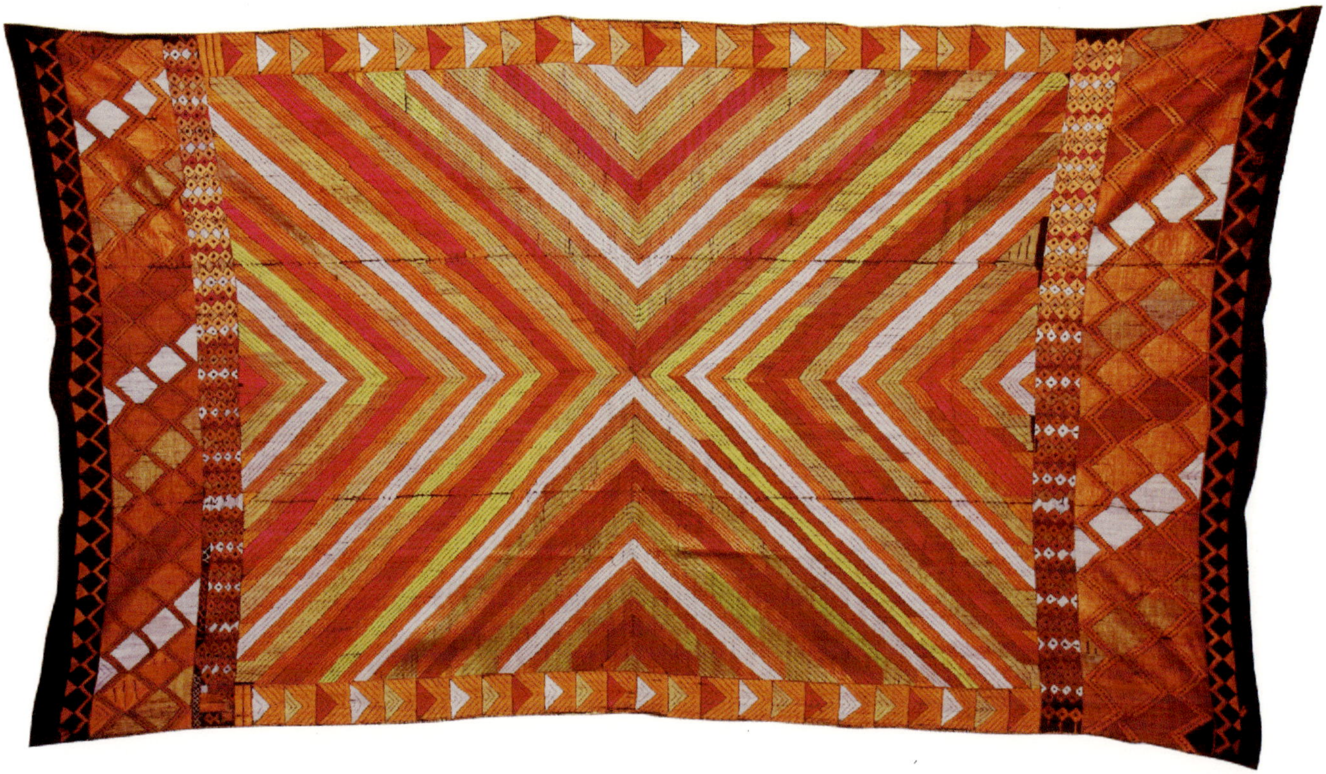

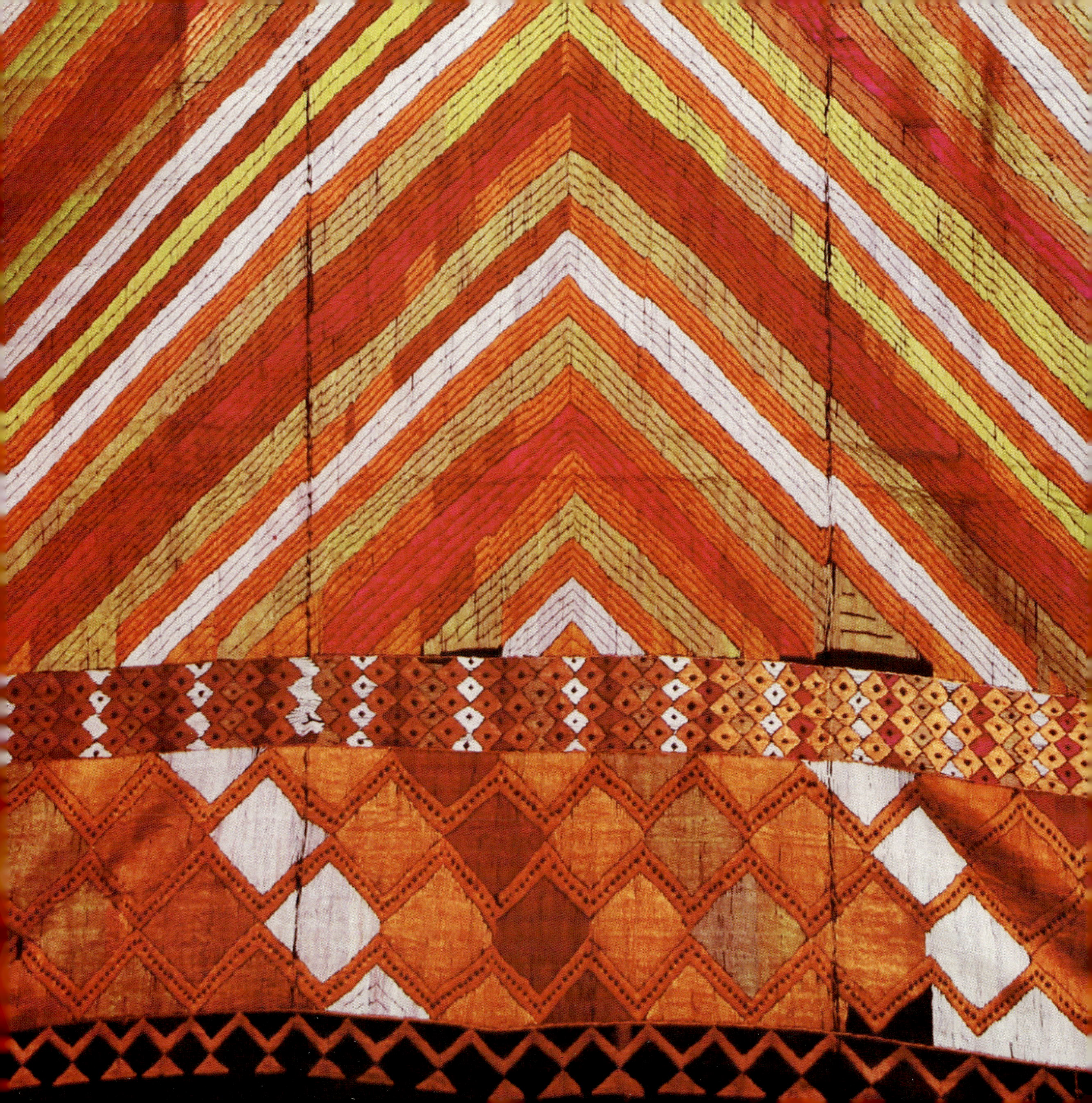

BAGH

Acc. No: 99.1.PH-45

Bagh with stylized geometrical pattern on the borders. The field is divided into four parts, each with a multicoloured cluster of rectangles.

Early 20th Century; Punjab

Size: L: 202 cm x W: 131 cm

Base fabric: Maroon khaddar.

Multicoloured stripes with zigzag motifs in blue, magenta, orange, green and white silk threads are used in the embroidery.

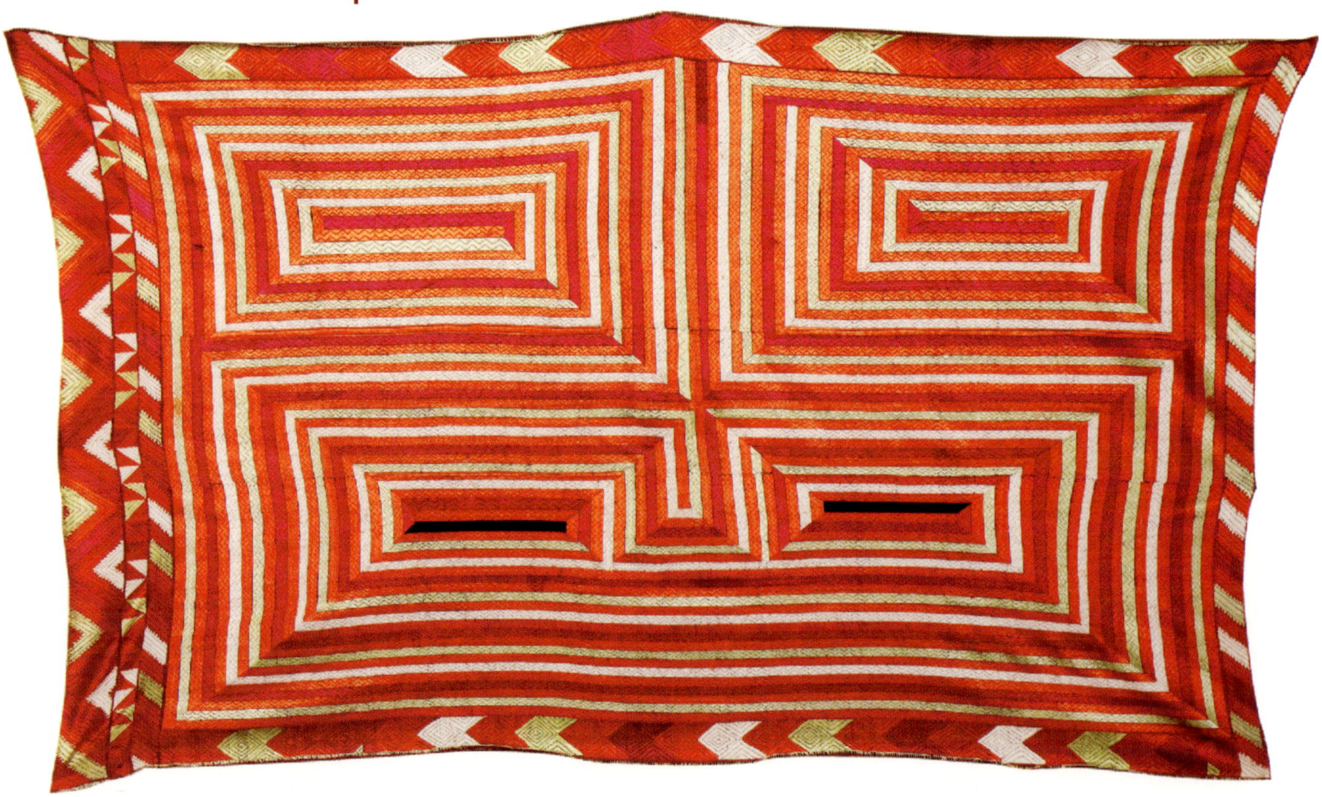

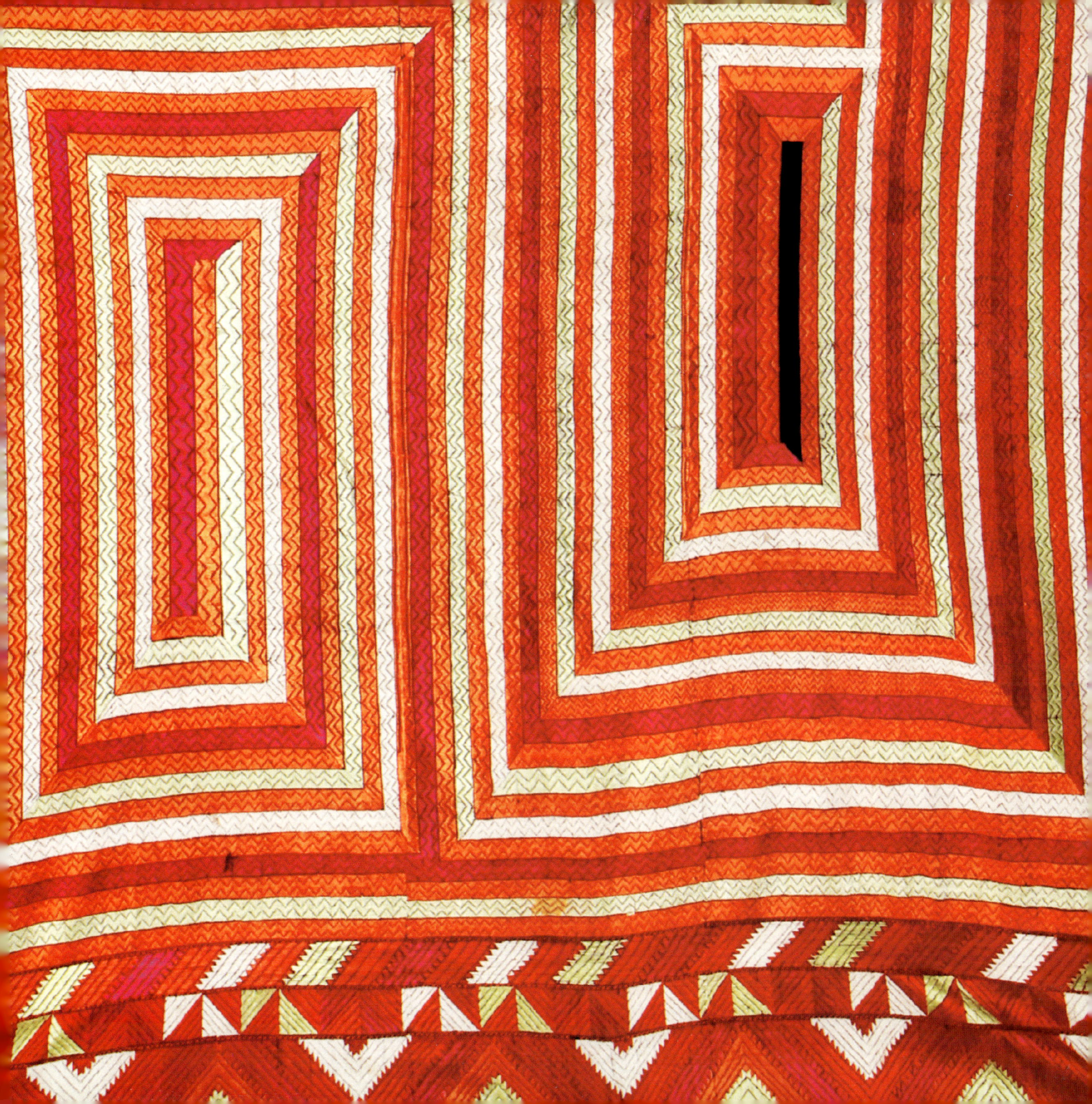

BAGH

Acc. No: 99.1.PH-46

Bagh embroidered with multicoloured diamonds on the border on one side, small diamonds surrounded by large diamonds are embroidered uniformly all over the field. This particular bagh is made by joining the two pieces of different coloured embroidery.

19th Century; Punjab

Size: L: 223 cm x W: 138 cm

Base fabric: Maroon khaddar.

Contrast silk threads are used alternatively with black lining and piping on both sides of the embroidery.

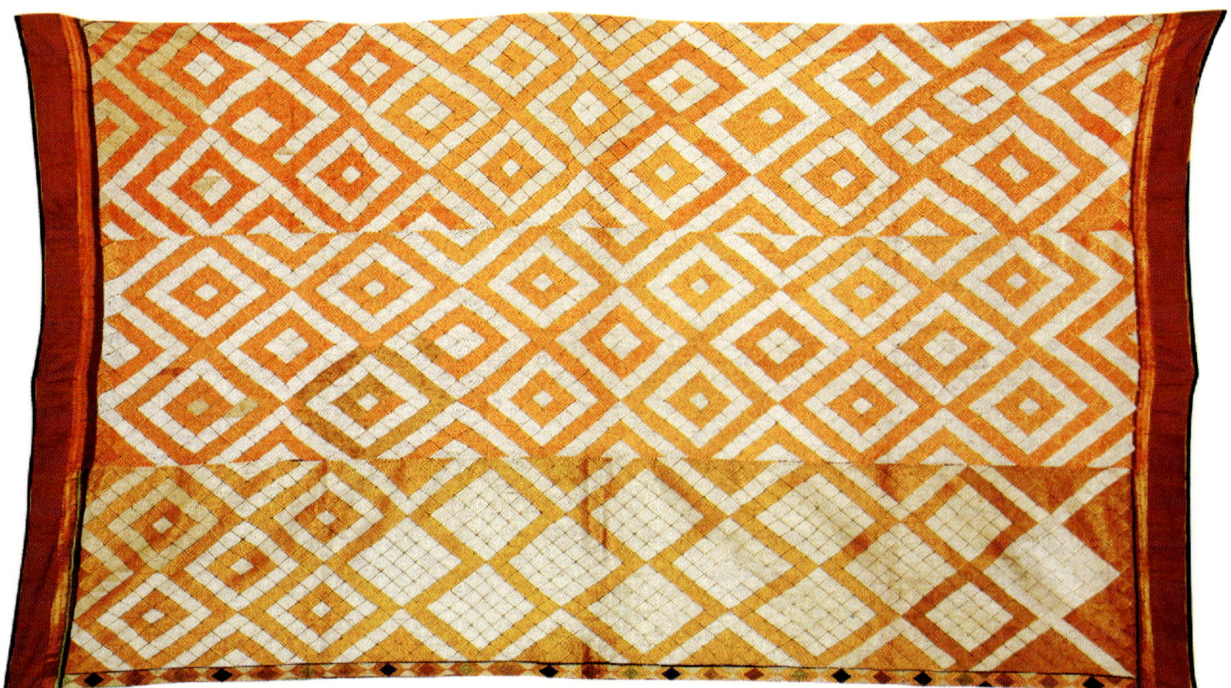

PATTI DA BAGH

Acc. No: 99.1.Ph-47

Patti da Bagh which looks more like Vari da Bagh is embroidered in two parts. Borders are in multicoloured triangles. The field depict small and big diamond motifs arranged in horizontal lines.

Early 19th Century; West Punjab

Size: L: 243 cm x W: 123 cm

Base fabric: Maroon khaddar.

Embroidery is in magenta, green, purple, white and beige silk threads.

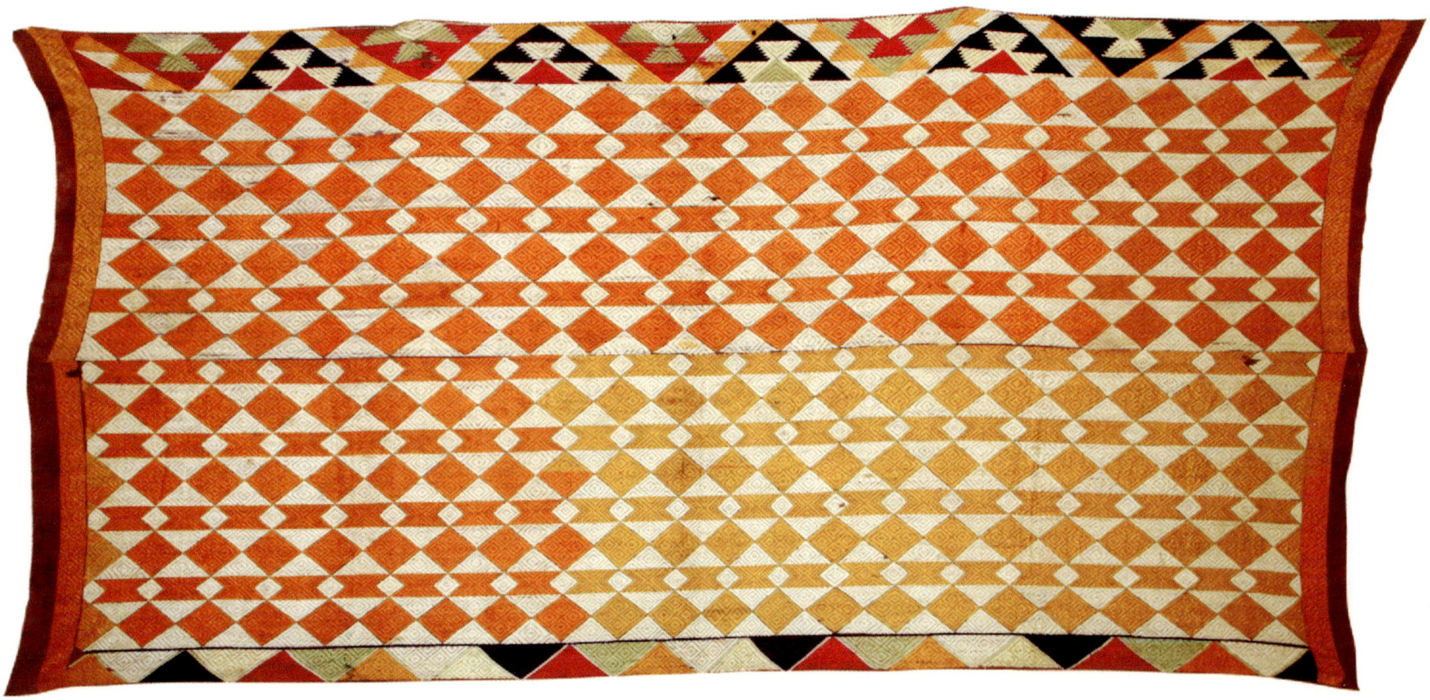

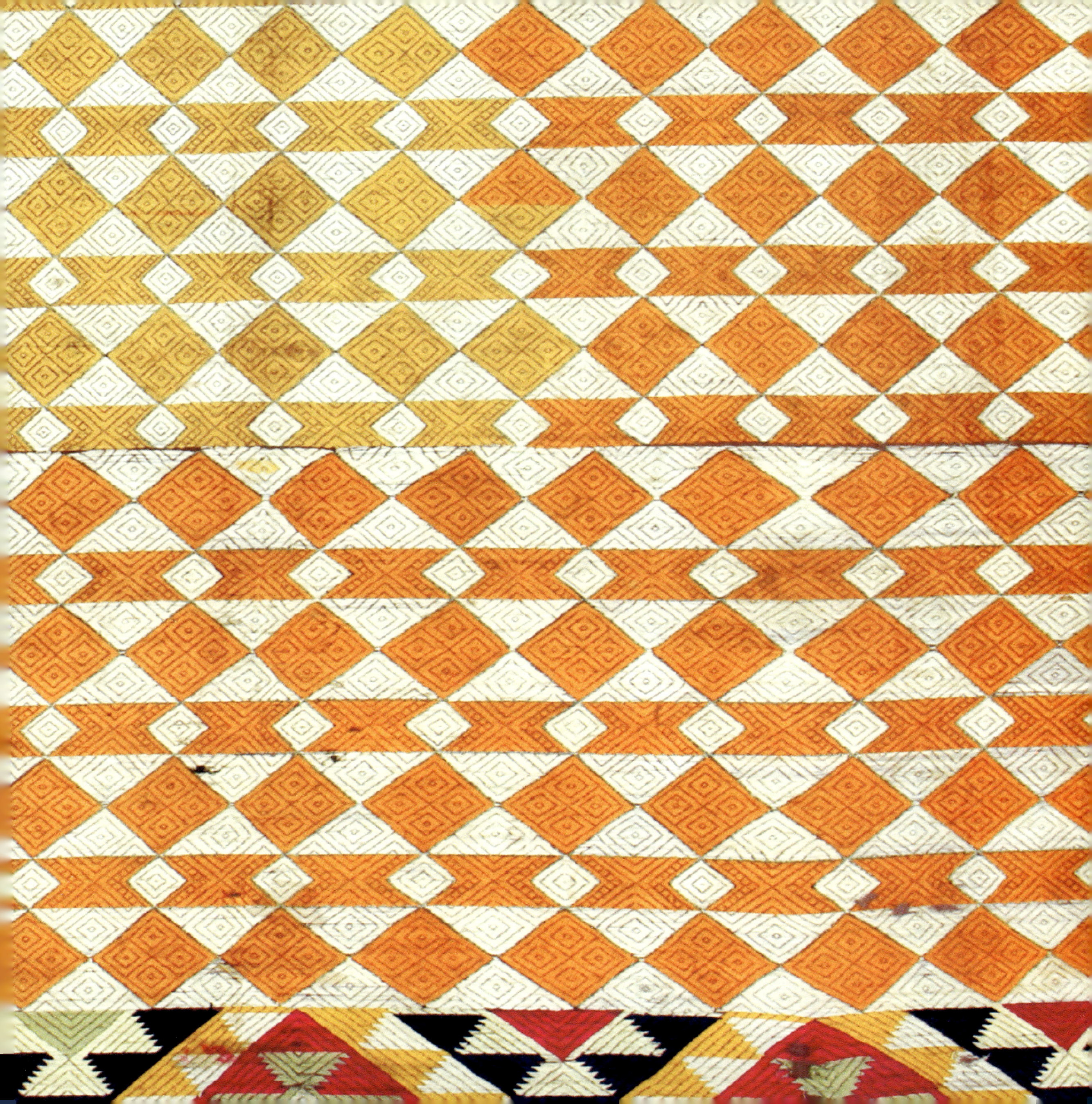

TOTA BAGH

Acc. No: 99.1.PH-48

Tota (parrot) Bagh with stylized geometrical design and squares on the *pallus* surmounted by a row of birds. The borders also have single bird pattern. The entire field is embroidered with parrots arranged in diagonal lines.

Late 20th Century; Haryana

Size: L: 260 cm x W: 156 cm

Base fabric: Maroon khaddar.

Embroidery is in green, magenta, white, black, and purple silk threads on orange field.

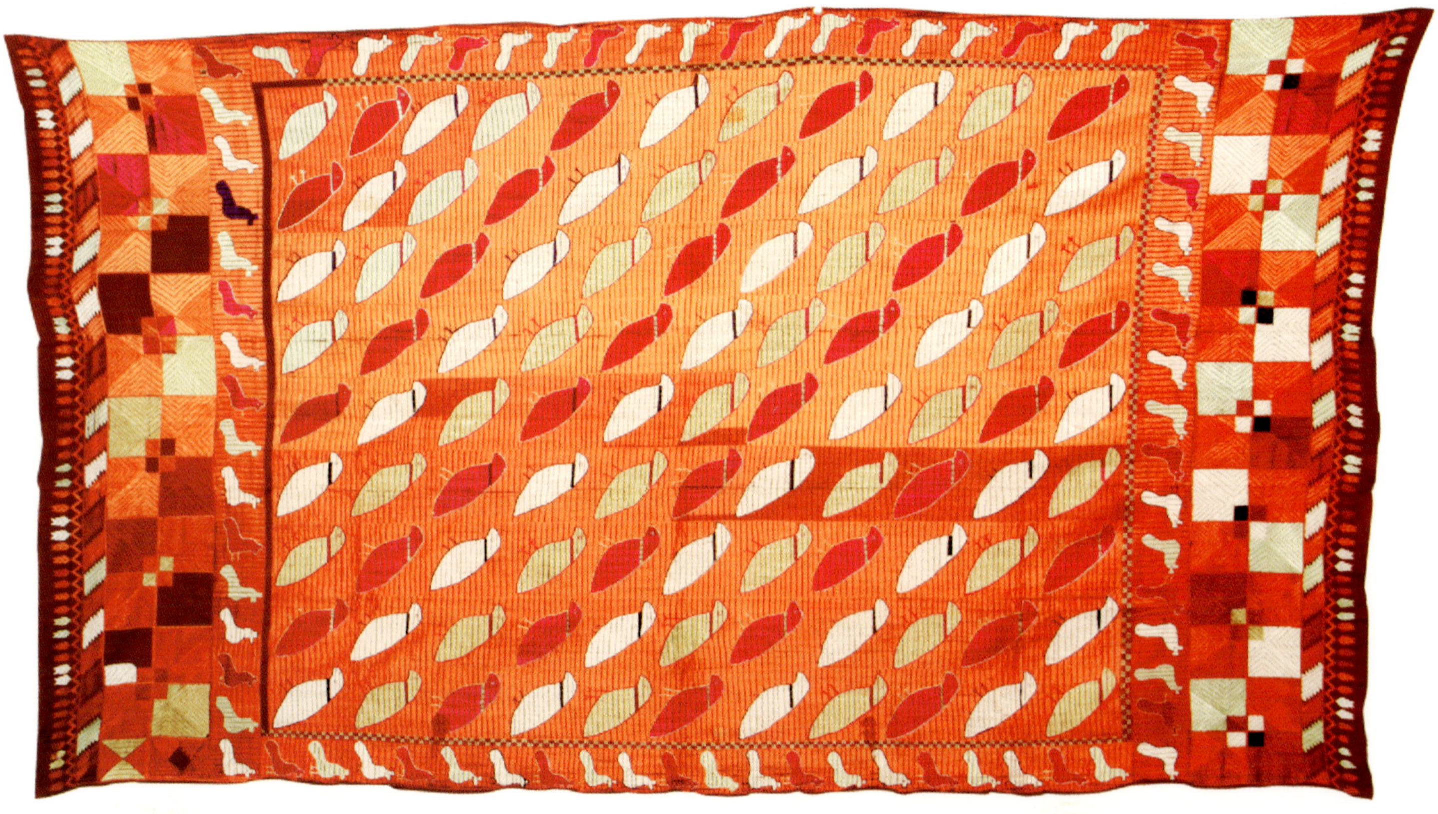

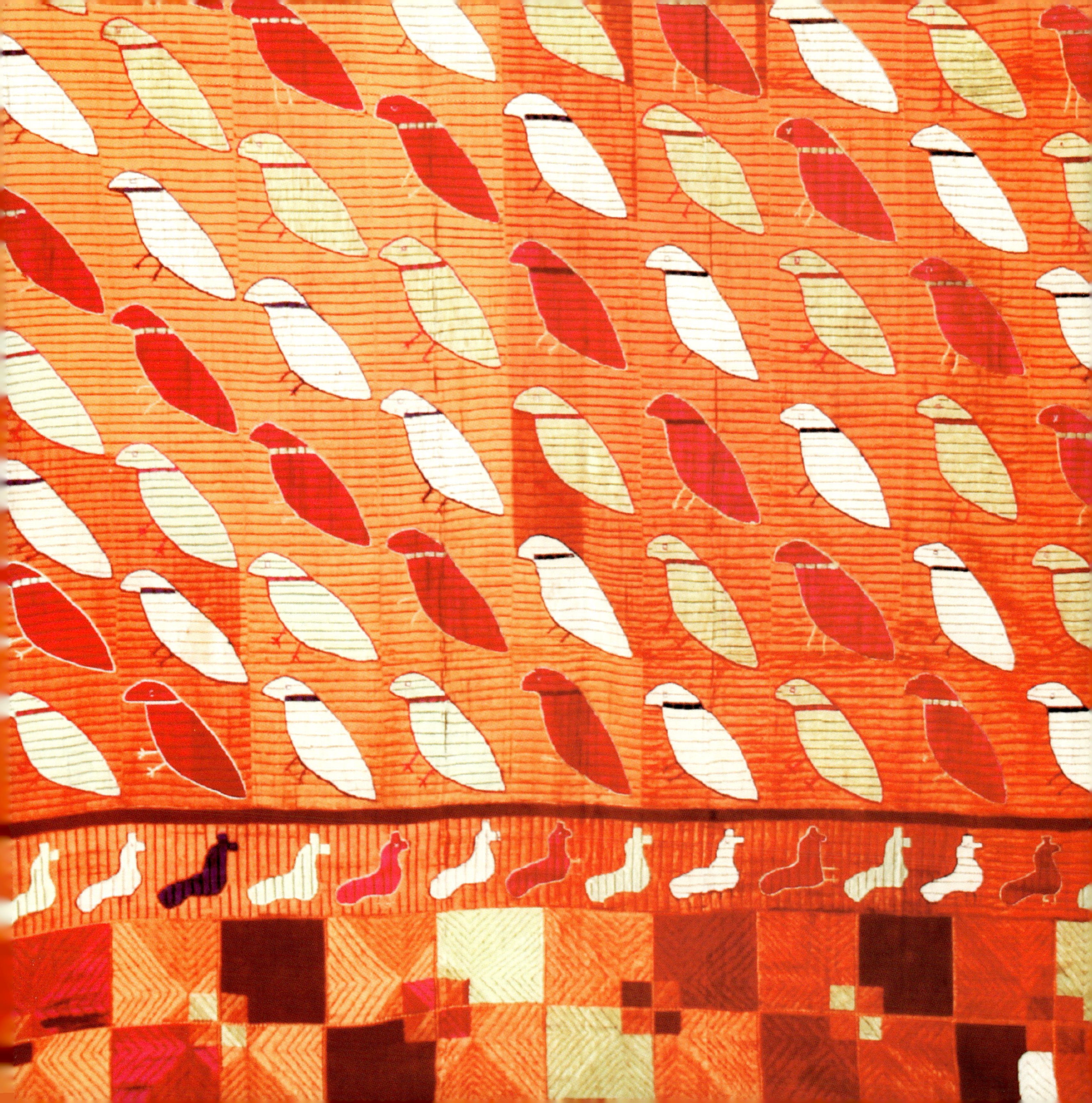

BAGH

Acc. No: 99.1.PH-49

Bagh with two *pallus* and borders in stylized geometrical patterns. The entire field is embroidered with small diamonds enclosed in bigger diamonds with six *pattis* (horizontal lines) in between.

Early 20th Century; Punjab

Size: L: 237 cm x W: 130 cm

Base fabric: Maroon khaddar.

Green, orange, magenta and white silk threads are used in the embroidery.

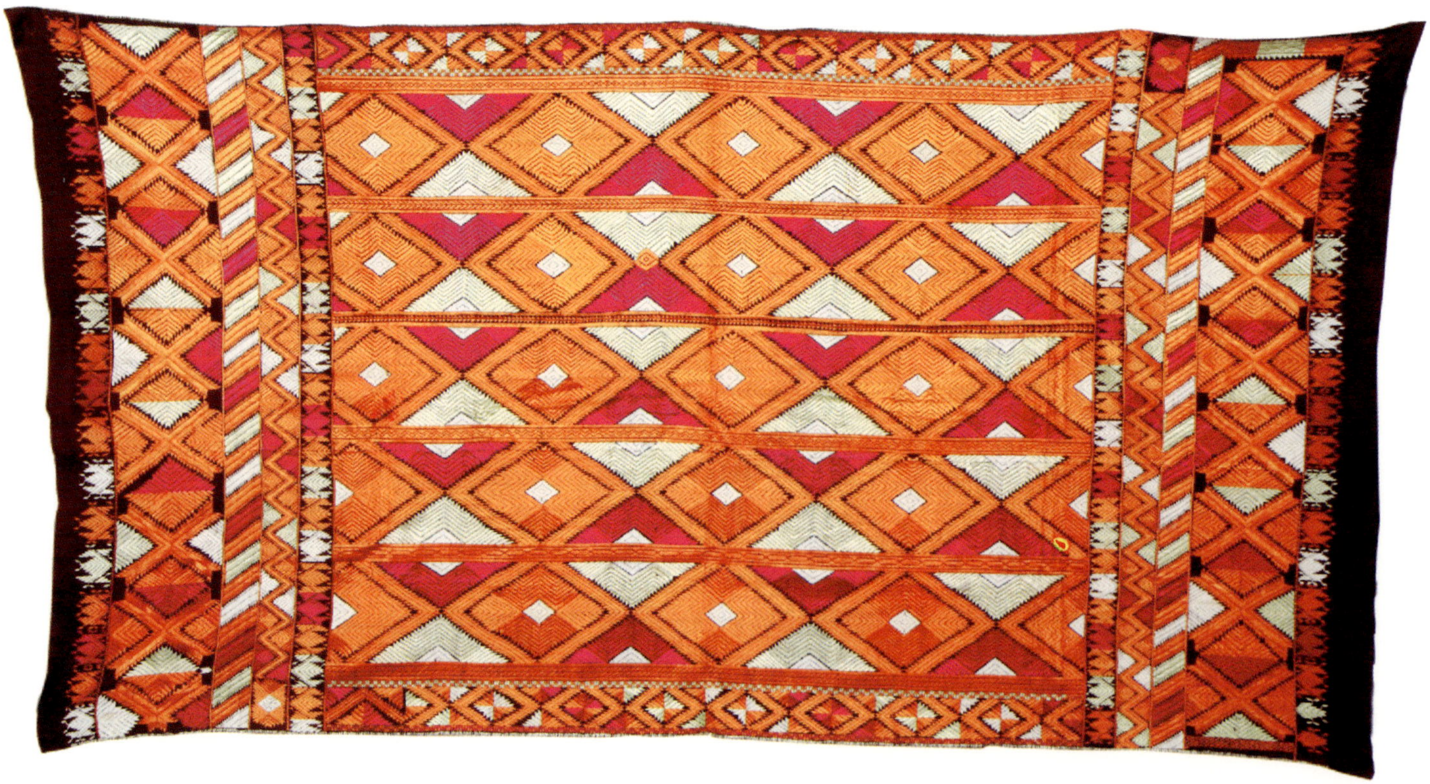

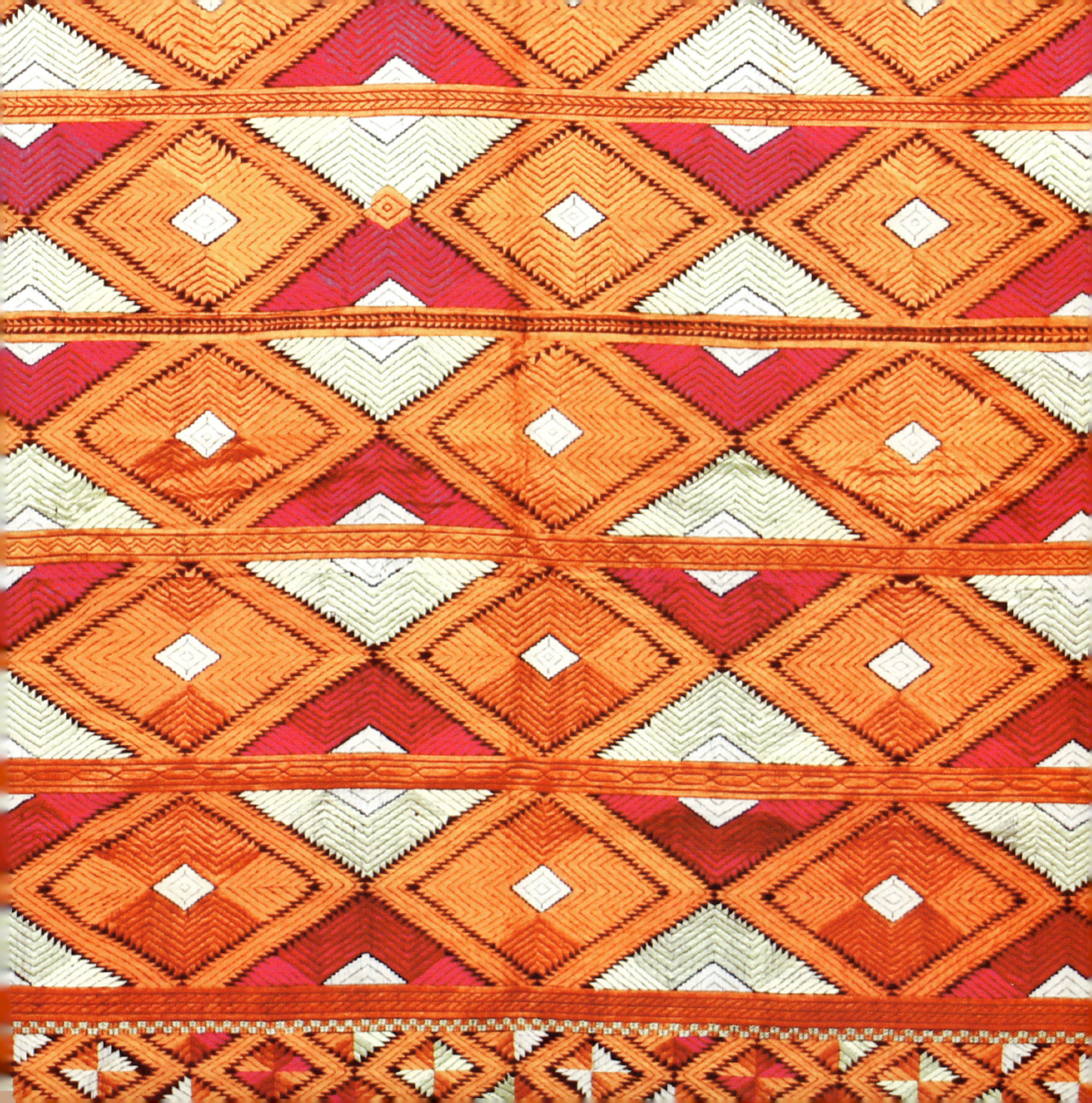

PANCHRANGI PATANGI BAGH

Acc. No: 99.1.PH-50

Panchranga Patangi Bagh with two *pallus* in multicoloured horizontal lines, zigzag triangular pattern and arrow heads. The two borders have diamond patterns with vertical lines in between. The entire field has kite pattern and lines, alternately arranged in vertical rows.

Late 19th Century; Punjab

Size: L: 245 cm x W: 154 cm

Base fabric: Maroon khaddar.

White, mustard, orange, magenta and green silk threads are used in the embroidery.

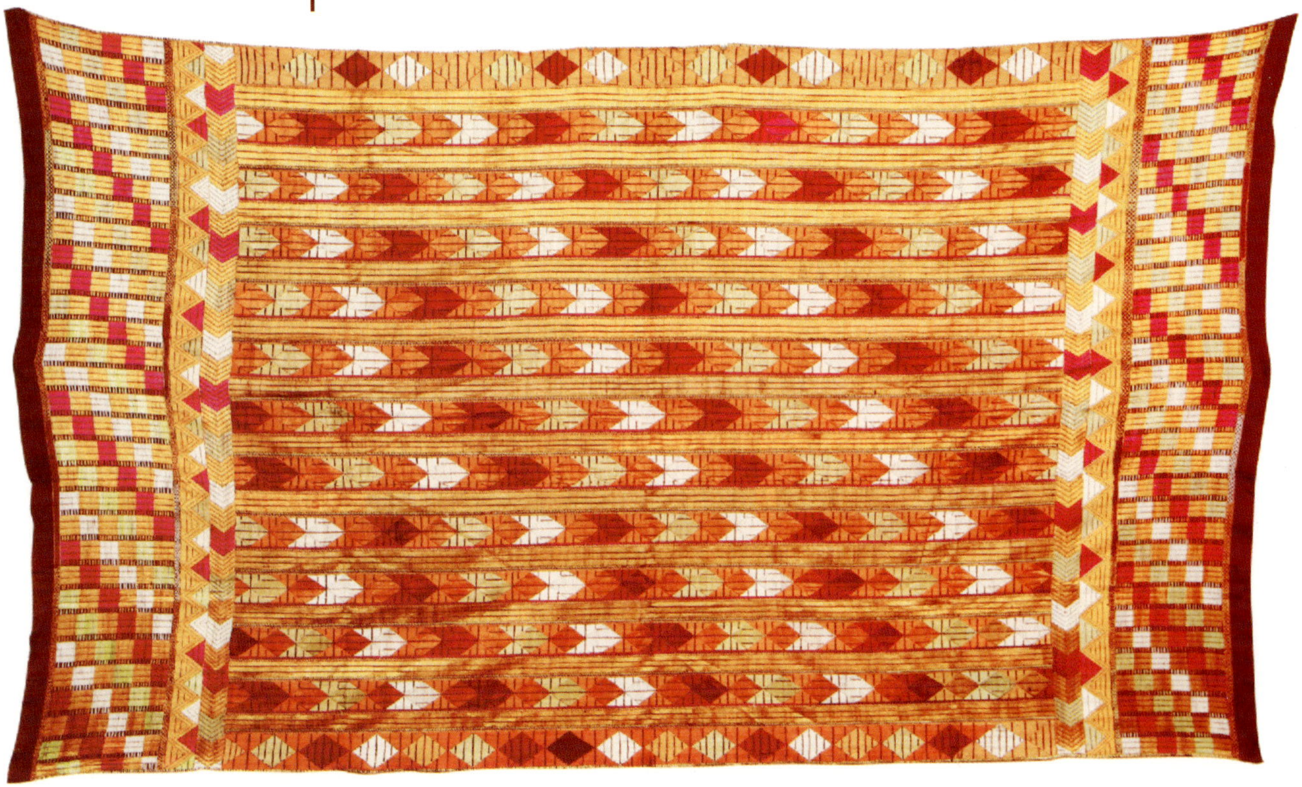

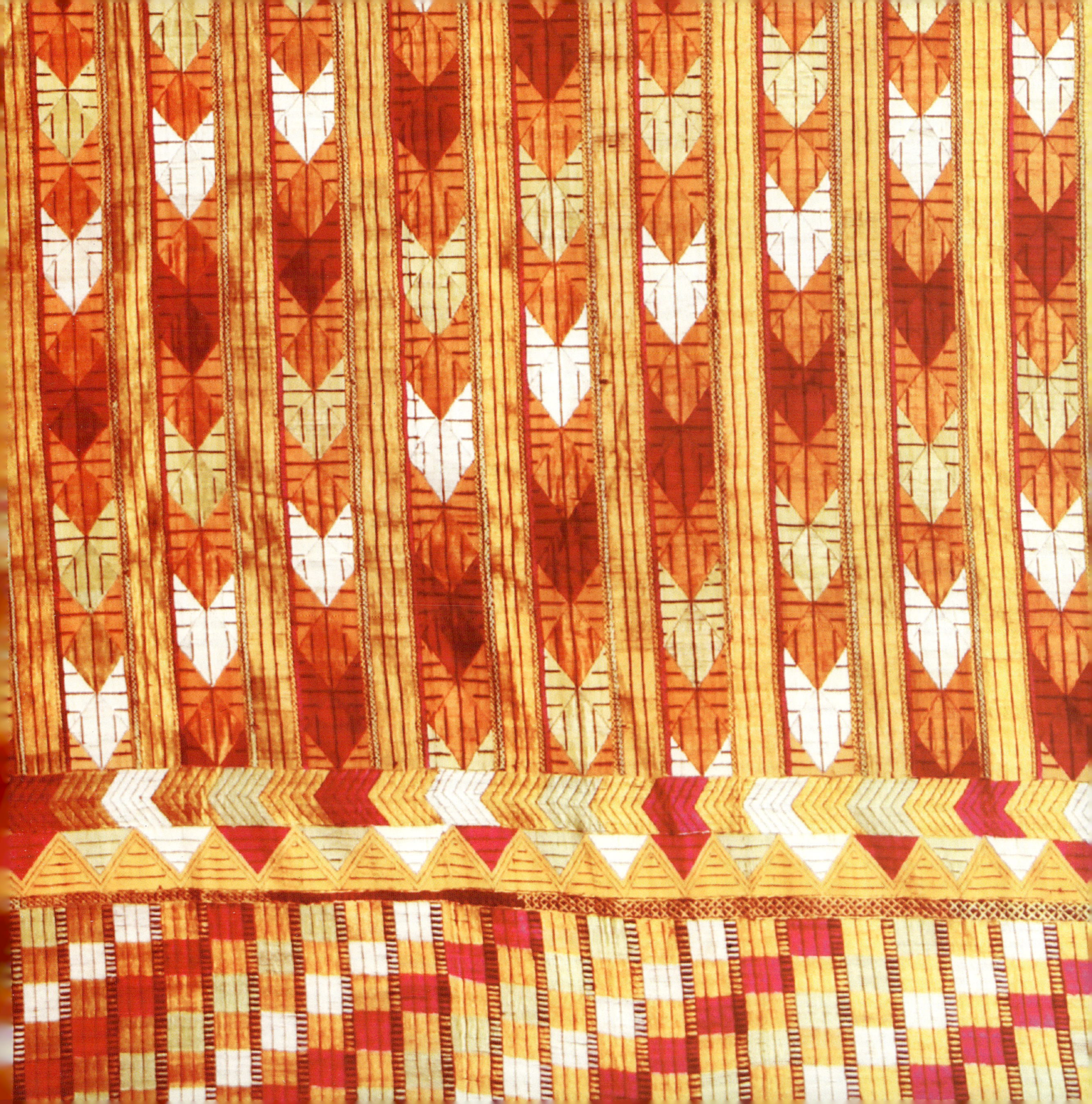

BAGH

Acc. No: 99.1.PH-51

Bagh with stylized geometrical cum floral motifs, diagonal lines, triangles, stylized pyramids and kites on the *pallus*. One pallu has a square in Char Bagh style. The entire field is embroidered with horizontal lines and small multicoloured squares, arranged in geometrical shapes.

Early 20th Century; Punjab

Base fabric: Maroon khaddar.

Orange, white, magenta, green, and mustard silk threads are used in the embroidery.

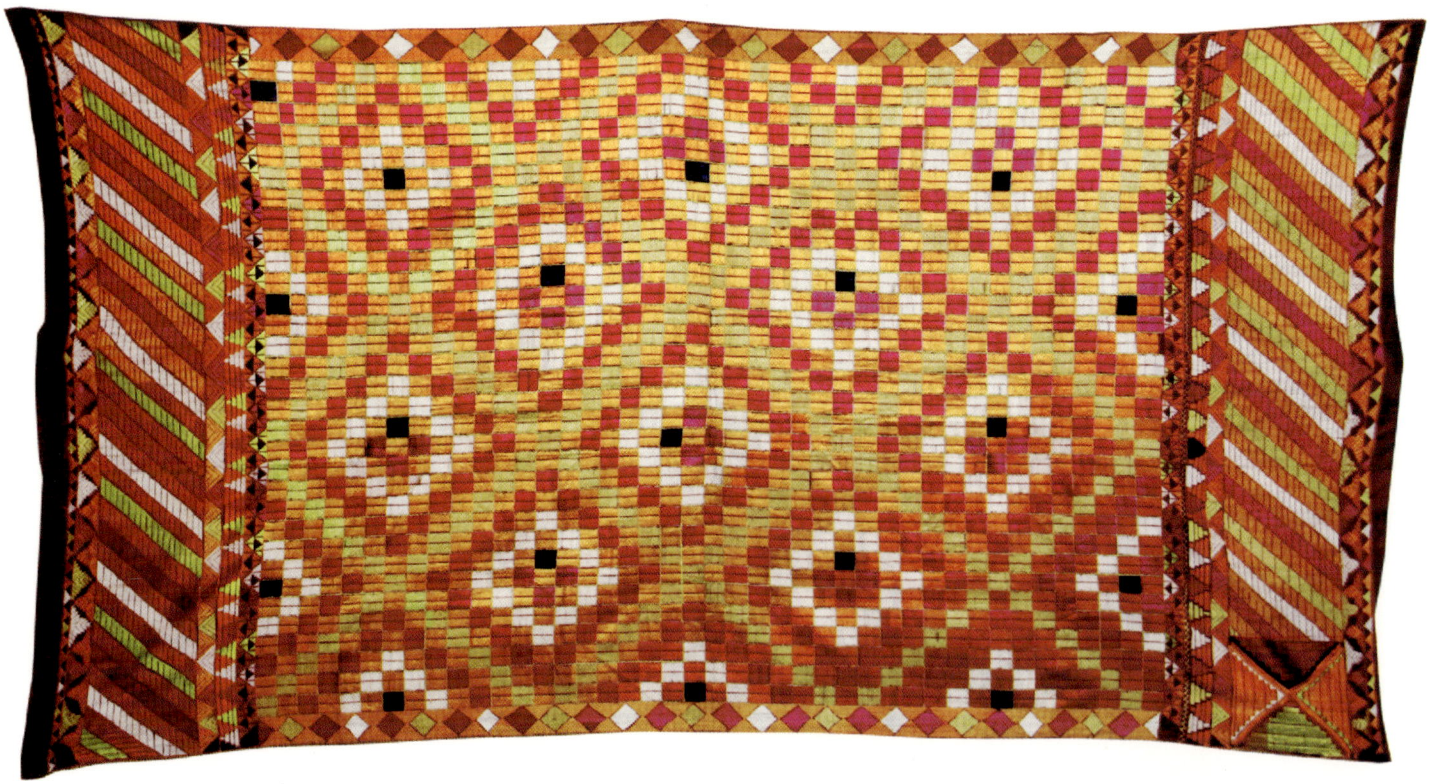

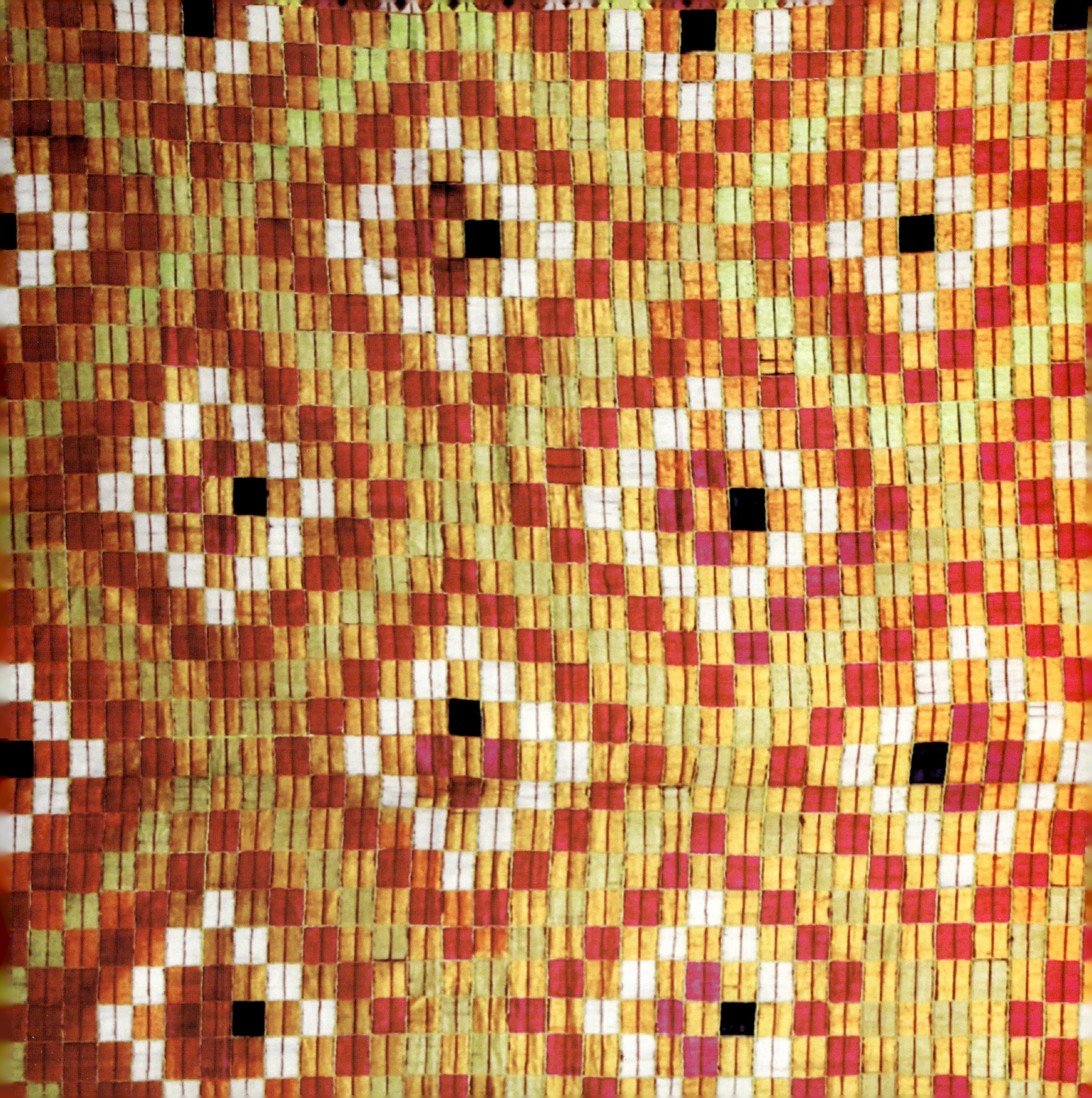

CHHOPE

Acc. No: 2008.1.PH-52

Chhope embroidered with double-sided line stitch in orange colour, which appears identical on both sides. The two outer panels consist of very large triangles with their base towards the salvage. The entire embroidery has been done with triangles with their base in opposite directions. The two panels are closely embroidered without leaving much space between them. The centre part has three or four rows of small triangles with base facing inwards. Each triangle is embroidered with different geometrical pattern. Borders are embroidered with lozenges. The two ends are kept open with no borders, symbolizing unlimited prosperity to the bride, the entire embroidery is done in double line stitch.

19th Century; West Punjab

Size: L: 310 cm x W: 200 cm

Base fabric: Maroon khaddar.

White, green and magenta silk threads are used on the borders in cross stitch.

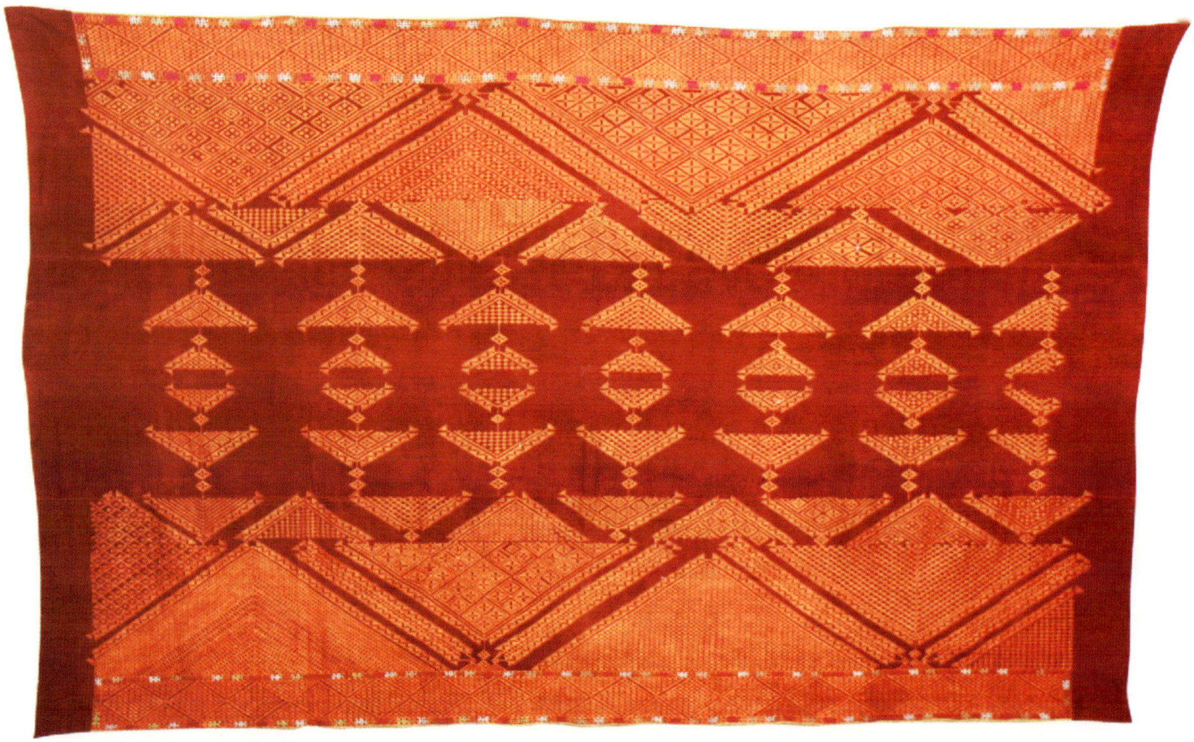

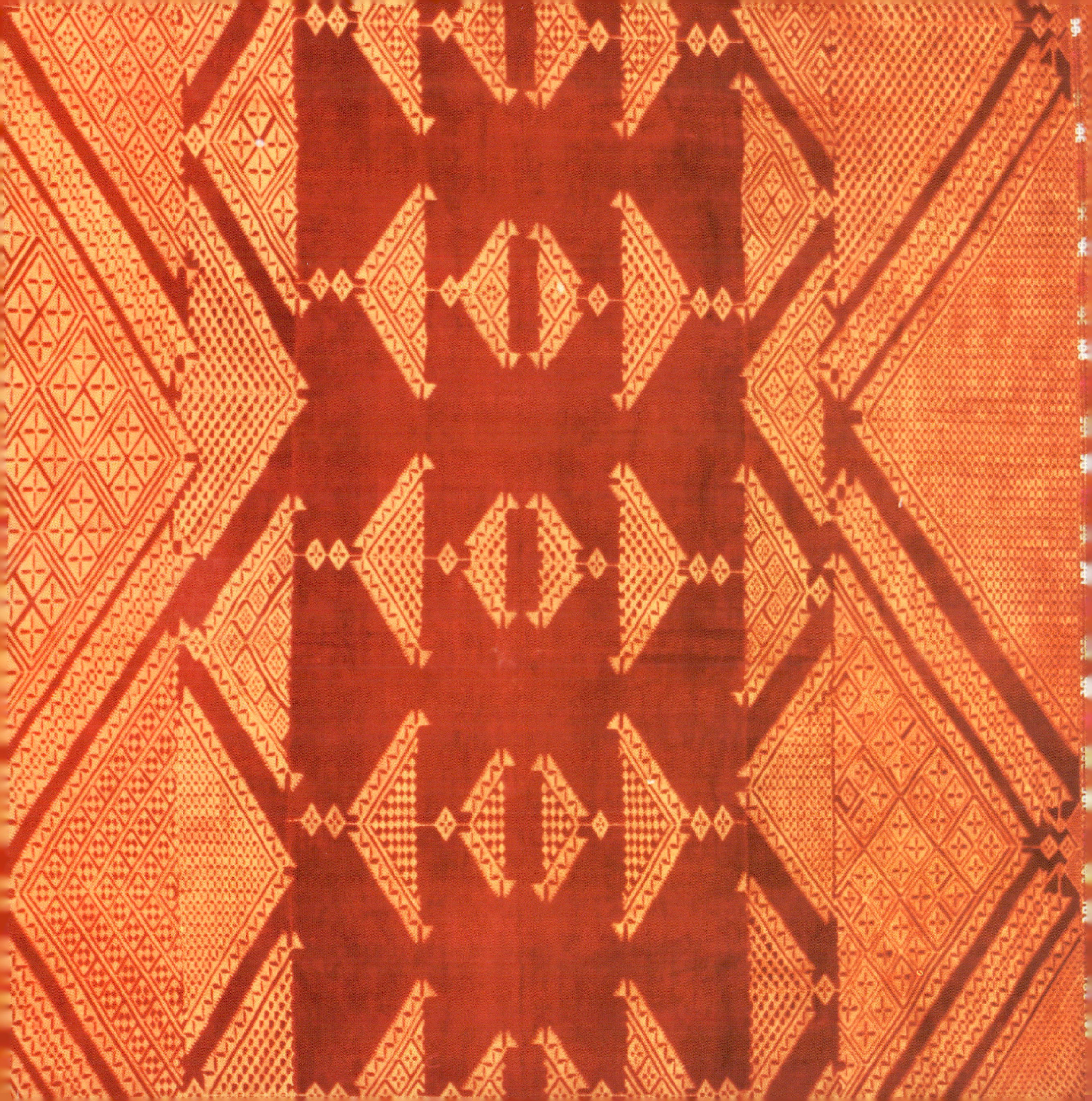

BIBLIOGRAPHY

Agrawala, V.S., *India as Known to Panini,* Lucknow, 1953.

Anand, Mulk Raj, 'Embroidery', *Marg,* Vol. 28, No. 1, 1974-75.

Balu, Shakuntla, 'Textiles of Karnataka', *Eve's Weekly,* Special Textile Issue, August 24, 1974.

Banabhatta, *Harscarita*, E.B. Cowell and F.W. Thomas (translated), Delhi, 1961.

Banerjee, Adris, 'Phulkari, a Folk-art of the Punjab', *Marg,* Vol. 8, No. 3, 1955.

Chattopadhyay, Kamaladevi, *Indian Embroidery*, New Delhi, 1977.

Chattopadhyay, Kamaladevi, 'Origin and Development of Embroidery in Our Land', *Marg,* Vol. 17, Bombay, March, 1964.

Coomaraswamy, Ananda K., *Arts and Crafts of India and Ceylon*, London, 1913.

Dahiya, B.S., *Jats – The Ancient Rulers,* New Delhi, 1980.

Dhamija, Jasleen, 'The Survey of Embroidery Tradition', *Marg,* Vol. 17, No. 2, Bombay, 1964.

Dhamija, Jasleen, 'Bagh and Phulkari', *Marg,* Vol. 17, No. 2, Bombay, 1964.

Doongerkery, Kamala S., *The Romance of Indian Embroidery,* Thacker & Co. Ltd, Bombay, 1951.

Elliot, H.M. and John Dowson, *History of India as Told by Its Own Historians,* 1867-77, Vol. I.

Epigraphia Indica, Vol. 20.

Gill, Harjeet Singh, *A Phulkari from Bhatinda,* Punjabi University, Patiala, 1977.

Graham, Joss, *Phulkari and Bagh: The Embroidery Shawls of Punjab*, Abhinav Publications, New Delhi, 2004.

Hitkari, S.S., *Phulkari–The Folk Art of Punjab*, New Delhi, 1980.

Ibbetson, Sir Denzil, *A Glossary of the Tribes and Castes of the Punjab and North West Province*, 1883, now reprinted by Languages Department, Punjab, Patiala, 1970.

Irwin, John & Margaret Hall, *Indian Embroideries*, Ahmedabad, 1973.

Kipling, J.L., 'The Industries of the Punjab', *Journal of India Art,* No. 20, London, 1887.

Mitradutta, Devyani, *A Catalogue on Phulkari Textiles in the Collection of Indian Museum,* Calcutta, 1985.

Mukherjee, Tinkari, 'Phulkari', *Rooplekha*, Vol. 24, No. 1-2, 1953.

Pal, Rampa, *The Phulkari: A Lost Craft,* Delhi, 1955.

Parihar, Subhash, 'Punjabi Phulkari', *Woman's Era*, April (second), 2004.

Saraswati, S.K., *Indian Textiles,* Govt. of India, Ministry of Information & Broadcasting, Delhi 1961.

Singh, Chanan, 'Phulkari from Phillaur', *Jan Sahit* (Punjabi), Vol. 20, Bhasha Vibhag, Patiala, September, 1979.

Singh, T.G., 'A Warp of Blessings' in *Embroidery in Asia: Sui Dhaga – Crossing Boundaries through Needle and Thread*, Kapila Vatsayan (ed.), New Delhi, 2010.

Steel, F.A., 'Phulkari Work in the Punjab', *Journal of Indian Art and Industry,* Vol. 2, No. 24, London, 1888.

ACKNOWLEDGEMENTS

Organizing Committee:
Chairperson & Chief Advisor
Mrs. Dipali Khanna, Member Secretary, IGNCA

Advisors
Shri V.B. Pyarelal, Joint Secretary, IGNCA
Prof. Molly Kaushal, Head, Janapada Sampada Division, IGNCA

Project Advisor
Mrs. Krishna Lal, Consultant, Cultural Archives & Ethnographic Collection, IGNCA

Catalogue Text
Mrs. Krishna Lal

Editor & Project Coordinator
Dr. Richa Negi, J.R.O., IGNCA

Academic Support
Prof. A.K Das, Consultant, Ethnographic Collection, IGNCA
Dr. Ramakar Pant, R.O., Janapada Sampada, IGNCA

Exhibition Curatorial Support
Dr. Achal Pandya
Shri Virendra Bangroo
Dr. Sangeeta Dutta
Shri Rajendra Taragi

Exhibition, Print, Publicity & Catalogue/Book Design
Neeraj Sahai, Pallavi Sahai
Picture Street

We deeply acknowledge:
Shri Chhotelal Bharany, for lending Phulkaris from his personal collection for the Exhibition. Images of these have been printed on pg. 12 (Ghungat Bagh), pg. 13 (Sainchi Phulkaris) and pg. 14 (Reshmi Sheesh Bagh & Bawan Bagh).
Smt. Lajwanti for lending Phulkaris from personal collection.
Shri Virendra Bangroo for photographs on pages – 4, 6, 9, 10 & 11

Printing, Distribution and Book Display
Shri Vikas Arya, Aryan Books International, New Delhi

ACKNOWLEDGEMENTS

Technical & Adminitrative Support
Shri Jayanta Chatterjee
Smt. Geeta Rawat
Smt. Sumitra Takkar
Shri Narayan Hari
Smt. Kavita Pande
Smt. Nandi Rawat
Shri Murari
Shri Saurabh Jain
Md. Danish Rehan

We are thankful to the following Divisions for their support
Sutradhara Division (Accounts Section, S&S, I&PR Unit)
Media Centre
Cultural Informatics Lab
Kala Darshana
Kala Nidhi
Conservation Unit
EMU

Important Telephone Numbers:
Mrs. Dipali Khanna, Member Secretary, IGNCA
011-23383895
Shri V.B. Pyarelal, Joint Secretary, IGNCA
011-23389675
Prof. Molly Kaushal, Head, Janapada Sampada, IGNCA
011-23388821

Programme Information:
Dr. Richa Negi, Janapada Sampada, IGNCA
011-23388448